T0350634

All Edge

All Edge

Inside the New Workplace Networks

CLAY SPINUZZI

The University of Chicago Press
Chicago and London

Clay Spinuzzi is professor of rhetoric and writing at the University of Texas at Austin. He is the author of *Tracing Genres through Organizations: A Sociocultural Approach to Information Design*; *Network: Theorizing Knowledge Work in Telecommunications*; and *Topsight: A Guide to Studying, Diagnosing, and Fixing Information Flow in Organizations*.

The University of Chicago Press, Chicago 60637
The University of Chicago Press, Ltd., London
© 2015 by The University of Chicago
All rights reserved. Published 2015.
Printed in the United States of America

24 23 22 21 20 19 18 17 16 15   1 2 3 4 5

ISBN-13: 978-0-226-23696-4 (cloth)
ISBN-13: 978-0-226-23701-5 (e-book)
DOI: 10.7208/chicago/9780226237015.001.0001

Library of Congress Cataloging-in-Publication Data

Spinuzzi, Clay, author.
    All edge : inside the new workplace networks / Clay Spinuzzi.
        pages cm
    Includes bibliographical references and index.
    ISBN 978-0-226-23696-4 (cloth : alk. paper) — ISBN 978-0-226-23701-5 (e-book)
1. Business networks.   2. Knowledge economy.   3. Business enterprises—
Technological innovations.   4. Business communication.   I. Title.
    HD69.S8S674 2015
    302.3'5—dc23

                                            2014027724

♾ This paper meets the requirements of ANSI/NISO Z39.48-1992
(Permanence of Paper).

Contents

Acknowledgments

In 1997, I took a summer internship at Schlumberger Well Services's Austin Product Center, where I conducted my first workplace study: a field study of how and when software developers in Austin and Houston chose to reuse code in software libraries. By the end of the summer, I knew two things: I wanted to keep conducting workplace studies, and I wanted to live in Austin.

Put those two passions together and you get this book: a book that identifies long-term workplace trends that are manifesting now in this extraordinary city, that theorizes these trends, and that spells out their implications for the future of work.

Along the way, I met some extraordinary Austinites. I especially thank my study participants, who generously opened their workspaces, and in some cases their homes, to me. Particular thanks go to the proprietors of Austin's coworking spaces who took part in the study described in chapter 5: Martin Barrera at Brainstorm; Jon Erik Metcalfe, Dusty Reagan, Cesar Torres, and David Walker at Conjunctured; Andrew Bushnell, Kirtus Dixon, and Pat Ramsey at Cospace; Blake Freeburg at Cowork Austin; Steve Golab at GoLab Austin; Liz Elam at Link; Lisa McTiernan at Perch; Sonya Davis and Laura Shook at Soma Vida; and Sam Lee and Paul Wang at Space12. The anonymous participants at Conjunctured, Cospace, and Link also generously gave of their time, as did participants in nonemployer firms across Austin and at Semoptco. They patiently described their working tips and tricks to me and they encouraged me to tell these stories.

My academic colleagues have also provided me with plenty of feedback and encouragement. In particular, I have discussed most of the book's components with Mark Zachry and Bill Hart-Davidson, both the case studies and the theoretical pieces. When I described the book idea to them at SIGDOC

2012, they gave me detailed feedback that helped to shape the book considerably. I also benefited from Skype, e-mail, and face-to-face conversations with many other scholars, including Eva-Maria Jakobs, David Ronfeldt, Catherine Schryer, Brian McNely, Saul Carliner, and Andrew M. Jones. Other valuable feedback came from the audiences at multiple conference presentations and talks, including talks at South by Southwest Interactive, SIGDOC, the Conference on College Composition and Communication, the Association for Teachers of Technical Writing Conference, Empirikom, Genre 2012, Lavacon, Writing Research Across Borders, Interactive Austin, RISE Austin, the Austin Society for Technical Communication, NetImpact Austin, the Austin Entrepreneur Scene, the University of Texas School of Information, and the Austin Chamber of Commerce, and from the students in the 2013 Helsinki Summer School course on activity theory and formative interventions.

My employer, the University of Texas at Austin, provided me with a spring 2013 fellowship that gave me the time to write much of this book.

At the University of Chicago Press, David Morrow has provided both encouragement and critical advice since I first mentioned this project to him in spring 2013. Two anonymous reviewers provided encouraging and substantial comments, which improved the book considerably. Logan Smith and Kelly Finefrock-Creed guided the project along expertly during the production and editing process.

Finally, my deep thanks to David R. Russell, mentor and friend. David told me in 2008 that I should write a book like this one: more broadly accessible, more attuned to practical applications of theory. As usual, he was right. This book is dedicated to him.

1

Becoming All Edge

Maas was small, fast, ruthless. An atavism. Maas was all Edge.

GIBSON (1986, p. 114)

In this quote from William Gibson's short story "New Rose Hotel," a character describes Maas Biolabs, a multinational corporation focused on research. Unlike other multinationals, Maas was stripped down to its essentials, composed of a small core of specialists, forming a "small, fast, ruthless" organization. "Edge" referred not just to the intellectual edge of Maas's specialists but also to the high-speed links that they could form with each other in order to swarm and innovatively address unique problems.

Such an organization was thinkable in 1986, when Gibson published *Burning Chrome*. In fact, it was thinkable even in 1970, when Alvin Toffler described such organizations in *Future Shock* as "adhocracies": rotating teams of specialists who could come together to swarm a project, disperse at the end of it, and re-form in a different configuration for the next project. But such organizations are now more than just thinkable, they are becoming commonplace. And their "edge" is their ability to form links both inside and outside an organization.

That is, this edge comes not through sheer ruthlessness and extreme talent, as in Maas's case, but through something much more ordinary and accessible: changes in how we communicate, coordinate, and collaborate with others. It's a function of communication changes that we have noted and theorized in fields such as business and technical communication (e.g., Dicks 2010; Spinuzzi 2007, 2009; Swarts & Kim 2009), computer-supported cooperative work (e.g., Czarniawska 2013; Kolfschoten, Herrmann & Lukosch 2013), and communication (e.g., Castells 2003, 2009; Rainie & Wellman 2012). But as we'll see, these changes have far-reaching effects on how we organize our work and ourselves, how we live and think, and how we interact with others.

We often tend to think of organizations as having an edge and an interior. The *interior* is where the real work happens—inside the hierarchy, inside the offices and bullpens, inside the factory, inside the company's databases and records, away from customers, clients, and partners. Those outsiders come in contact with the *edge* of the organization, its interface: marketing and advertising, customer service, liaisons, spokespeople, interface designers, and technical communicators. But that distinction between interior and edge has more to do with the historical limitations and costs of information and communication technologies (ICTs), especially texts, than it does with a necessary division of organization. When ICTs are slow and costly, it's more efficient to limit the edge and create an interior, restricting forms of communication via a hierarchy. In fact, that's the environment in which many of our business and technical communication genres developed (e.g., Jakobs & Spinuzzi 2014; Yates 1989). But when ICTs are rapid and cheap, the picture changes. Put a phone in everyone's pocket, a mobile computer in everyone's bag, and you have the potential for an organization to become *all edge*: able to rapidly link across organizational boundaries, combine into temporary work groups, swarm a project with a team of specialists, and disperse at the end of the project, often to re-form in a different configuration, with some different members, for the next project.

We don't all work that way right now, and it's likely that most organizations will not become purely all edge. But many will, and many others will be overlaid with all-edge capabilities, due to these changes in ICTs. Many of us do have a mobile phone in our pocket and a tablet in our bag; we can instantly pull information off the Internet; we're more likely to Google for answers than open a software manual (cf. Novick, Elizalde & Bean 2007); we spend considerable and increasing amounts of time on social networking sites. We can videoconference; many of us can do our work on laptops in coffee shops, hotel lobbies, and airports. We can, and do, read and write constantly in a remarkable range of genres and media. And these capabilities have changed how we work together: how we communicate, coordinate, and collaborate; how we define our work, our projects, and our products; how we set our goals and objectives; how we manage our time; how we learn on and off the job; how we trust—and doubt—each other.

This change has had remarkable effects on how we organize ourselves. In the twentieth century, we were all about hierarchies. We built bureaucracies to command and control our work; we established specific relationships and regulations and channels; we created training programs and operations manuals and forms so that we could nail down and regulate our work, our relations, our communications. Communicating across a large organization was so difficult and expensive that we reduced the communication channels, forcing people to go through the proper channels to communicate. We did everything we could to make work generic, routine, so that we could train people to do it quickly and produce similar results. And as we made it generic, we made it exportable: once work was reduced to a program, we could train a new worker, or a worker overseas, or (increasingly) a machine to do that work. Bureaucratic hierarchies have shaped much of what we do, and they certainly have shaped how we think about business and technical communication.

Such bureaucratic hierarchies have their place, and probably always will. But for an increasing number of jobs, bureaucratic hierarchies simply don't cut it. They're too rigid, too inflexible, too focused on protocol, too unconnected and clumsy. They don't respond well to rapid change. They don't innovate well. They don't allow strong cross-connections across different parts of the organization. In fact, they emphasize hierarchy too much, walling off agents that have to coordinate with each other across departments, specializations, companies, and locations. Bureaucratic hierarchies sharply limit the organization's edge.

Near the end of the twentieth century, and accelerating during the first decade of this century, we have begun to see less bureaucratic, more agile ways for people to connect—ways that expand that edge, putting nearly everyone on the organization's edge (cf. Spinuzzi 2008). These adhocracies are loose, spontaneously forming, often temporary arrangements that reach across an organization. Adhocracies are less stable than bureaucracies, but they aren't (necessarily) chaotic either, and in fact we're seeing some remarkably intricate, connected work structures emerge. They're certainly not the bureaucratic hierarchies that dominated so much of the previous century. They're more connected, more flexible, more open. They're temporary and interdependent. They excel at creativity and innovation—although they don't do as well at producing reliable, predictable outcomes. Adhocracies ignore the old borders between organizations, between disciplines, between locations, between work and leisure and family. They are enabled by new ICTs, certainly, but they also represent a different kind of work with different values and principles. They aren't based on hierarchies; they're based on networks that simply route around these old borders, creating new capabilities and new characteristics of work.

Moreover, these adhocracies are increasingly all edge, temporarily connecting specialists across organizations rather than just within an organization. They form briefly around a defined project, swarming it, then dispersing once it's completed. They change composition. They communicate, coordinate, and collaborate constantly, usually through digital information technologies. And they bring a level of flexibility, agility, and innovation that is unmatched by institutional hierarchies.

Such organizations quickly made the leap from Toffler's futurism to Gibson's cyberpunk to real life. We read about them in books such as *The Starfish and the Spider* (Brafman & Beckstrom 2008), *Smart Mobs* (Rheingold 2003), and *Networked* (Rainie & Wellman 2012). Yes, digital ICTs change the way we relate. But *how?* What shapes do these all-edge adhocracies take?

That's what I address in this book. Instead of speaking in general terms, I examine real incidents, in real organizations, talking to real people, demonstrating real changes in how people work. I look closely at all-edge adhocracies, comparing them and speculating on how they'll develop in the future.

Throughout the book, I present case studies of all-edge adhocracies in creative fields focused on communication and design, since we are seeing the most movement in those fields (for reasons that I discuss in chapter 2). I specifically examine them in terms of technical communication, although I discuss other aspects of the work as well. These case studies are set in Austin, Texas, a rapidly changing city whose economy has been rated the number one metropolitan economy in the United States, leading in the creation of middle-class jobs (see Barr 2013, Kotkin 2013a, 2013b; Olivieri 2013). But the changes represented in these case studies are happening across fields and sectors as work becomes more informated (Zuboff 1988), so I also touch on how all-edge adhocracies are moving into other fields (such as software development, health care, entertainment, administration, international development, and the enterprise) and into the public sphere (in areas such as parenting and growing up, politics, disaster recovery, and warfare).

In the remainder of this chapter, I first discuss what I mean by *communicate, coordinate,* and *collaborate.* Then I discuss how changes in information technology have opened up—and required—new ways to organize our activities. Finally, I preview the rest of this book.

Communication, Coordination, and Collaboration

The terms *communication, coordination,* and *collaboration* are often used broadly. Here, I follow Clarence A. Ellis, Simon J. Gibbs, and Gail L. Rein (1991) by understanding them in broad terms related to computer-supported cooperative work.

By *communication* I mean the act of transferring information from one person or group to another—broadly speaking. That information can be highly abstract, such as a mathematical formula, or highly concrete, such as a face-to-face demonstration in an apprenticeship. It can be highly codified, such as the Internet protocols that allow digital communication, or highly uncodified, such as face-to-face communications over Skype (see Boisot, Nordberg, Yami & Nicquevert 1991). It can be synchronous, such as a telephone call, or asynchronous, such as a message left in a time capsule. It can be textual, like an e-mail, or nontextual, like flashing one's headlights at oncoming cars to warn them of a speed trap. And it can be directed, like a telephone call, or ambient, like signage.

Communication encompasses business and technical communication, and throughout this book, I specifically look at examples of textual communication that can be classified under that heading. But I also discuss examples that go beyond the familiar business and technical communication genres, examples that respond to changes in ICTs and organization.

By *coordination* I mean the act of meshing our efforts with those of other people in the same or connected activities: ordering and integrating them so that they build on each other rather than conflicting. As Ellis et al. put it, "Coordination can be viewed as an activity in itself, as a necessary overhead when several parties are performing a task" (1991, p. 40). Coordination requires communication. We coordinate when we wave another car on at a four-way stop, when we set an appointment with someone, and when we set a completion date on a project we're trying to achieve with (or for) other parties.

Collaboration involves working with others toward a shared objective (Ellis et al. 1991, p. 40), particularly when bringing different kinds of expertise to bear (see Sherlock 2009; Swarts 2000). As Charles Heckscher puts it, collaboration involves "a shared objective that cannot be reached without the contribution of all. Thus it necessarily implies processes of dialogue and negotiation, of exchanges of views and sharing of information, of building from individual views toward a shared consensus" (2007, p. 2). When we work together with others to define a project objective, when we develop a shared understanding of a problem, and when we find ways to make sure that everyone gains an advantage from our shared work, we are collaborating.

Notice that although collaboration and coordination often go together, they don't always. I might collaborate with someone else on a project by doing what I think is my part but without coordinating with him or her to make sure that our efforts mesh. I might coordinate with someone (say, by waving them on at a four-way stop) but without meaningfully engaging in a shared, mutually defined activity. But collaboration and coordination both involve the necessary substrate of communication.

So it shouldn't be surprising that collaboration and coordination have changed radically as we have learned new ways to communicate. As we develop and learn to use new ICTs, we open new possibilities for coordination and collaboration. New ICTs create additional communication channels, allowing us to coordinate and collaborate across broader swathes of time, location, and activity. These new opportunities create new needs for coordination: for ordering and integrating our actions, especially when we don't entirely understand each other's specialties. They also create new needs for collaboration: for pulling others into shared, mutually defined objectives. Each time a new ICT is introduced, it presents the possibility for fundamentally changing our work.

ICTs and Writing: A Historical Sketch

In 1870, 20 percent of the people in the United States above the age of fourteen were illiterate—unable to read or write in any language. By 1979, that number dropped to only 0.6 percent (Snyder 1993). The CIA World Factbook similarly estimated that 99 percent of the US population was literate in 2003 (CIA 2013). That is, about 99 of every 100 people in the United States can read and write to some extent. And we do—everywhere: from professional documents to shopping lists to bathroom walls.

It's hard to overstate how extraordinary that fact is. For about 98 percent of human history, writing didn't even exist. And until very recently, writing was an elite and rare skill, practiced by a tiny percentage of the population.

Writing is our most protean tool, fundamentally changing how we communicate, coordinate, and collaborate. But those changes aren't uniform: different information and communication technologies inflect writing in different ways, creating new possibilities and affordances, and sometimes nudging people in unexpected directions.

BEFORE WRITING

Before writing, communication, coordination, and collaboration looked very different. Our ancestors tended to live in smaller preagricultural communities, simple societies with low population density (Fried 1967). These societies were often nomadic. In those societies, they mostly communicated face-to-face. Although they had developed symbolic artifacts such as art and some rudimentary counters (possibly calendars; see Schmandt-Besserat 1992, 1997), these were context bound, not generally meant to communicate with others outside a limited context. It was not until *prewriting*—which included symbolic systems such as hieroglyphs, petroglyphs, and counters—that human beings were able to communicate beyond these contexts.

Our ancestors were able to count, but only through correspondence counting, which was concrete rather than abstract: they might match a counted item (say, a sheep) with a counter (say, a pebble), but they had not yet separated the number from the counter. That is, if a herdsman had five sheep, he would match each sheep to a pebble: "sheep, sheep, sheep, sheep, sheep." He didn't think of the number as an abstract concept to apply to different kinds of items: "five sheep, five pebbles, five goats."

That system was adequate for small, simple societies that did not practice mass agriculture, especially nomadic societies. But eventually people stopped moving from place to place and started banding together to grow things. And when that happened, their information needs changed.

THE BIRTH OF WRITING

We are used to thinking of writing as a basic and incredibly useful kind of information. So it might be surprising to realize that writing, by some accounts, has been invented *only three times* in the history of the human race: in Mesopotamia (circa 3200 BCE), in China (about 1250 BCE), and in Mesoamerica (about 650 BCE; Schmandt-Besserat and Erard 2008). As Denise Schmandt-Besserat and Michael Erard emphasize, writing is neither intuitive nor common: "the cognitive steps that led from logography to numerals and phonograms occurred only once in Mesopotamia" (pp. 13–15), and similarly the alphabet was invented only once (p. 15).

Let's look at the first invention of writing, the one that underpins all Western writing systems. According to Schmandt-Besserat (1997), it came in three stages. First, people began using tallies—such as notches in pieces of bone—somewhere between 30,000 and 12,000 BCE (p. 98). These tallies likely helped them record time (p. 101).

Next, when people invented agriculture, they stopped roaming and started staying put. Land was no longer a setting but a commodity. New tools (such as polished stone) and new materials (such as clay) became available. And people had to organize their work in different ways so that they could grow and distribute goods. Specifically, "agriculture brought about a need for accounting" (Schmandt-Besserat 1992, p. 102), including an elite that could oversee and control the redistribution of resources (Schmandt-Besserat 1992, p. 170; 1997, pp. 104–5). So in Sumer in about 8,000 BCE, tokens appeared: small geometric shapes, generally made out of fired clay, representing different quantities of goods (Schmandt-Besserat 1992, p. 102). For instance, a sphere represented a bushel of grain, while a cylinder represented an animal. These tokens were perhaps based on still older systems of counters made of natural materials (stones, seeds). And since the tokens were part of an open system, this system could be expanded: as the state developed, people developed more tokens to describe processed goods such as oil and textiles (Schmandt-Besserat 1997, p. 107).

Interestingly, tokens were not initially used for trade. That is, they weren't used like coins. They were instead used by central authorities for accounting: tracking debts and redistributing goods. Eventually, by the early fourth millennium BCE, they began bundling these tokens by putting them in clay "envelopes"—actually hollow clay balls that were fired to harden them (Schmandt-Besserat 1992, pp. 108–10). One's debt would be represented by the tokens in the ball: perhaps eight sheep tokens and three wheat tokens, for instance.

Of course, the problem with clay envelopes was that the accountants couldn't see through them; to get an accurate count, the accountant had to break the envelope. Eventually, the Sumerians solved this problem: before putting the tokens in the soft clay envelope, they would make an impression of each token on the outside of the envelope. (Sometimes we see something similar when buying a calzone: some vendors will put representative ingredients from the calzone's interior onto the exterior so that they don't confuse the veggie calzone with the pepperoni calzone.) Soon—"soon" in archaeological time, anyway, around 3100 BCE—accountants realized that the outer markings made the tokens superfluous. They began producing solid clay balls with token markings on them, then began using a stylus to imitate the imprinting of tokens. "The signs were not pictures of the items they represented," Schmandt-Besserat tells us, "but, rather, pictures of the tokens used as counters in the previous accounting system" (1997, p. 7).

The solid clay balls were a turning point because the markings, although superficially the same, "assumed an entirely new function. Whereas the markings on envelopes repeated only the message encoded on the tokens held within, the signs on the tablet *were* the message" (p. 55; original emphasis). After the envelopes gave way to the clay balls, it took about two hundred years (eight generations) to move from token impressions to additional pictographic representations (p. 57).

The Sumerians had invented writing—not to tell stories, record histories, or express themselves, but to solve a novel accounting problem that resulted from the invention of agriculture. And in doing so, they had created a system for making information more codified and abstract—a system that allowed people to communicate more effectively across time and distances.

The system, however, was still very young. Over the centuries, it would develop into a number of different writing systems couched in an ever-expanding number of genres and carried by various media. As Frederick Kilgour (1998, p. 4) chronicles, the book—meant broadly, as a storehouse of information—has gone through five basic stages: the clay tablet (2500 BCE–100 CE), the papyrus roll (2000 BCE–700 CE), the codex (100 CE), and the electronic book ("currently in the process of innovation"). The codex, which we know best as a printed book, itself went through three major stages of reproduction: "machine printing from cast type, powered by human muscle (1455–1814)"; "nonhuman power driving both presses and typecasting machines (1814–1970)"; and "computer-driven photocomposition combined with offset printing (1970–)" (p. 4). Historically, Kilgour says, the book follows a "pattern . . . in which long periods of stability in format alternate with periods of radical change" (p. 4). These radical changes went far beyond the presentation of information, influencing the way people worked, lived, and thought.

PRINTING

One of these radical changes happened around 1450 CE. With the development of the printing press (Eisenstein 1980), writing became central to economic pursuits—and, in western Europe, to religion. Literacy gave people access to the Bible, allowing Protestants to study the sacred texts for themselves and engendering a different understanding of their relationship to God, to authorities, and to work (Weber 2002). Literacy spread, and with it, the ability to use texts in more ways. Texts facilitated better and more-systematic calculations, enabling the distributed control over distances (O'Leary, Orlikowski & Yates 2002) that became the hallmark of the corporation (Bazerman 1999; Popham 2005; Yates 1989). Writing became central to work and business.

Throughout the twentieth century, writing both encouraged and was supported by universal schooling and universal literacy (e.g., Hernandez 1995). Literacy efforts were so widespread and so successful in Europe and North America that much work was textualized. Writing, perhaps the most protean tool at our disposal, became a crucial resource for problem solving and self-mediation as well as communication: quotidian texts became widespread even in "nonliterate" activities (Karlsson 2009) as work and leisure became increasingly textualized (Johnson-Eilola 2005).

After World War II, writing took on other roles as industrial- and information-age expansion required more people to learn new skills quickly, leading us to develop a knowledge society in which the economy was increasingly driven by the analysis and processing of information (Drucker 1994).

Record keeping became a vital way to ensure accountability and protect against legal issues (Schryer and Spoel 2005). Report writing became crucial for conveying complex information within and across large organizations (e.g., Miller and Selzer 1985; Pogner 2003; Sauer 2003), while proposal writing supported complex arguments for value (Broadhead and Freed 1986). Engineers found that they had to produce and read documentation of various types, including manuals, reports, and forms (Artemeva and Freedman 2001; Winsor 1996).

LONG-DISTANCE COMMUNICATION INFRASTRUCTURE

Meanwhile, people developed other forms of long-distance information: first roadways and waterways, then railways and mail services, then the telegraph, telephone, and broadcast media. These media supported significant developments in how people organized themselves and their work: as Max Weber argues, modern bureaucracy "requires the services of the railway, the telegraph, and the telephone, and becomes increasingly dependent on them" (1978, p. 224). That is, communication and transportation technologies create the conditions under which bureaucracies can flourish. After all, "bureaucratic administration means fundamentally domination through knowledge," including both "technical knowledge" and "knowledge growing out of experience in the service" (p. 225). Indeed, "telecommunications infrastructure has strong explanatory power for why some countries have industrialized and others not" (Isakkson 2010, p. 3).

These new communication and transportation technologies made it much easier to move information across distances—as long as information was highly structured. That meant more education, more types of literacy, and more genres.

DIGITAL COMMUNICATION

Finally, in the second half of the twentieth century, people began to use digital technologies to share and analyze information. At first, these uses were restricted and relatively closed, such as internal message boards (Zuboff 1988) and, later, e-mail and forums (e.g., Castells 1997). But as more people gained Internet access and as digital technology spread and developed, these uses differentiated: we could connect with strangers, friends, or coworkers through e-mail, instant messaging, message boards, social media, and our ubiquitous mobile phones (Castells, Fernández-Ardèvol, Linchuan Qiu & Sey 2007; Rainie and Wellman 2012). We increasingly became "always on."

And like the other milestone changes in ICTs, this one is having an enormous effect on how we live, work, and organize.

ICTs and New Capabilities

Digital technologies and telecommunications aren't just about moving information faster and more easily. They provide qualitatively different connections.

COLLAPSING TIME AND SPACE

ICTs have led to the possibility of being "always on," always available to communicate, coordinate, and collaborate. As Howard Rheingold predicted in 2003, mobile phones, and especially texting, have changed how we live, work, and organize. The growth in this sector is remarkable. In December 2012, the world topped 6.7 billion active mobile subscriptions, which reached 4.3 billion human beings, 61 percent of the planet's population. Of these subscriptions, 5.6 billion included texting (Ahonen 2012). Mobile subscriptions are on the rise across the globe, especially in China, India, and the rest of the Asian Pacific region (Ericsson 2013). As of May 2013, more than 61 percent of US mobile phone subscribers owned smartphones (Nielsen 2013). As of April 2013, a quarter of US teens accessed the Internet mainly through their smartphones (Madden & Lenhart 2013).

This broad connectivity means that people can increasingly communicate, coordinate, and collaborate across time, space, and other barriers (Rainie & Wellman 2012; Spinuzzi 2007, 2009; Sun 2012; Swarts & Kim 2009). It entails a new social logic (Castells et al. 2007). An always-accessible social layer means that we can be continually available to our friends, family, and collaborators—simultaneously. As former US secretary of state Hillary Clinton declared in 2010, "The spread of information networks is forming a new nervous system for our planet."

Of course, this social layer also means that we are increasingly expected to be available anytime for work. So we get a workforce that is increasingly mobile (iPass 2011), increasingly incentivized to work remotely (Dixon & Ross 2011), with increasing opportunities to work in looser arrangements. We get a workforce that is increasingly distributed, increasingly able (and incentivized, and conditioned) to work independently (Mettler & Williams 2013). This workforce increasingly works in virtual environments (Bullock and Klein 2011) and collaborates in virtual teams (Solomon 2012; Yoo & Alavi 2004), often in temporary groups (Dwyer 2011; Lister & Harnish 2010). Workers are sometimes "on call" continually, and that continual on-call status sometimes works its way deeply into their personal lives: during the October 2013 government shutdown, for instance, the *Washington Post* ran a story about furloughed government workers who found it nearly unbearable to put down their smartphones (Rosenwald 2013). As Jason Swarts and Loel Kim put it:

> Our personal information technologies can help us turn our cars into extensions of the office, help engineers turn work zones into extensions of design space, and help doctors turn exam spaces into extensions of lab space (see Mol, 2002). The boundaries between different places do not overwrite one another but instead simultaneously include, distribute, dispel, and merge with one another, resulting in what Mol and Law (1994) referred to as "fluid spatialities . . . [where] space behaves like a fluid" (p. 643) and where the identities, relationships, and objects of work that concern the inhabitants of those spaces seamlessly change and transition from one state to another without disruption as people attune to different information objects and information flows. (2009, pp. 218–19; original ellipsis, brackets, and parenthetical material)

Lee Rainie and Barry Wellman similarly argue that ICTs extend work across spatial and organizational boundaries:

> People often work in multiple projects with different teams. This allows firms to assemble ad hoc teams with diversified talents and perspectives. As workers shift among teams, they can develop cumulatively larger networks of expertise that are "glocal," with both local interactions and global connectivity. Instead of submitting to the traditional hierarchical mode of authority, workers have more discretion about the work they jointly accomplish. Networked organizations have advantages for boundary spanning, as employees work and network between work groups and organizations—and at times, between continents. (2013, p. 181)

ICTs overlay other spaces, creating new possibilities and merging different sorts of activities (Swarts & Kim 2009, p. 212). One result is *nomadism*, in which people are expected to work in impermanent settings such as buses, trains, airplanes, coffee shops, or the offices of clients (Büscher 2014; Costas 2013; Czarniawska 2013; Humphry 2013; Mark & Su 2010; Su & Mark 2008).

CREATING AMBIENT AWARENESS

Since we are increasingly working in different spaces at different times, one might assume that it would become more difficult to coordinate. But lower communication costs lead to greater *ambient awareness* (Cornejo, Tentori & Favela 2013): the ability to maintain peripheral knowledge of relevant events in others' lives, work, and activities. This ability has been developed in various ways. For instance, social media allow us to monitor each other's expressed statuses across organizations, families, and other groups (Backhouse 2009; Baehr & Alex-Brown 2010; Brzozowski, Sandholm & Hogg 2009; Cummings, Massey & Ramesh 2009; Jacobs & Nakata 2010; Kolfschoten 2013; Reimer & Richter 2010; Ruppel, Gong & Tworoger 2013; Walton 2013; Wu, DiMicco & Millen 2010; Zhao & Rosson 2009). Members of a distributed workgroup once told me that they would start Skype each workday so that they could talk to each other as if they were at the same desk. Social media also support back-channeling in more-structured activities (McNely 2009). But more-formal systems for ambient awareness have also been developed: For instance, Jacob McCarthy, Jeffrey Grabill, William Hart-Davidson, and Michael McLeod (2011; see also Hart-Davidson, Zachry & Spinuzzi 2012) developed a system to "workstream" writing activities and revisions within a writing group—itself an incremental improvement over document histories in wikis and publicly available online systems (cf. Bhatti, Baile & Yasin 2011; Divine, Morgan, Ourada & Zachry 2010; Divine, Hall, Ferro & Zachry 2011; Ferro, Derthick, Morgan, Searle & Zachry 2009; Wagner 2010) and content management systems (see Spinuzzi 2007 for a review).

MAKING NEW CONNECTIONS

In creating a social layer that can reach beyond preexisting groups such as work and family, and across geographic barriers, new ICTs create the potential for new connections. Such connections are often in the form of *loose ties*—that is, connections who are not close friends or coworkers but who might be able to provide information in unusual situations (Granovetter 1973). Those loose ties are important because we are increasingly connected to those outside our organizations—and we have to be. We are at the edges of our organizations, and part of the value we provide is in connecting to the edges of other organizations.

In knowledge-work organizations, it's relatively easy to extend one's networks in formal and informal ways. That's because, although these organizations also do physical work, most of their work involves circulating, analyzing, and synthesizing information. And information is increasingly inexpensive to circulate, as we'll see in chapter 2.

In knowledge work, strength comes from combining sets of expertise in unique ways. That means crossing borders—borders between fields/disciplines/trades, borders between organizations, borders between countries and agendas. Workers must be able to learn at least a little bit about each other's work. Furthermore, cross-organizational work often means less leverage over aspects of the work—you can command, but not control, people in different organizations. Temporary, project-based, cross-networked organizations multiply, and they work differently, often tactically rather than strategically. Due to these new, loosely structured connections, we are seeing organizational transformations in various places.

Parenting and growing up   New ICTs are changing how parents parent and how children interact. For instance, in 2013, a quarter of teens in the United States mostly accessed the Internet through their smartphones (Pew Research 2013). These ICTs make long-distance parenting more practicable: in a poignant example, foreign domestic workers in Singapore use mobile phones to parent their children at a distance (Chib, Malik, Aricat & Kadir 2014). And as teens become college students, they find that, like mobile workers with their smartphones, they are always on call, a "tethered generation" whose members are connected via social networking "to the extent that that they find it increasingly difficult to distinguish relationships that exist in their pockets from those that exist in their physical surroundings" (Mihailidis 2014). That tethering, however, can end up strengthening their family network as they themselves become adults (Cornejo et al. 2013).

Leisure and sociality   Along those lines, ICTs have deeply affected leisure and sociality, from the mobile phones that have refigured personal and family relationships (Castells et al. 2007; Rheingold 2003) to online games and their ecosystems (D. L. Jones 2012; Moore, Ducheneaut & Nickell 2006; Nardi 2010; Sherlock 2009) to social media (Ugander, Karrer, Backstrom, Marlow & Alto 2011). They have also reformed how existing social organizations such as clubs and fraternities are run (Ferro 2012; Pennell 2007).

Politics   ICTs, particularly social media, have had an impact on politics in democracies. For instance, Michael Xenos, Ariadne Vromen, and Brian D. Loader (2014) suggest that social media could be considered "the great equalizer" because they exhibit a strong relationship with political engagement and may lead young people to become politically engaged. Sheetal D. Agarwal et al. (2014) investigate how stakeholders in the Tea Party and Occupy Wall Street have adopted and contested various technological tools in accordance with their values. John Jones (2014) examines how people of different political persuasions used Twitter hashtags to engage with those of other persuasions.

Disaster recovery   Hastily formed networks (Denning and Dunham 2010, p. 345) address natural disasters, allowing strangers to coordinate their rescue and relief work (D. L. Jones & Potts 2010; Mark & Semaan 2008; Potts, Seit-zinger, Jones & Harrison 2011; Sarcevic et al. 2012; Starbird 2011, 2012; Starbird and Palen 2013; Starbird, Palen, Hughes & Vieweg 2010).

Warfare People in areas of warfare or low-intensity conflict can similarly provide information to each other—information that can sometimes be co-opted by the aggressors (Collings & Rohozinski 2008; Monroy-Hernández, Counts, Way & Wa 2013; Oh, Agrawal & Rao 2011).

Work But especially affected is the way we work. As we'll see throughout the rest of this book, ICTs transform work—and also how we organize work and create value. They make it easier to move information and also provide in-creased value in combining and synthesizing different types of information. New ICTs push us to the edge of the organization, where we can connect with people in other organizations who can supply that information.

And in some cases, organizations become all edge: comprised of connec-tions across other, more-permanent organizations, forming temporarily to swarm a project before dispersing again. All-edge adhocracies may have been possible under older ICTs, but with the new social layer afforded by digital ICTs, they are becoming more and more common. This reveals how they tick: I examine their characteristics and dynamics to better understand how they work, how they develop, and how they will change the way we work.

The Rest of the Book

All-edge adhocracies are increasingly viable and common—but they're still so new that we have trouble seeing them, understanding why they occur, and supporting them so that they can flourish. To better understand them, I describe three case studies that involve all-edge adhocracies in communi-cation and design work. These cases themselves are not so extraordinary—you might have seen similar cases in your work or your everyday life—but I examine each one carefully to see what it tells us about work trends, first in communication and design work and then across sectors. That examination is based on activity theory (Engeström 2008) but draws from many other strands to make sense of this phenomenon.

As we move through the book, we'll encounter some key ideas:

People have new ways to work together. What are they? I mentioned the seismic shift from bureaucratic hierarchies to all-edge adhocracies. But how does each work? Why is this shift happening? In chapter 2, I look at the shifts in work organization that we've seen over the last forty-odd years, and especially how all-edge adhocracies have developed to attack new kinds of work.

People in all-edge adhocracies have to pull together a flexible team-for-today, but they also have to provide a stable interface for other contexts. How do they do it? By design, all-edge adhocracies are temporary and constantly changing. But they also have to interface with more-stable organizations, including bureaucratic hierarchies. Sometimes they even have to look like those organizations in order to gain trust. In the case study in chapter 3, we'll see how nonemployer firms handle that tricky dynamic.

All-edge adhocracies represent a structural shift in organizations—and society in general—from hierarchies to networks. What are the characteristics of networks? Hierarchies and networks play by different rules. In chapter 4, I get into the details of organizational networks, which are the foundation of adhocracies, seeing the principles by which they work.

All-edge adhocracies require a different kind of workplace. What does it look like? Whereas institutional hierarchies tend to cluster people in departments by specialization, all-edge adhocracies need to put specialists in unstructured contact with others from different specializations. In the case in chapter 5, I look at one class of workplaces that do this—coworking spaces—and see how they help all-edge adhocracies to form.

All-edge adhocracies are kinetic, but they're not chaotic. How are they structured? Even though they aren't stable in the same way institutional bureaucracies are, all-edge adhocracies are still structured. In chapter 6, we'll find out how to understand their moving parts and how to see order in the chaos.

All-edge adhocracies aren't just free-floating—they can show up in, and add capabilities to, other sorts of organizations. But how? If an organization has networks, an all-edge adhocracy can spring up in it, even alongside an institutional bureaucracy. And when it does, it can add key capabilities—if the combination doesn't tear itself apart first. In the case in chapter 7, we'll see how all-edge adhocracies surface in a hybrid organization, making that organization capable of feats it would otherwise be unable to perform.

Hybrid organizations are the rule, not the exception. And the internal dynamics of such organizations can drive innovation and expand capabilities. How do all-edge adhocracies enhance those dynamics? In chapter 8, I look at how four basic organizational forms—hierarchies, markets, clans, and networks—have developed to meet different needs and transform different kinds of objects. I take a second look at the case from chapter 7, showing how these different organizational forms interact and how all-edge adhocracies play a role in tying them together.

All-edge adhocracies integrate work across organizations, specializations, and locations. How? In chapter 9, I look at three ways they do this, three integrations that provide these kinetic organizations with the stability they need in order to get anything done.

All-edge adhocracies have an important function to play in work. But what is that function? All-edge adhocracies aren't good at everything. In fact, they're quite bad at a lot of things. But for certain applications, they can't be beat. How do we support them in their strengths, shore up their weaknesses, and use them to their potential? In chapter 10, I draw lessons for the care and feeding of all-edge adhocracies.

That's a lot to cover in one book. So let's get started. First up: discussing what all-edge adhocracies actually are.

2

What Are All-Edge Adhocracies?

Let's start with three people, each twenty years apart. They're fictional, but the changes they see are real.

It's 1970, and "A" is a graphic artist working for an advertising agency. Like most agencies and firms, this one is divided into major departments (in this case, Account Services, Account Planning, Creative, Finance, Media Buying, and Production). Different specializations go in different departments—for instance, A works alongside and talks with other creatives, not with accountants. He also shares the same equipment, such as drafting tables and clip art. When A does have to communicate outside his department, it's mostly through managers or through meetings set up by managers.

It's 1990, and "B" is a graphic designer working for the same advertising agency. The same departments are in place, but B knows quite a few people in other departments because he recently served on a cross-departmental task force. The task force was assembled because the agency had a tough problem to solve: what computer and networking equipment should it purchase in the coming years? The task force, which was composed of a cross section of employees at the agency, provided perspectives from across the company. For his part, B is relieved that he was able to convince the task force that the creatives needed Macintoshes, desktop publishing software, and color printers. He now feels that others in the organization understand his work a little better—and he has a better idea of how their departments are run too.

It's 2010, and "C" is a graphic designer working out of her home office. She freelances for a lot of different organizations, including the advertising agency, which now has just a couple of in-house graphic designers left: the advertising agency shed a lot of its noncore functions in the last twenty years, relying instead on independent contractors for much of that work. She works with several clients and subcontracts out a lot of her work. In fact, some of these independent contractors are in C's city, but others are around the globe— just like her clients. Her relationships with her clients and subcontractors are driven by the project, not the department. And she relies on consumer products she purchases herself—her laptop, her home broadband connection, and her mobile phone—to keep her connected with all of these people and to do her work. In fact, C could work anywhere: just last month, she completed a job for the advertising agency while vacationing in Oregon. The agency neither knew nor cared.

What happened in the space of forty years? No less than a fundamental shift in how certain types of work get done: a shift from 1970s institutional bureaucracies to 1990s budding institutional adhocracies to 2010s all-edge adhocracies. In A's 1970 advertising agency, organizations had *interiors*, departments full of people who didn't communicate or work directly with others outside the department. In B's 1990 agency, those interiors were starting to break down for special projects. And by 2010, C's work had no interior at all: her organization was *all edge*. She could potentially work with different organizations, different specialties, and different people in different locations.

That fundamental shift is obvious from C's point of view, once she thinks about it, because she works for herself. But even within organizations, this fundamental shift is affecting how people work, communicate, coordinate, collaborate, persuade each other, and develop trust with each other. If we're going to understand the new workplace networks, we have to start here. So let's get started.

What Happened in 1970?

In 1970—right about the time that A began working in the bureaucracy of his advertising agency—the famed futurist Alvin Toffler argued that bureaucracies were doomed. They were doomed, Toffler said, because workers were too transient and bureaucracies were too inefficient and inflexible to survive the rapid change he was seeing. Instead, he predicted, bureaucracies would give way to "the organization of the future": in it, "man will find himself liberated, a stranger in a new free-form world of kinetic organizations. In this alien landscape, his position will be constantly changing, fluid, and varied. And his organizational ties, like his ties with things, places, and people, will turn over at a frenetic and ever-accelerating pace" (1970, p. 125). Of course, Toffler had a mixed track record—he also predicted that by 2000 we would be living in space stations (1980, p. 143) and undersea villages (1970, p. 191) and leaning against pillows made of human mammary tissue (1980, p. 148). But when he described the "organization of the future," Toffler was right. (Well, mostly; we'll get to the differences in a moment.) He called this organization of the future the *adhocracy*.

Toffler argued that since organizations were facing higher turnover, the resulting high change in organizational relations would doom the bureaucracy by destroying fixed lines of authority and loyalty (1970, p. 128). It's easier to put up with a bureaucracy when you know that you have lifelong employment, but the 1974 recession spelled the end of lifelong employment in the United States (Heckscher 2007, pp. 186–87).

Furthermore, organizations were beginning to face problems that individual departments couldn't solve—think of B's 1990 agency, which had to develop a purchasing strategy for equipment that was fundamentally changing the way it operated. These organizations did the same thing B's agency did: turn to project or task-force management, in which "teams are assembled to solve short-term problems" (Toffler 1970, p. 132). Novel problems, such as ones involving innovation or customization, require novel organizational structures (p. 135). Such ad hoc teams don't necessarily replace permanent functional structures, Toffler conceded; but they do change those structures (p. 135). Simultaneously, traditional chains of command were breaking or being sidestepped, replaced with horizontal communication (p. 137), because vertical communication required too many steps to convey information (p. 139). For instance, once B worked with others on the task force, he knew them and knew what they did—and since every worker had a desk phone, it was not hard to talk to these new contacts. The walls between departments began to break down.

Finally, Toffler said, more of these workers are specialists—people like B, who has developed specialized skills through education and training, skills that his manager doesn't share. Specialists don't fit well into traditional chains of command. Indeed, Toffler argued, these specialists are "in vital fields so narrow that often the men on top have difficulty understanding them. Increasingly, managers have to rely on the judgment of these experts. . . . Such men are assuming a new decision-making function" (p. 140). Thus "managers are losing their monopoly on decision-making" (p. 140). They can command, but they cannot control. Toffler concluded, "This is a picture of the coming *Ad-hocracy*, the fast-moving, information-rich, kinetic organization of the future, filled with transient cells and extremely mobile individuals" (p. 144). We can sum up adhocracies with one simple comparison: adhocracies are to networks as bureaucracies are to hierarchies.

Adhocracies : Networks :: Bureaucracies : Hierarchies

To understand what Toffler was driving at—and why it's so important for understanding work in the early twenty-first century—we need to examine the difference between bureaucracies and adhocracies. And that means we have to understand their relationships, respectively, to hierarchies and networks.

1970: BUREAUCRACIES

The term *bureaucracy* literally means "rule by desks or offices." The word *rule* is key here: we can think of bureaucracy as the organizing principle that makes the members of an institutional hierarchy communicate, coordinate, and cooperate efficiently.

Yes, efficiently! We tend to think of bureaucracies as tremendously inefficient—and maybe we imagine specific bureaucracies with which we have had seemingly inefficient transactions, such as the DMV. But in a traditional institution, which is organized into a fairly rigid hierarchy and separated into different departments, the bureaucracy is a relatively efficient way of circulating information and commands (see Malone 2004, p. 22). Think of the bureaucracy as the "operating system" of an institution—the software that keeps the institution running and connected (see Rainie & Wellman 2012). The bureaucracy furnishes the operating logic for the hierarchy, the basic set of instructions that connects the hierarchy's "hardware" to its applications in different domains.

Max Weber famously described bureaucracy as a structure of domination (Weber 1978, p. 219). Weber listed its characteristics: "Precision, speed, unambiguity, knowledge of the files, continuity, discretion, unity, strict subordination, reduction of friction and of material and personal costs—these are raised to the optimum point in the strictly bureaucratic administration" (p. 973). In a bureaucracy, regular activities can be carried out reliably, methodically, and continuously under a stable, strictly delimited authority (p. 956). The bureaucracy demands calculable rules and little ambiguity—and therefore written documents (p. 957); the reduction to rules is "deeply embedded in its very nature" (p. 958). It connects people of different specialties; demands their full working capacity; and expects them to see their work as a lifelong vocation rather than just a job (p. 958).

The bureaucracy gives these lifelong workers particular tools and channels to communicate, coordinate, and collaborate. As Warren Bennis and Philip Slater (1998) later argued, bureaucracies tend to share certain characteristics:

- *A strong division of labor.* Bureaucracies overlay hierarchies, which tend to be divided into departments. For instance, recall A's 1970 advertising agency. Major departments might include Account Services, Account Planning, Creative, Finance, Media Buying, and Production. If the agency is large enough, it might also include departments such as Research, Human Resources, and Facilities. Different specializations go in different departments—and communicate largely through their managers, via well-defined chains of command.

- *Narrow specializations.* Implied in this strong division of labor are narrow specializations. Bureaucracies tend to compartmentalize specializations in departments. In A's advertising agency, for instance, creatives (such as graphic designers and copywriters) were sequestered in one department, while accountants were sequestered in another. That compartmentalization wasn't just on the organization chart either: departments tended to be physically clustered together. The result was that creatives talked to creatives, accountants talked to accountants, but when they talked across departments, it was mostly through managers or through meetings curated by managers.

- *Hierarchy and levels.* And that brings us to managers. In a rigid bureaucracy, the manager operates as the official communication and coordination point for his or her department. Although people in the department might informally chat with others in different departments, officially, they communicate via the chain of command. For instance, if A needed to communicate with an accountant (say, to seek a reimbursement), he would have to obtain a reimbursement form, fill it out, and turn it in to his manager, who would then convey it to the proper department. Furthermore, this hierarchical organization goes all the way up: managers have managers, culminating with the CEO.

- *Command and control.* Finally, bureaucracy assumes a command-and-control structure. In a hierarchy, people higher in the hierarchy are assumed to have more information by virtue of their positions. They also tend to have more experience in their given department, having worked their way up the hierarchy in that department. Thus they are assumed to be in a better position to make decisions than those lower in the hierarchy. The greater access to information gives them the ability to command effectively, while the greater experience gives them the ability to control those in their specialty due to their understanding of the job.

In their 1998 preface to the book *The Temporary Society*, first published in 1968, Bennis and Slater noted that bureaucracies are set up to control, order, and predict. Given a slow-changing hierarchy offering lifelong employment, bureaucracies provided a way to make sure those with the most experience got the most information and (theoretically) made the best decisions. Bureaucracies, as Toffler told us in *Future Shock*, are characterized by "permanence, hierarchy, and a division of labor"—and demand people who can work within those constraints (1970, pp. 144–45). They are fundamentally organized by department, and when people work together in a bureaucracy, they tend to focus on how to address the needs of that department.

Done right, bureaucracies can be very efficient. As Henry Mintzberg argued in his book *The Structuring of Organizations*, an organization structure is considered bureaucratic to the extent that its behavior is predetermined or predictable (i.e., standardized; 1979 p. 86). So bureaucracies rely on formalized behavior to achieve smooth coordination (p. 84): they work best when people follow rules, protocol, and established communication channels. That means that bureaucracies are good at executing routines under stable circumstances—but, as Weber suggested, they're not so good for innovation and adaptation (cf. Galbraith 1983).

Weber saw no real hope of escape from bureaucracy. But bureaucracies have plenty of limitations. And by the late 1960s, these were starting to become more obvious.

1990: INSTITUTIONAL ADHOCRACIES

Bureaucracies, as we've seen, simplify the communication, coordination, and collaboration challenges of an institutional hierarchy. They put people with similar specialties into "silos" where they interact mainly with each other rather than with people of different specialties. They limit the sorts of communication that happen across these silos. And they put the most experienced people in positions where they receive the most information and use that information to make decisions, creating bottlenecks (see Boisot, Nordberg, Yami & Nicquevert 2011).

Yet by 1970, bureaucracies were showing severe limitations. For instance, by separating specialties, bureaucracies limited innovations that could come from crossing silos. By rewarding workers for following commands, bureaucracies tended to promote rule followers rather than innovators, reinforcing silos and resulting in managers who focused on guarding their turf. Bureaucracy resulted in bureaucratic layers, procedures, and paperwork.

Moreover, bureaucracy proved unequal to so-called "wicked problems," ill-defined problems that require perspectives from different specializations. In response, some large organizations turned to cross-functional project teams—teams that brought together people from different specializations and different layers of the hierarchy, teams that were organized around a defined project rather than a department. In some industries, these teams were rare, used for strategic planning (as in B's 1990 advertising agency). But in other industries, especially in specialist-heavy industries such as aerospace engineering (e.g., Kent-Drury 2000), they became common.

In 1970, Toffler saw these cross-functional teams functioning as flexible and informal organization structures that avoided bureaucratic logic, policies, and procedures. Such adhocracies, he said, demand workers who are loyal to their professions rather than the organizations through which they cycle (p. 146); able to work in interdisciplinary, cross-functional groups (p. 147); oriented to the task or project rather than the job (p. 148); entrepreneurial (p. 148); risk-seeking and innovative (p. 150); able to move among slots in the organization (p. 150); extremely adaptable in terms of systems, arrangements, locations (p. 150); and in sum, "basically uncommitted to any organization. He [the adhocratic worker] is willing to employ his skills and creative energies to solve problems with equipment provided by the organization, and within temporary groups established by it. But he does so only as long as the problems interest him. He is committed to his own career, his own self-fulfillment" (p. 149). Weber said that bureaucracies demanded people who saw their work as a lifelong vocation dedicated to the bureaucracy rather than just a job. But Toffler saw specialists who separated their careers from any particular bureaucracy.

Toffler—and others who described adhocracies, such as Bennis and Slater in *The Temporary Society*, Mintzberg in *The Structuring of Organizations*, and Robert Waterman in *Adhocracy*—saw adhocracies as working within an institution, an alternate way to solve problems within a large corporation. These institutional adhocracies have characteristics that are very different from those of bureaucratic hierarchies:

- *A weak division of labor.* In bureaucracies, people focus on their own department, with its existing team and specific place in the hierarchy. But in adhocracies, people focus on a project, organizing a temporary team around it (something that's called *projectification*; I discuss it further in a moment). For instance, in his book *Adhocracy*, Waterman described how a senior VP at New York Life tasked a team with designing a new whole life policy (1993, pp. 14–15)—a specific, bounded project with a definite focus and endpoint. Similarly, in our example, B was involved in a cross-functional team that worked on one common problem and dissolved at the end of its project.
- *Teams of specialists crossing boundaries.* Since the focus shifts from the department to the project, teams become reconfigured around each unique project. That is, workers look beyond their departments for team mem-

bers who can bring unique value to that unique project. Typically this means specialists. For instance, the cross-functional team at New York Life included salespeople, designers, actuaries, technicians, a competition specialist, and a service person, all of whom had different specializations and perspectives to apply to the project (p. 15). Similarly, B's team drew from different specialties across the organization. These specialists come from very different education and work backgrounds; they represent different fields and functions, and thus they are able to provide complex, unique outputs (Mintzberg & McHugh 1985). They emphasized not the formal hierarchical relations that characterize the bureaucracy but the informal associational relations that cut across the bureaucracy's levels and silos (Heckscher 2007, pp. 26–27).

- *Rotating leadership.* Since team members are specialists in different things, their specialties often come to the forefront at different stages of the project; each might thus become the de facto leader at a given stage, then cede leadership to another specialist at the end of the stage. This arrangement can work because the organizational structure is relatively flat, with everyone in the team talking—and listening—to everyone else. Rather than coordinating through formalized behavior, as bureaucracies do, adhocracies are coordinated through mutual adjustment: team members are constantly in contact and constantly adjusting to a dynamic, complex environment (Mintzberg 1979, pp. 286, 449; Mintzberg & McHugh 1985). Adhocratic teams are like "guerilla units" (Mintzberg 1979, p. 449).

- *Command, not control.* Since leadership rotates among different specialists, rather than resting with people who have the most experience in one specialty, leaders in an adhocracy can command but not control. To put it another way, although a designated, permanent leader might command the team, providing broad parameters for success, the team members themselves must control the project when they are addressing their specialty; no one else on the team has the specialized expertise to do this. In an adhocracy, leadership is generative: "generative leaders get their power from authority granted by others" (Denning & Dunham 2010, p. 242; cf. Alberts & Hayes 2003).

Bennis and Slater claimed that in contrast to bureaucracies, which are set up to control, order, and predict, adhocracies are set up to acknowledge, create, and empower. Consequently, they are extremely flexible and innovative, uniquely able to tackle the wicked problems that bureaucracies seem so ill equipped to handle: "No structure is better suited to solving complex, ill-structured problems than the Adhocracy" (Mintzberg 1979, p. 463).

Think of these adhocracies as crosswiring the organizations, connecting departments and levels that had officially been kept separate. By cutting across the established divisions, they established networks that put people in direct contact with each other, networks that didn't follow the bureaucracy's established, restricted, departmentalized lines of communication. Such networks had to overcome the costs of pushing information around the organization, the costs that made bureaucracies attractive to begin with. In fact, networks have historically had trouble scaling precisely because information has been hard to move around. But by 1968, when Bennis and Slater were writing, information had become much easier to move around: a phone could be put on every desk, allowing people from different parts of the organization to contact each other easily. The technical capability to support networks was there; but in 1968, the organization was only just beginning to support it.

Later, organizations developed or adopted other ways to make communication easy, cheap, and constant across departments: fax machines, message boards, e-mail, instant messaging, social networks, videoconferencing. With each additional channel, organizations could more easily allow contact across individuals, who then begin to engage in mutual adjustment on a massive scale: they could achieve "the coordination of work by the simple process of informal communication" (Mintzberg 1979, p. 3), by staying in frequent informal contact, adjusting to each other's work actions on the fly, allowing them to do the institution's work more quickly.

In fact—and this is key—Bennis and Slater, Mintzberg, Toffler, Waterman, and others saw adhocracies as working only *within organizations*, sitting *on top of* preexisting institutional hierarchies. That is, they were institutional adhocracies. For instance, Waterman talked in great detail about how adhocracies must be pulled together across all parts of a corporation, preferably in a "diagonal slice" across the organizational structure so that the team members represent all departments and hierarchical levels (1993, pp. 37–38). (Think of B's 1990 task force.) Adhocracies, Waterman cautioned, won't work without the backing of upper management: "Adhocracy can flourish only in an environment that discourages bureaucratic excess and *uses the bureaucracy to structure team efforts*" (pp. 97–98; my emphasis; see Heckscher [2007, chap. 1] for a much more thorough discussion of hierarchical versus associational relations). And to cultivate adhocracies, he told his 1990s-era audience, we must resist downsizing and outsourcing: "In the rush to downsize and de-layer, most companies don't have the human resources to make adhocracy work as it should. If you agree that rapid change is here to stay and that team efforts work only when staffed with good people, then it's hard not to conclude that there is such a thing as being too lean and too mean" (Waterman 1993, p. 45).

Companies did get leaner and meaner. They did not resist downsizing and outsourcing; instead, they embraced these changes. But adhocracies didn't disappear. They thrived—in a different form. Let's call these *all-edge adhocracies*.

All-edge adhocracies are adhocracies without the bureaucratic structure. That doesn't mean that bureaucracies disappear—as I discuss in later chapters— but it does mean that all-edge adhocracies become somewhat indifferent to them, routing around them and facilitating different configurations of communication, coordination, and collaboration. All-edge adhocracies differ from institutional adhocracies in key ways:

- *They're interorganizational by nature.* Whereas earlier adhocracies functioned within the organization, all-edge adhocracies function interorganizationally, linking other organizations together—like C's freelance work, which temporarily brought subcontractors to bear on a given agency's project. (In fact, the project may be the only thing that holds them together.)
- *They're interdisciplinary by necessity.* In all-edge adhocracies, the borders among fields, specialties, disciplines, trades, and organizations are porous, allowing disparate people to be linked. And they're linked not in special circumstances, as in B's 1990-era task force, but in normal circumstances, as in C's 2010-era freelancing. They're not the exception but the rule.
- *They're alliances.* People aren't assigned to all-edge adhocracies via a diagonal slice in the organizational chart. They enter into these alliances voluntarily. And as in any alliance, they each pursue their own motivations, values, and ideal outcomes as well as those of the alliance. Those motivations, values, and outcomes might come from their individual situations, from the fields and disciplines to which they are loyal, or from other sources, but they have to reconcile these to some extent as they do the work of the all-edge adhocracy. And they reconcile these the same way that they reconcile other aspects of their work: through constant mutual adjustment.

Why have these all-edge adhocracies thrived in an era of downsizing and outsourcing?

Earlier I said that bureaucracies provided the "operating system" of a hierarchy—the software, the organizational logic, that keeps the hierarchy running and connected. People like Toffler and Waterman saw this operating system breaking down and concluded that it needed an upgraded operating system, one that could crosswire the existing hierarchy, exploiting associa-

tional links (Heckscher 2007) so that it could tackle problems that the bureaucracy couldn't. But the basic architecture on which the operating system
ran—the hierarchy—remained unchanged. As Waterman reckoned it, if the
hierarchy started breaking down (say, by outsourcing and downsizing), the
adhocracy would no longer function.

But in reality, the hierarchy has changed. It hasn't disappeared, as we'll
see in chapter 8. But it's been superseded by a different form of organization. Whereas the bureaucracy was the operating system for the hierarchy,
the adhocracy is the operating system for the network. And as the hierarchy
has broken down, organizations have become more networked, and adhocracies have thrived. They've specifically thrived interorganizationally, linking together temporary networks of organizations—some of which are very
small indeed.

Thomas Malone (2004) called them "e-lancers"; Chris Bilton (1999)
called them "new adhocracies"; Timothy Dolan (2010) saw them moving toward postadhocracies modeled after free-form "smart mobs" (cf. Rheingold
2003). Rainie and Wellman (2012) described them as "permeable." Here, I
call them *all-edge adhocracies*, because they rely on always-on, all-channel
connections among specialists in open networks. Everyone in an all-edge adhocracy is potentially connected to everyone else, at any time, across specialties and divisions. This is what gives an all-edge adhocracy its agility—as well
as its weaknesses, as we'll see.

Let's look at how we got from institutional adhocracies to networked all-
edge adhocracies. Writing in 2001, but echoing a distinction that Toffler made
in his 1980 book *The Third Wave*, Alan Burton-Jones noted a pronounced
shift away from work as growing things (agriculture) or making things
(manufacturing) and toward knowledge about things: "As both goods and
services become more knowledge and information intensive, the distinction
between them is becoming both less apparent and in many cases less relevant.
Knowledge is becoming the defining characteristic of economic activities" (p. 4;
my emphasis). So "*knowledge* is transforming the nature of production and
thus work, jobs, the firm, the market, and every aspect of economic activity"
(pp. 4–5; original emphasis; see also Drucker 1994). Indeed, Burton-Jones
said, "In 1900, less than 18 percent of the total workforce in the USA were
engaged in data- and information-handling tasks. By 1980 it had risen to over
50 percent. . . . On present trends, over 80 percent of the workforce are likely
to be involved in information-handling tasks by 2020, of whom a higher proportion than at present are likely to be engaged in knowledge-building and
decision-making activities" (2001, pp. 8–9). Sounding like Toffler in 1970,
Burton-Jones added that workers are orienting to their own careers rather

than their jobs: industry-wide standardization (e.g., a standard word processing package used by secretaries across all companies) has led to less firm-specific knowledge, resulting in more circulation among jobs. "In effect, careers owned by individuals will progressively replace jobs owned by firms. By the same token, firms are becoming less dependent on the idiosyncratic knowledge of particular workers, when the same/similar knowledge can be obtained more cost effectively, either through automation or on the open market" (p. 20).

Knowledge products—symbolic goods such as data and analysis—are much easier to move around than physical products; and with ubiquitous mobile phone access, inexpensive laptops and software, and plentiful broadband access, much knowledge work can be done anywhere. A graphic designer, for instance, doesn't actually need to be in the same building as the people for whom she provides design work, and she can afford to buy her own tools and infrastructure. Indeed, she doesn't need to be in a specific department in the hierarchy—or in the organization at all. As Timothy Dolan argued, "The administrative core, a key feature to adhocracy, is diminished, often to a single individual and a hard-drive" (2010, p. 44). Indeed, Thomas Malone argued that "technologies allow us to gain the economic benefits of large organizations, like economies of scale and knowledge, without giving up the benefits of small ones, like freedom, creativity, motivation, and flexibility" (2004, p. 4). He asked: "What if . . . many tasks currently done by large companies were done instead by temporary combinations of small companies and independent contractors? Taking this idea further, what if most businesses consisted of only a single person?" (p. 74). He answered the question: "In an e-lance economy, the fundamental unit is not the corporation, but the individual. Tasks are not assigned and controlled through a stable chain of management, but rather are carried out autonomously by independent contractors. These freelancers join together into fluid and temporary networks to produce and sell goods and services. When the job is done—after a day, a month, a year—the network dissolves, and its members become independent agents again, circulating through the economy, seeking the next assignment" (p. 75).

That's a perfect description of C's work—and very similar to the work of the nonemployer firms we'll meet in chapter 3. No wonder an increasing number of organizations, like C's advertising agency, have decided to do just what Waterman feared: outsource noncore functions to the flexhire market, the mediated services market, the dependent contractors market, and the independent contractors market (Burton-Jones 2001, p. 58). And no wonder the nature of employment contracts is changing from relational to transactional contracting: contracting driven by output-based performance, focused on results rather than time, and independent of location (p. 52). If you contract out your firm's graphic design work, who cares if your contractor works in pajamas, sleeps in late and works until 2:00 a.m., and lives in Bangalore or Boston—as long as she performs her work competently and on deadline?

Burton-Jones isn't the only one to have noticed this shift away from centralized hierarchies and toward far-flung, changing networks of specialists. Long-term employment trends (e.g., Castells 2003; Malone 2004; Rainie & Wellman 2012; Zuboff & Maxmin 2004) and developments in mobile technology have tended to encourage more work from remote locations, more cooperative work that is not collocated, and more work that is federated rather than permanent. Examples include independent contracting and other forms of contingent labor (Burton-Jones 2001) but also nomadic work (Mark & Su 2010; Su & Mark 2008), distance work and telework (Bradner & Mark 2002; Paretti, McNair & Holloway-Attaway 2007), peer production (Benkler 2006; Mueller 2010), and other forms of distributed work (Spinuzzi 2007). One recent industry report estimates that "the modern contingent labor umbrella encompasses over 22 percent of the average organization's total workforce" (Dwyer 2011, p. 2): that is, 22 percent of the people working for a given organization are not permanent employees. Especially in certain project- and campaign-oriented, limited-engagement sectors, such as web design and development, freelancing and sole proprietorships have thrived; people have gotten used to flexible hours, to working on projects that interest them, to choosing people with whom they would like to collaborate, and to supplying or foraging infrastructure. At the same time, social software has begun to support opt-in collaboration on a broader scale, and workers have increasingly begun using publicly available online services to communicate, coordinate, and cooperate (Divine, Hall, Ferro & Zachry 2011; Ferro, Divine & Zachry 2012), providing a substrate for supporting adhocratic work. At the same time, necessary support for virtual teams has not grown so quickly, with virtual team members reporting difficulties in training, building relationships, developing leadership styles, and making swift decisions (Solomon 2012)

I said a moment ago that whereas the bureaucracy was the operating system for the hierarchy, the adhocracy is the operating system for the network. As I discuss in chapter 8, networks have been around for a long time, but they have often had trouble scaling: information has traditionally been expensive to push around an organization, and thus hierarchies—which set up orderly chains of command and communication—have tended to scale better and less expensively. But as sociologist Manuel Castells pointed out, the twentieth century introduced information and communication technologies that could literally connect anyone in the organization with anyone else: first telephones, then computer-mediated communication such as message boards, and now mobile technologies and social media. In such an environment, Castells said, networks can come into their own: information and communication technologies allow networks to become more flexible and adaptable, to coordinate tasks better and faster, and to manage complexity more easily. "This results in an unprecedented combination of flexibility and task performance, of coordinated decision-making and decentralized execution, of individualized expression and global, horizontal communication, which provide a superior organizational form for human action" (2003, p. 2).

Furthermore, Castells argued that the reorientation to networked organizations creates new relationships, both internal and external. Internally, organizations are acting more like networks, forming the institutional adhocracies that Toffler and others began to see in the late 1960s. But externally, spontaneous, temporary, project-based organizations spring up, swarm projects, then disperse when their work is done. As Castells put it, "What is emerging is not a dot.com economy, but a networked economy with an electronic nervous system" (2003, p. 65).

One example, Castells said, is "e-business": "By using the Internet as a fundamental medium of communication and information-processing, business adopts the network as its organizational form" (2003, p. 66). This transformation "permeates throughout the entire economic system" (p. 66). So "*the network is the enterprise*" because "business practice is performed by *ad hoc* networks" that "have the flexibility and adaptability required by a global economy subjected to relentless technological innovation and stimulated by rapidly changing demand" (p. 67; original emphasis). These networks are created not just to communicate but to outcommunicate. They are adaptive, open-ended, and multiedged, and they are meant to circulate information, which has become the product of the production process (p. 65, 172). And information and communication technologies allow them to scale and to customize processes (p. 76).

Such capabilities do not rest easily within the hierarchies where bureaucracies thrive, "in a traditional, rigid, business environment." Rather, "the e-firm, on-line or off-line, is based on a flat hierarchy, a teamwork system, and open, easy interaction between workers and managers, across departments and between levels of the firm. The network enterprise is enacted by net-workers, using Internet capability, and equipped with their own intellectual capital" (p. 91). And these "net-workers" also tend to be operationally autonomous, particularly in small businesses and consultant-subcontractor networks (p. 92). Like C, "these business entrepreneurs own their means of

production (a computer, a telephone line, a mobile phone, a place somewhere, often at home, their education, their experience, and, the main asset,
their minds)" (p. 92).

In corporations such as the ones Waterman discussed, an adhocracy is
a modification, a tool that managers can use to solve problems that are ill-
suited to the bureaucracy. But in a pure networked organization, there is no
bureaucracy—that is, managers can't fall back on the authority and muscle
of the hierarchy, because it either doesn't exist or is too weak to help. Rather,
these all-edge adhocracies are the way to get things done in networked organizations. They are not add-ons, they are the operating system.

To truly understand all-edge adhocracies, and to see how much they differ
from bureaucracies, let's look a little more deeply at their key organizational
principle: projectification.

Projectification

Projectification is the organizing principle of adhocracies: the organization
of work around project teams oriented to defined projects, as opposed to
departments oriented to narrow functions (the organizing principle of bureaucracies). The adhocracy is organized around a specific, defined project
objective with a specific endpoint. Adhocracies swarm projects, with actors
clustering around the project, working on it until it is completed, then dispersing at the end of the project (cf. Edwards 2005).

Christophe Midler, a management professor, coined the term "projectification" in a 1995 paper in which he studied Renault's shift from 1960s functional organization to 1990s project teams. In the 1960s, he says, Renault "was
divided . . . into powerful compartmentalized and skill-based departments:
engineering design, methods, production and so forth. No direct link existed
between the operational divisions" (p. 364). But by the late 1980s, Renault had
largely reoriented its work around projects, creating dense pathways for horizontal communication across parts of its hierarchy so that cross-functional
teams could communicate, coordinate, and cooperate on specific projects.

Writing in 2004, economic geographer Gernot Grabher noted that although projects have long served as an organizing principle in certain industries (such as ship building), projectification has recently spread across
a range of industries that were traditionally organized by function. For this
to happen, he said, networks were key: "Projects, in fact, hinge on a dense
fabric of lasting ties and networks that provide key resources of expertise,
reputation and legitimization." Furthermore, "the practice of temporary

and episodic collaboration, phrased differently, relies on an intricate *project ecology* . . . of enduring ties and institutions." He added, "The notion of the project ecology, in other words, signifies not just a passive institutional environment but denotes the networks and institutions that constitute integral ingredients in the practice of temporary collaboration" (2004, p. 104; original emphasis). That is, shifting from functions to projects entails shifting (at least in part) from hierarchies to networks. As management professor Charles Heckscher later argued, shifting to a project focus can support adaptive collaboration, focusing resources such as knowledge around focused problems; such organizations "reduce hierarchy considerably and emphasize project teams generated around opportunities. Size is not so important because this strategic approach narrows the focus to a small number of 'core competencies'" (Heckscher 2007, p. 63).

Building on Midler's and Grabher's work, education professor David Guile argued in 2012 that projectification in interprofessional work involves a lot of boundary crossing between professions, and thus a lot of recontextualization: if people of different professions hope to work together, they must become good at explaining their professions' rules, tools, and assumptions to each other, "making their implicit reasoning explicit" (p. 94; see also Guile 2010; Tuomi-Gröhn & Engeström 2003). Without this essential boundary crossing, projectification doesn't work.

But projectification in all-edge adhocracies comes at a cost. In particular, because all-edge adhocracies are geared to be nimble and reactive, coalescing around a temporary project, they tend to be weak at strategy (Dolan 2010). Power over strategy making is diffused in an adhocracy, tending to form implicitly via reactive decisions (p. 621) and tending to be regarded as "disposable" (p. 623). With this in mind, let's revisit the characteristics of all-edge adhocracies.

The Characteristics of All-Edge Adhocracies

Earlier, we looked at the characteristics that Bennis and Slater listed for adhocracies. But as we've seen, Bennis and Slater, Toffler, and Waterman were all describing institutional adhocracies that overlay existing bureaucracies in hierarchies. As organizations shift from hierarchies to networks, work becomes more projectified and the new all-edge adhocracies become less anchored to legacy hierarchies.

Now let's look at what these changes do to the key characteristics of all-edge adhocracies:

- *A weak division of labor.* Institutional adhocracies (such as B's task force) allowed institutions to cut across silos and hierarchical levels: the institutions could organize some of their work around a project instead. But in networks, all-edge adhocracies don't crosswire existing silos and levels; rather, they are project-oriented, connecting people in a relatively flat organizational structure. For instance, if you contract C to build your website, C isn't in your hierarchy, doesn't belong to one of your departments, and doesn't answer to you for anything outside the project. Similarly, if C subcontracts people to help her with the project, she only directs their labor for this particular project; next time they might subcontract her. The project doesn't serve as an alternate organizing principle; it's the main or only organizing principle. The project may be the only thing that keeps the all-edge adhocracy together.

- *Teams of specialists crossing boundaries.* We've seen that in an institutional hierarchy, an adhocracy involves assembling cross-functional teams around each unique project. In a networked environment, this tendency goes further. Here, the teams are customized for each project, staying together only for the duration of the project—if even for that long. In fact, each team can change in composition and size during different phases of the project. These factors make the project team agile, flexible, reconfigurable, and mobile. Of necessity, specialists are not only expert in their own specialty, they learn to cross boundaries among specialties, fields, and organizations; across these boundaries, they must interpret clients' (or contractors') requests and apply these requests to their own specializations. This constant border crossing makes them innovative. As Guile (2010) said, these specialists become expert in reinterpreting their work for others and vice versa. This boundary-crossing skill becomes a key part of their work. The adhocracy becomes all edge, with each member potentially in contact with others across what are increasingly porous organizational boundaries.

- *Rotating leadership.* As we've seen, since team members are specialists in different things, their specialties often come to the forefront at different stages of the project; each might thus become the de facto leader. (For instance, C's subcontractors might subcontract her next week.) In an institutional hierarchy, this flat organization has to be constructed and nurtured, as Waterman cautions. But in a network, there's no other way. The team comes together to attack the project, not because they are assigned but because they are allied—voluntarily joined in an alliance of different specialists with their own motivations, expectations, home organizations, and values. And the allied specialists have to direct their own efforts because no one else has the expertise to direct them. This arrangement means that they must coordinate by mutual adjustment rather than by fixed rules and procedures, leading to far more communication among members (cf. Mintzberg 1979, pp. 206, 463), but new information technologies keep the cost of this constant communication low (Beniger 1989; Malone 2004). Leadership takes new forms, including initiating, scheduling, and integrating (Yoo & Alavi 2004).

- *Command, not control.* In an institutional adhocracy, leaders can command but not control; they can tell the other specialists what they want to achieve, but not how to achieve it. Control is decentralized. In an all-edge adhocracy based on a network, again, there's no other way. In fact, as we'll see in chapter 3, any given team member tends to have very limited authority or leverage over the other members of the team. For the most part, then, the team members are autonomous, able to exercise their own freedom, flexibility, and creativity as long as they can produce results (Castells 1997). As Malone (2004, p. 129) put it, they no longer respond to command-and-control; they respond to coordinate-and-cultivate.

These changes mean that adhocracies are more flexible than bureaucracies, more able to attack unique projects, and more innovative (Cameron and Quinn 2011; Mintzberg 1979). They allow members to communicate anytime, anywhere, across organizations; to coordinate rapidly, in ad hoc configurations, via mutual adjustment; and to collaborate via projectification. But let's not praise all-edge adhocracies too fulsomely. They have their own limitations, their own growing pains, and their own struggles. In the next chapter, we'll see adhocracies at work and get to know some of their strengths and weaknesses.

Stage Management: The Case of Nonemployer Firms

In chapter 2, we saw how three fictional people—A, B, and C—worked in a 1970 bureaucracy, a 1990 institutional adhocracy, and a 2010 all-edge adhocracy. But we only got a general idea of how C communicated, coordinated, and collaborated in her all-edge adhocracy. In this chapter, I use actual examples from actual people working in subcontractor networks, described in two studies that I conducted in 2007–2008 and 2010.

In 2007, I visited a graphic design partnership in Austin, Texas. The two principals and an intern were working on their laptops at a kitchen table. One principal—Bob, the one who owned the condo in which they were working—read an e-mail from a web developer whom the partnership had subcontracted. "Alan Adams emerges from the depths," he announced. "He doesn't want to meet with me. 'Do you think it will take more than a phone call?'" Around the table, eyes rolled. Later, Bob delivered his frank assessment: this subcontractor is a "douche bag." The other principal, Tom, added: "He will only talk to you over speakerphone," and later opined that "all web developers are douche bags."

A few miles away, Sophie was the principal of a sole proprietorship, also in graphic design, also working out of her home. She had worked for years at a publisher before striking off on her own. When I asked her how she handled poorly performing subcontractors, she explained that it was much easier than handling them in a formal organization: "It's a lot easier to do that working with a freelancer. 'Cause you can just say, 'Yep, we're wrapping this up [early], just send me your files and [bill me for the work completed].' You don't even have to tell them why." In contrast, as a manager, she had felt less

This chapter is based on Spinuzzi (2014). All names are pseudonyms.

empowered: "There's a process, you have to see people the next day, they sulk, they think you are supposed to be their cruise director." As a sole proprietor employing subcontractors, she is far more autonomous than she was in her old job, and that means that she can more easily maintain the friendships that bind her and her subcontractors—even when they have not served her well in a particular engagement.

Bob, Tom, and Sophie have all worked in larger, more permanent, more hierarchical organizations. But for various reasons, they have decided to form their own nonemployer firms; now they do project-oriented contract work for larger organizations. Most of their projects are one-off rather than continuing relationships, and they work several projects at the same time.

In fact, 2007 was a good year to do project-based work, since companies were (and are) tending to contract out noncore functions. That means that these companies cannot handle certain projects in-house; in the case of graphic design, such projects include logos and identity systems, website design, publication design, brochure design—all of which involve work that cuts across specialties (e.g., graphic design, copyediting, photography and photo editing, web development, printing). This work gets contracted out to nonemployer firms such as the ones that Bob, Tom, and Sophie own.

And that's the way they like it. Sophie, who started her own nonemployer firm because she wanted to spend more time with her son, wanted more time flexibility. Bob and Tom, who were (at the time) unmarried and childless, were more interested in the freedom to select projects that were interesting to them and that would allow them to be creative. And all of them wanted to be able to choose whether or not to work with a given client.

But nonemployer firms have a built-in limitation. They do not retain enough capacity or expertise to tackle each contract: as specialists, graphic designers typically don't handle the copywriting, illustration, photo retouching, and web development work involved in their contracts. So these businesses draw on specialists whom they know from past engagements in order to assemble small, light, transient organizations for each contracted project (and in other projects, those specialists may subcontract them in turn). That is, they build all-edge adhocracies for each project. These adhocracies form, swarm the project, then disperse when the project is complete.

As we saw in the last chapter, these all-edge adhocracies share several characteristics. They are project-oriented, forming around a given project and dispersing at the end of it. Because they are built around each project, they are agile, including only the people who can move the project forward. Those people are specialists, so control over the project is decentralized, and thus each subcontractor can be innovative in how she or he pursues each specialized piece of the project. Since no one is a permanent employee, everyone is autonomous rather than completely dependent on others in the adhocracy; the adhocracy is allied, made up of people who agree to work with each other, rather than people who work together because they occupy the same part of a hierarchy. In fact, today's contractor might be tomorrow's subcontractor.

Such organizational networks are not entirely new: this is how movies are made and houses are built. But they have now spread to knowledge work, such as graphic design, copywriting, web design and programming, and other pursuits that can now be accomplished with a laptop, broadband connection, and mobile phone. And that means a basic, qualitative change in how knowledge work can be organized. In the 1990s, Sophie would have needed access to large and expensive physical infrastructure to do her work; in the early twenty-first century, she can do her work in a home office, and Bob and Tom can pursue their partnership around the kitchen table in Bob's condo. They control their own time, select their own projects, and choose their own subcontractors—subcontractors who don't even need to be in the same country.

But here's the thing. Even though their all-edge qualities are what give these nonemployer firms their competitive advantages and strengths, these qualities aren't part of the front they want to present to clients. To understand why, let's take a little detour and talk about simulated wood.

Simulated Wood and Nonemployer Firms

In the 1930s and 1940s, it was common for the sides of automobiles to be made partly of wood. These "woodies" were popular, but wood turned out not to be a very good material for constructing automobiles: it's not durable, it's not as strong or light as materials such as steel, and—to put it mildly—wood doesn't crumple well under impact. So by the mid-1950s, genuine "woodies" were no longer being produced.

But "woodies" still caught the public's imagination. So in the mid-1960s, Chevrolet and Dodge came out with simulated wood grain siding and other manufacturers soon followed suit. The siding was sometimes textured vinyl, sometimes just a film appliqué.

Simulated wood grain was a transitional marker. It wasn't meant to fool us. (How could it? It obviously wasn't real wood.) Instead, it was meant to reassure us that an automobile belonged to a certain class and maintained a certain level of quality. Ironically, simulated wood grain actually covered a material far superior to the wood it represented.

Just as automobiles used simulated wood grain to reassure buyers without fooling them, nonemployer firms often set up an appearance—a "front stage," if you will (Goffman 1959)—that makes them look like larger, more stable firms. This appearance is transitional, reassuring clients that the nonemployer firm will behave in familiar ways, but not deceiving the clients into thinking that these firms are larger. In fact, this veneer hides the fact that in some ways, these all-edge organizations are superior to the ones they mimic: faster, more agile, with less overhead, and more able to leverage specialists.

Despite these advantages, these nonemployer firms face two challenges that larger companies don't—two challenges that are two sides of the same coin. One, they have to *assemble the right team* for each project, and since those team members are temporary subcontractors, nonemployer firms have very little leverage over them. And two, they have to *stage-manage those subcontractors*; to gain the trust of employers, nonemployer firms must make the temporary, project-bound adhocracies appear to be larger, more stable organizations. That is, when a company hires Sophie's firm for two projects, they expect Sophie's firm to be the same in both projects. And it won't be. To better understand the challenges, let's look a little more deeply at nonemployer firms: how they act and how they've multiplied in the last several years.

Background: What Is a Nonemployer Firm?

Imagine that you represent a company that needs a new identity system (logo, business cards, letterhead, website design, etc.). You go to an advertising and design agency, where you meet the project lead and her team. Together, you and the team discuss your needs, then the team puts together a timeline and writes up an agreement. Throughout, the design team strives to appear professional: unified, competent, imaginative, trustworthy, and able to execute your project within the parameters to which you've agreed. Their office is the front stage for this performance. And their fate is bound up with their performance: as full-time employees, these performers know that if they don't get your business, they may lose their jobs.

But as we've seen, services, such as design and advertising, that once required considerable overhead, no longer do; work that once required a studio full of equipment can now be done with laptops and mobile phones. That fact has affected how teams work. For instance, many design agencies are now actually nonemployer firms (NEFs) like Sophie's or Bob and Tom's: self-employed individuals or small partnerships whose firm has no paid employees, has business receipts over $1,000, and is subject to federal income taxes (US Small Business Administration Office of Advocacy 2011). NEFs typically take on a client, then enlist a temporary network of subcontractors to handle parts of the client's job. These subcontractors could be anywhere—in town or across the globe—and they may not have even met the person running the NEF. Just as importantly, unlike traditional employees, these subcontractors work in multiple networks and have multiple income streams. And that means that if they don't perform well, at worst, they may lose one of these many streams of income. Their fate is not necessarily bound up in their performance for any one contractor, and that fact gives them considerable autonomy.

As you can imagine, NEFs have tremendous advantages over traditional hierarchies, and these advantages help to explain the recent remarkable growth of NEFs. But at the same time they face unique challenges, challenges that they are still feeling their way through.

First, let's look at their growth. Then we'll see how NEFs wrestle with problems that never occurred to people like Alvin Toffler and Robert Waterman—and we'll see how they meet those challenges.

The Growth of Nonemployer Firms

We've seen strong growth in NEFs, thanks in part to the long-term employment trends and developments in mobile technology that I discussed in chapter 2. These developments have led to more work from remote locations, more distance collaboration, more independent contracting and other forms of contingent labor, more peer production, and in general, more work that is organized around temporary projects (or projectification, as we saw in chapter 2).

These employment trends favor the growth of nonemployer firms. Consequently, NEFs have increased in the United States, especially in Austin, where I conducted my studies. For instance, in 2002–2008, the number of these firms increased by 21 percent in the United States—and by 41 percent in the Austin–Round Rock Metropolitan Area. In the information sector, which includes "(a) producing and distributing information and cultural products, (b) providing the means to transmit or distribute these products as well as data or communications, and (c) processing data" (US Census Bureau 2011a), NEFs have grown remarkably in number (64 percent in the Austin–Round Rock Metropolitan Area versus 32 percent in the United States) and in receipts (105 percent in the Austin–Round Rock Metropolitan Area versus 46 percent in the United States; US Census Bureau 2011b). These changes all far outpace the population change in the Austin–Round Rock Metropolitan Area (22.2 percent) and the United States (5.8 percent) during the same period (US Census Bureau 2011c). And despite the economic difficulties that began in late 2008, Austin led the nation in small-business growth in 2008–2009 with a 0.43 percent growth rate: it was one of only three major markets in the United States to add small businesses during that time (*Austin Business Journal* 2011). In 2013, Austin was named the friendliest city for small business (*Austin Business Journal* 2013).

Beyond the employment trends, other factors have been favorable to NEF growth. For instance, consumer-level information and communication technologies have both improved and dropped in price; thus, work that once required a desktop computer and a fixed-line telephone—such as graphic design or technical writing—can now be accomplished with less expensive, more mobile technologies such as laptops, mobile phones, and consumer-grade wireless broadband (cf. Mettler & Williams 2013). And since these technologies are mobile, NEFs can avoid the overhead of a leased office or studio by working out of home offices, coffee shops, coworking spaces (see chapter 5), or other low-cost spaces. Another factor is that professionals have found strong motivations to strike out on their own, such as autonomy and the ability to work flexible hours. These characteristics distinguish this sort of work from more traditional forms of contracting, such as builder contracting or movie making (cf. Zuboff & Maxmin 2004).

But to flourish, as we've seen, NEFs must take on jobs that are sometimes too large or too complex for one person or partnership to handle. To do this, NEFs must assemble networks of subcontractors to which they subcontract for capacity (i.e., to offload work they do not have time to do) and for skill (i.e., to perform work outside their expertise). (Grabher [2004] calls these "project ecologies.") To take on and execute jobs reliably, they must have access to a large enough network of subcontractors. When an NEF considers taking on a job, the first question it must answer is, can I find reliable people in these specialties whom I can trust to perform quality work within this time frame and budget? How do NEFs stage-manage this work?

The Nonemployer Firms

To find out, I conducted in-depth interviews with seven nonemployer firms in Austin, examined their web and social media presence, and observed two of them at work (see appendix). Before we get to the interviews, let's see how they presented themselves to clients via their websites. We've already met two:

- Sophie, who described herself as the principal of a studio specializing in web and graphic design; and
- Bob and Tom, who described themselves as co-owners of a creative agency.

In addition, I interviewed

- Albert, who described himself as president of an agency specializing in digital services;
- Benny, who described himself as president / creative director of a service specializing in content management systems and social media;
- Cory, who described himself as owner and designer of a company specializing in web and graphic design;
- Denise, who described herself as owner of a company specializing in technical writing and copywriting; and
- Ed, who described himself as a web developer, consultant, and strategist in a consultancy focused on web development.

Titles such as *president, owner,* and *creative director* may seem to indicate that these firms are larger than they are, and in fact some of these firms' websites strongly implied that the firms included other people. But in fact these firms were all nonemployer firms, with no permanent employees, just a rotating cast of subcontractors.

Think of these firms in terms of a theater performance (Goffman 1959). They actively constructed a front stage for their audience (clients) so they could attract projects. Once they identified a potential project, they held a casting call to find the right subcontractors, subcontractors who could not just do the work but also sustain the performance of a larger firm. When they got the project, they had to coordinate backstage with the subcontractors to make sure that the performance went off well. Like an actual theater performance, the performances of these NEFs were tricky. How did they pull them off?

The Front Stage: How Do NEFs Represent Themselves to Clients?

I really am representing [subcontractors' work] as my own work to the client. Because it's more seamless. I mean, not like it's a lie because I am very responsible for the work. So there's no blaming the freelancer anymore.

SOPHIE

Sophie was in business by herself, running her graphic design firm from her home office. But her website and collateral materials repeatedly used "we" to describe her business. Like the other NEFs, Sophie reported that she had to construct and maintain a particular representation for her firm: one that allowed it to project the capacity and skill of a larger firm, and therefore engender the trust of clients. To do that, Sophie chose to represent subcontactors' work as coming from her firm—and consequently, her firm took both the praise and the blame for their work.

Sophie isn't trying to fool her clients, any more than people were fooled by the simulated wood grain paneling on the 1966 Chevrolet Caprice. (They might not even think about it.) But most of the time she was able to present a reassuring front stage of enduring stability for her firm, a front stage that hid the complex, ever-changing all-edge adhocracies that she had to coordinate for each job. Here's how she and others maintained that front stage.

PRESIDENT OF A ONE-PERSON FIRM: PRESENTING COLLATERAL MATERIALS

All of the NEFs promoted themselves on their websites and social networking sites—especially LinkedIn—not as individuals, but as firms. For instance, the NEFs' professional titles suggested that they headed larger organizations: "principal" (Sophie), "president" (Albert, Benny), and "owner" (Bob and Tom, Cory, Denise). Of the NEFs, only Ed presented himself as an individual agent on his LinkedIn page. But even Ed used "we" on his company's website and stated that "we are a team." In addition, the NEFs' websites—even Ed's—never stated how large their firms were. In fact, Cory's original website listed two employees; when I asked him about this, he confessed that they were a regular subcontractor and an intern, and that he had added them "to look a little more professional, I guess, so I'm not the only one on the site." Similarly, Ed's site stated that he "works with" two others.

NO MEETINGS AT THE DINING ROOM TABLE: TAILORING CLIENT INTERACTIONS

The NEFs also tended to tailor their interactions with clients to engender trust and to cultivate a professional persona. For instance, at one point Sophie told a client on the phone that she could not meet that afternoon because she had a conflicting meeting; later, she confessed to me that the "meeting" actually entailed taking her preschooler to the library. Sophie also avoided meeting clients in her home office. But she did meet often with clients at their own offices, using a range of techniques for trust building in meetings, including choosing a seat near the head of the table and taking notes even when they were not necessary. Similarly, Bob and Tom avoided meeting clients in their office, which was in the dining room of Bob's condo.

These graphic designers frequently conducted face-to-face meetings with clients, a vital strategy since they focused on local work. But the other NEFs didn't necessarily do this. They were involved in aspects of web design, and their clients were sometimes local (e.g., Denise, Ed), often regional (e.g., Al-

bert, Benny, Cory), and sometimes out-of-state (e.g., Ed). Although these
NEFs told me that they did sometimes conduct face-to-face meetings for local work, for much local and regional work and all out-of-state work, they relied on conference calls and e-mail with clients. In fact, Cory reported that for
about one-third of his engagements, he never even met clients; for the other
two-thirds, he held initial and concluding meetings with clients but rarely
saw them otherwise. Consequently, these nonemployer firms relied mostly
on other ways to represent themselves: websites, LinkedIn profiles, e-mails,
and conference calls.

Sometimes the NEFs had to let their subcontractors interact directly with
clients—but even then, they heavily stage-managed the interactions. For instance, when Bob and Tom trusted a subcontractor to interact properly with
clients, they would give that subcontractor an e-mail address strictly for those
interactions—an e-mail address from their firm's Internet domain. Albert
reported that when he worked with one trusted local designer, he would allow
that designer to take part in conference calls and make promises to the client
within a particular set of parameters. Benny also allowed subcontractors on
conference calls, though reluctantly and only when their expertise exceeded
his. Cory had his subcontractors relay questions through him rather than
allowing them direct access to clients. Sophie typically did not discuss subcontractors at all, but when she was preparing for a vacation, she transpar-
ently connected her client to a trusted subcontractor. And Albert and Bob
and Tom reported allowing subcontractors to interact with clients through a
project management system.

NO BLAMING THE FREELANCER:
STAGE-MANAGING MISTAKES

Since the NEFs chose to represent themselves as firms rather than individuals, they had to stage-manage failure. That is, they had to absorb the blame
for mistakes the subcontractors made—since blaming subcontractors would
mean letting clients see the back stage, undermining their self-representation
as firms. As Sophie put it, there's "no blaming the freelancer." Indeed, Sophie,
Benny, Cory, and Ed all told me stories about having to cover for subcontractors' mistakes and failings. In Benny's case, he had hired one subcontractor
who made a "bonehead" mistake—promising functionality that turned out
to be too immature to deploy on the customer's website—forcing Benny to
"go back to the client and beg for forgiveness and hope that I'm not going
to get sued." In Ed's case, he hired a friend, only to find that the friend made
an unreliable partner: "I can't ever afford to let that happen to me again. I

had two clients that were pissed off about this guy. I had two clients that fired me because of this guy, because of his inability to deliver. They were very unhappy clients, and I have never had unhappy clients before. So it was not a mistake I would want to repeat."

But the NEFs told me that they didn't have much leverage over poorly performing subcontractors during a project. After all, these subcontractors weren't employees, and they had other contracts as well. So if the subs didn't perform well, all the NEF could do was refuse to pay them. And that wasn't much of a threat, since these subs had multiple income streams due to the nature of their work—and that meant that the NEF could threaten only a small part of their income. On the other hand, this arrangement made the NEF's team much more flexible. As Sophie explained, she could drop (not fire) a subcontractor without explanation or warning, instantly reconfiguring the all-edge adhocracy—a degree of flexibility that she valued in comparison to the more formal firing process she had had to follow when working in a bureaucratic hierarchy.

So these NEFs pulled together all-edge adhocracies for each project, organizations that changed composition even during the project. But they still managed to project a unified front stage. We've seen some of the ways they presented this performance. Every stage production has actors. Where did they find the right actors for this performance?

The Casting Call: How do NEFs Find the Right Subcontractors for Their Performance?

[I met one copywriter] at a seminar. And just happened, when she contacted me, I was like, "Hey, I do need a copywriter." The second one, who I've used a number of times, is a copywriter that's actually in my networking group.
ALBERT

It's really because everything is so trust- and relationship-based in this business. I can't just say "You're a bonehead. You just screwed me."
BENNY

In chapter 2, we saw how Robert Waterman described how to pull together adhocracies across hieararchies: A manager draws a diagonal slice across the organizational chart, pulls the indicated workers into a cross-functional team, incentivizes them via bonuses, and gives them hierarchical support so that they have the resources and latitude to accomplish their project. At the end of the engagement, they go back to their own departments. Oh, and if they don't pull their own weight, the manager can demote or fire them.

But, as Sophie explained to me, she didn't fire subcontractors. They were not employees, they were allies who had chosen to work with her in a tempo-rary, cross-organizational team. In fact, the NEF had very little control over them—as Benny noted—and just as Sophie could drop them, they could drop Sophie by prioritizing other projects or simply abandoning hers. Where could Sophie and the other NEFs find allies that they could trust? What lever-age did Sophie have over these allies, since she couldn't threaten to fire them and she knew she would have to take the blame if they dropped the ball? Here, the flexibility of all-edge adhocracies becomes a double-edged sword—as we see in other studies of virtual teams (Bullock & Klein 2011; Solomon 2012). Let's see how Sophie and the other NEFs handled it.

WHERE NEFS FIND SUBCONTRACTORS

Manuel Castells (1997) argues that the network society is characterized by the "flexibility and instability of work, and the individualization of labor" (p. 1; see also Castells 2009). NEFs and their subcontractors have traded stability for flexibility and autonomy (Castells & Cardoso 2006). For instance, Sophie reported that she started her NEF so she could have the flexibility to spend time with her family, while Albert relished being his own boss. But the result-ing instability means that NEFs must pull together ad hoc teams-for-today, almost like a pickup basketball game.

Every game has tactics. So what tactics do NEFs use to pull together to-day's team, today's all-edge adhocracy? The NEFs I interviewed mentioned four tactics for finding subcontractors: networking, affinities, referrals, and market solutions.

Tactic 1: Networking   Like Albert, most of the NEFs mentioned using pro-fessional contacts that they developed through networking groups, jellies (in-formal coworking sessions), special interest groups, previous engagements, and previous coworkers. They especially used this strategy for locally based work that involved local nuances.

For instance, Sophie and Bob and Tom all discussed subcontracting out to people with whom they had worked previously (at a publisher and an adver-tising firm, respectively). Albert, Benny, Denise, and Ed all said that they had subcontracted people they had met via professional networking opportuni-ties. These sorts of opportunities allowed the NEFs to prescreen subcontrac-tors by getting a sense of how they worked with others in the network. As Denise put it, she looked for "people who [at least share a] referral network and we've kind of shared clients with each other."

Tactic 2: Affinities   Beyond professional networking, some NEFs reported looking to nonprofessional affinities. For instance, Sophie said that she only worked with people she considered friends: "It's hard to just hire somebody out of the blue if you don't really know them and this job's gotta get done, and I mean even if you have a great recommendation, that's a scary thing to do." Sophie's criteria for friendship and subcontractors were similar: "I'm friends with people with whom I share similar values about respectfulness and responsibility. Basically, if I don't like and trust someone enough to come over to my house and hang out with me and my son, I also don't want my design project hanging out with them." (In contrast, Bob and Tom did not consider their subcontractors to be friends; as we saw earlier, Tom described their web developer as a "douche bag.") Ed also reported subcontracting someone whom he had considered trustworthy because of their friendship—although that trust unfortunately turned out to be unfounded.

Friendship was not the only affinity. For instance, Cory reported meeting subcontractors through a Christian organization. One of these subcontractors became a close friend and consequently became Cory's chief subcontractor. Similarly, Benny told me how he met a designer when they were waiting to pick up their children from school.

Tactic 3: Referrals   Albert, Benny, Cory, Denise, and Ed all discussed hiring subcontractors on the basis of referrals. For Albert, Benny, Cory, and Ed, a trusted party's referral was typically enough—although Benny, Cory, and Ed each reported being burned by a subcontractor who did not live up to the reference. Denise was more cautious: "I had someone recommended and I'm going to meet with her soon, in the next few days. See some of her work and maybe look at some client references. Check her out on LinkedIn." Bob, Tom, and Sophie did not mention using referrals.

Tactic 4: Market solutions   Finally, some of the NEFs reported turning to market solutions for finding appropriate subcontractors. For instance, Albert and Ed took advantage of global arbitrage by outsourcing some technical jobs to "the Philippines" (Ed) and "Poland, Pakistan, the Philippines, and St. Louis" (Albert), either directly (Ed) or via the virtual work-team service oDesk (Albert). This trend of micromultinational outsourcing is becoming increasingly common, allowing small businesses to "enter markets with a minimum of bureaucracy and overhead" while retaining their "unparalleled ability to respond promptly to changing market developments, a collaborative DNA that often translates into superior innovation performance and the

lack of the institutional inertia and legacy relationships plaguing larger organizations" (Mettler & Williams 2013, p. 2). Albert added that he typically
used market solutions for technical work, while reserving "creative things
such as graphic design or copywriting" for local contacts "because I feel that
it really helps with the nuances." Multinational collaboration wasn't the only
market solution: Benny reported finding a subcontractor by taking out a
Craigslist ad.

HOW NEFS BUILD TRUST WITH SUBCONTRACTORS

As I said earlier, these NEFs didn't have much leverage over their subcontractors, who have other income streams and often only a temporary relationship
with the NEF. This arrangement, although ideal for quickly forming and dis-
solving teams, also poses problems for team performances. As Tom put it, "I
think that's a lot more difficult with contract labor, because contract laborers
don't necessarily have a vested interest in your company. I mean, they have a
vested interest in doing the best work they can to get paid, but there's not an
investment in the company itself."

Without the traditional recourse available to managers in hierarchies—
threatening to demote or fire workers—the NEFs had to rely on swiftly developing trust. And this was the trust of allies: the NEFs weren't running a
bureaucratic hierarchy, where loyalty was enforceable. They were forming
all-edge adhocracies, where "people may be working on multiple tasks and
initiatives with multiple accountabilities, and they frequently find themselves
in situations where they are pulled in several directions at once"(Adler &
Heckscher 2007, p. 52; cf. Heckscher 2007, p. 95), pulled by different projects,
different loyalties and obligations. In such an environment, the NEFs had to
be able to trust their subcontractors to come through.

So how did the NEFs establish this trust, which was so vital to maintaining their front stage? They discussed several trust-building moves, which
we can organize into five categories: previous engagements or relationships,
background research, agreements, social capital generated during the engagement, and reviews.

Trust building through previous engagements or relationships   First, the
NEFs sought out subcontractors whom they knew from previous engagements
or relationships: previous subcontractors or coworkers, people alongside
whom they had served as subcontractors, friends, and those with whom they
shared a network. As we've seen, these previous engagements and relationships
are one of the main avenues for finding subcontractors in the first place, but

they also serve as a key way to assess and lend trust to subcontractors. That is, the NEFs had to find people and trust people—two sides of the same coin.

Sophie reported that friendship was her key criterion in trusting a subcontractor. After all, she said, "It's hard to just hire somebody out of the blue if you don't really know them and this job's gotta get done . . . even if you have a great recommendation, that's a scary thing to do." Like Sophie, Cory and Ed reported hiring friends—though Ed pointed out that this approach was hardly foolproof: "Trust isn't based on whether I like them or not. . . . The guy was my friend, but I can look back now and see there were warning signs that he might not be a really good worker."

In contrast, Bob and Tom relied more heavily on previous work experience. Most of their subcontractors had been coworkers at the ad agency where they had worked previously. Similarly, Denise said that she considered subcontractors on the basis of previous projects in which she and the subcontractor had both bid and/or worked together: these projects allowed her to assess not only their work but also their interpersonal skills and honor, maturity, and reliability.

When an NEF did not have direct experience with a subcontractor, it would sometimes rely on other relationships. For instance, Denise reported that she would consider "people who [at least share a] referral network and we've kind of shared clients with each other." Albert, Benny, and Ed also described variations of this strategy, considering friends of friends, contacts of contacts, and members of professional societies. This strategy helped them to find reliable, skilled subcontractors, but it also gave them some badly needed leverage: if they hired a subcontractor who underperformed, they could report that fact to the referral network. (More on that in a moment.)

Trust building through background research   For such referrals, some NEFs did additional background research on recommended subcontractors. For instance, Denise planned to check a subcontractor's client references, examine her work, and scrutinize her LinkedIn page. Similarly, Bob and Tom carefully checked the portfolio of each prospective subcontractor.

Trust building through agreements   One way to deal with the lack of leverage in subcontracting might be to have subcontractors sign formal contracts. However, none of the NEFs reported using these with subcontractors (although some signed contracts with customers). The NEFs certainly took on risk by not requiring formal contracts, but they saved time and legal fees, and perhaps more importantly, they were able to put together teams faster and more flexibly. So, instead of formal contracts, the NEFs used what Albert and Benny both characterized as handshake agreements. Handshake agreements were a better fit for the highly agile, constantly changing all-edge adhocracies they had to assemble; but as Benny ruefully added, "A handshake doesn't mean what it used to anymore."

Trust building through social capital during the engagement   Trust is a two-way street. So during the engagement, the NEFs built trust in different ways. For instance, Albert and Benny both made a point of paying subcontractors promptly and sometimes even ahead of schedule. As Albert put it, "I think that by paying people promptly and fairly, then I think that when you ask them to be a little bit more flexible, then they are willing to do that." In some cases, such as when he works with a steady and trusted subcontractor, "then I'll go ahead and pay fifty percent up front, I'll go ahead and pay him 100 percent, because I have a good relationship with him, I know he's not going to jet on me." Because he does this, Albert can occasionally ask this subcontractor to work without an advance when "things are a little lean."

Trust building through reviews   After the engagement, the NEFs used the one form of leverage they had: reviewing the subcontractor. Benny reported that he intended to apply this leverage to a problematic subcontractor: "If anybody asks me, I will give him the bad review. 'But don't hire him, you'll be sorry.' And so, you break your trust, then you deserve what you get." Yet the NEFs did not express confidence that this method of recourse would be successful.

Collaboration was critical, then, and the NEFs' "casting calls" focused on finding the right collaborators. They needed to cast the right people for each performance—that is, create the right configuration of subcontractors for a given project—and sometimes they needed to change the cast during different phases of each project. They needed to rotate their cast from a pool of voluntary subcontractors. And thus they needed to establish swift trust for each project. This is, to put it mildly, a very different situation from that of a bureaucratic hierarchy, in which people are placed by a manager into long-term functional teams or short-term cross-functional teams. But to achieve the collaboration, they had to also execute. And that brings us to the next issue.

The Back St'age: How Do Nonemployer Firms Coordinate the Performance?

So if somebody said, "Well we need a website, but we also really need a logo because our old logo is crap. . . . And we don't have anyone to write content for this website so can you do that." So I would . . . reach out to my copywriter, my designer, and my developer, and say, "OK guys, here's the project." And we would all sit down together, generally over Skype or something like that, and go through the project and all the items and figure out from each person. OK. My portion is this and it's going to take me these many hours to do it, and I'll throw it all out on a spreadsheet basically. OK, here is this person's column, here is this person's column. . . . Here's their hourly rate at the bottom. And I can show you all of this if you want to see it.

BENNY

Once they pulled together their all-edge adhocracies as a trusted alliance, the NEFs had to coordinate that alliance behind the scenes. And there's a lot of coordination in all-edge adhocracies: As we saw in chapter 2, adhocracies coordinate via mutual adjustment—and mutual adjustment becomes even more critical in all-edge adhocracies, which are temporary and interorganizational, and which involve coordinating both front and back stages. So the NEFs found that they had to coordinate very frequently, as Benny indicated above. And that coordination had to enable their backstage work while avoiding interference with the front stage.

Traditionally, mutual adjustment can be expensive, not just in terms of infrastructure, but also in terms of time: each worker has to send and process more messages than she might in a hierarchical bureaucracy. But for these NEFs, the infrastructure is cheap—Skype is free, for instance—and time is, if not more plentiful, at least more flexible for them. So they could feasibly coordinate their subcontractors. Of course, they had to, since poor coordination could badly disrupt the team's performance. As Cory lamented about one subcontractor, "It was supposed to be like four hours . . . and it took him like two to three months." Ed similarly told me that one subcontractor "overcommitted himself because he wasn't just doing my work; he had other work he was doing. And he couldn't get all the work done. So, he would let projects slide." One subcontractor could hold up an entire project. To avoid that problem, the NEFs turned to two ways to mutually adjust: coordinative texts and backstage meetings.

COORDINATIVE TEXTS: GETTING
EVERYONE ON THE SAME PAGE

As the face of the organization—and the one with the most to lose—the NEF had to coordinate the team's work. As Albert put it, "It's my job . . . to send them out to the subcontractors, to hire the right people, to make sure that the graphic designer is aware of the schedule, of the timeline. Make sure that he knows that, hey, we are going to have a conference call on this date."

The NEFs used many texts to coordinate their teams, including project management software; spreadsheets, forms, and notes; and e-mails and instant messages. These constellations of textual technologies tended to be pulled together ad hoc, like the subcontractor networks themselves (cf. Rossitto, Bogdan & Severinson-Eklundh 2013).

Coordinating through project management software   Many NEFs coordinated their all-edge adhocracies with project management software. For instance, Albert and Bob and Tom used Basecamp, while Denise used Privia, which was specialized proposal management software for bids and proposals. Bob and Tom also used OmniFocus for tracking tasks. As Albert explained, project management software served as a way to communicate the project's parameters without micromanaging the subcontractors—and it doubled as a communication medium. Similarly, Bob and Tom sometimes brought clients into their Basecamp project so that the clients could see their firm's progress.

Coordinating through spreadsheets, printed forms, and notes   The other NEFs coordinated via other texts. For instance, Benny used a spreadsheet to plan and coordinate tasks, while Cory used sticky-note software to track basic tasks that his contractors were completing. Finally, Sophie tracked tasks by filling out printed forms.

Coordinating through e-mails and IMs   Beyond communicating with subcontractors, Cory used his e-mail in-box for tracking progress, while Bob and Tom coordinated with their contractors over instant messaging—common coordinative tools for virtual teams (cf. Pazos, Chung & Micari 2012; Solomon 2012, p. 4).

BACKSTAGE MEETINGS: MAKING SURE EVERYONE HAS THE SAME STORY

In addition to texts, and frequently in concert with them, the NEFs often conducted backstage meetings with their subcontractors. In these backstage meetings, the NEFs coordinated work—often in informal ways—but they also took the opportunity to build the relationships and trust that were so vital to the team's performance. These meetings sometimes happened over telecommunications and sometimes in person.

Coordinating through video and phone conversations   The NEFs sometimes made direct phone calls (Albert, Benny, Cory, Sophie, Bob and Tom), conference calls (Benny, Denise), and Skype calls (Benny) to coordinate sub-contractors, especially when the subcontractors were not local. In these conversations, they often focused on how to divide the labor and develop the timeline. For instance, Benny told me that at the beginning of a project, he would assemble his team on Skype, discuss the project, then record the tasks and time estimates on a spreadsheet. The finished document served to coordinate the project and set client expectations.

Coordinating through face-to-face meetings For local subcontractors, the NEFs sometimes held face-to-face meetings (Denise, Ed, Sophie, Bob and Tom). For instance, I once sat in as Sophie met with a subcontractor at her dining room table, where they went over and discussed client documents, then planned tasks and a shared timeline. Sophie also used the meeting to coach her subcontractor extensively on how to present herself to the client—that is, she used the backstage meeting to coordinate the front-stage performance.

As I've discussed, all-edge adhocracies are not embedded in hierarchies; they form across different organizations. And part of what has enabled this shift has been the steadily falling cost of communication, including the NEFs' main tools: laptops, broadband Internet access, mobile phones so inexpensive that even tweens can afford them. Put these together and you get the possibility of a new way to organize work: via all-edge adhocracies, which require frequent, inexpensive communication to coordinate these allied teams. But the organizational adjustments lag the technical ones.

Conclusion: Stage-Managing All-Edge Adhocracies

So what have we learned about all-edge adhocracies in this chapter? Critically, each of the NEFs studied here had to reach three hard-to-achieve objectives, made even harder because of the tensions among them. And they had to achieve these for every project in which they were simultaneously involved—as did their subcontractors.

First, they had to achieve the *project objective*: the job that the NEF had been hired to do, the job that the NEF assembled the specialists in the adhocracy to swarm: the web design, the identity, the document that they were hired to produce. They achieved this work by rapidly assembling and coordinating temporary teams of trusted subcontractors, held together as trusted alliances.

Second, they had to achieve the *front-stage performance*: a performance of unity, stability, and competence, one that hid the decentralization and autonomy that characterized the adhocracy. Like the wood grain paneling in a Chevy Caprice, this front-stage performance was meant to give a new innovation — the all-edge adhocracy — the appearance of the old and familiar. They achieved this front-stage performance, in part, through strategies such as developing professional websites, carefully wording their LinkedIn profiles, and controlling where and when meetings with clients took place.

Third, they had to achieve the *backstage collaboration*: the mutual adjustment that allowed the allies in the adhocracy to work together and remain incentivized. They achieved this collaboration through various avenues, including communication technologies and face-to-face meetings, that let them achieve mutual adjustment throughout each project.

On each front, these all-edge adhocracies took advantage of the lower costs of communication, communicating almost constantly with clients, collaborators, and potential collaborators. This rapid communication, which enables mutual adjustment, is the lifeblood of all-edge adhocracies; it's what makes them viable. And consider that we see remarkable levels of communication even within a single project; but each NEF pursues several opportunities, and pulls together several all-edge adhocracies, simultaneously.

We've caught a glimpse of how NEFs handle each of these challenges. But we can't really understand these challenges until we delve down to the foundations of the all-edge adhocracy: the underlying network.

4

The Foundation of All-Edge Adhocracies: Organizational Networks

In chapter 2, I said that adhocracies are to networks as bureaucracies are to institutions. That is, adhocracies and bureaucracies both sit on top of more fundamental organizational structures—networks and institutions, respectively—and provide an "operating system" or set of rules by which people in those organizational structures communicate, coordinate, and collaborate. As we saw in chapter 3, the set of adhocratic rules in a subcontractor network might differ dramatically from the bureaucratic rules in an institution. And when institutions and networks interface, we see some important adjustments, including the stage management that Sophie, Albert, and the others had to conduct in chapter 3.

Network is an overused term. We're told that we use computer networks; that we engage in networking; that we are socially networked with weak and strong ties; that Al Qaeda is a network. So what *is* a network? And what does it actually mean when we say that all-edge adhocracies operate on top of networks?

In this chapter, I pin down what I mean by *networks* in this book, using examples from the nonemployer firms in chapter 3. This is an important step, since—as I said in chapter 2—organizational networks are the very foundation of all-edge adhocracies. Understanding that foundation is critical for understanding why all-edge adhocracies don't work—or communicate—the way we might expect. As we'll see throughout this chapter, organizational networks (such as the subcontractor networks in chapter 3) possess a flat structure, a changing composition, flexibility, and adaptivity.

Organizational networks have been around for a very long time—in fact, they have been a staple of unconventional warfare (Arquilla 2011)—but they have traditionally not scaled well due to the cost of sharing information. Thus, most organizations have historically used different forms: institutions (as we saw in chapter 2), but also tribes and markets (as we'll see in chapter 8). But with the rise of digital communication technologies, networks have become far more common, and consequently, we are seeing tremendous changes in how people organize and execute their activities.

Organizational Networks May Not Be What You Think

"Network has become a trendy term," Milton Mueller tells us in his book *Networks and States*. But he asks, "When we talk about 'networks' are we talking about technologies, or societal organizations, or both? Or are we simply projecting the latest metaphor into any and every kind of social relationship we can see?" (2010, p. 36.)

It's a fair question, since *network* is used in many different ways and you may have heard it in different contexts. In fact, at least three distinct understandings of the term exist in the social sciences and humanities. These three understandings have developed from distinct traditions, involve distinct concepts and theories, and produce distinct analyses. In this chapter, I focus on organizational networks, but let's clarify the differences between organizational networks the other two sorts of networks: social network analysis and sociotechnical networks.

ORGANIZATIONAL NETWORKS AREN'T SOCIAL NETWORK ANALYSIS

You may have heard of networks in the context of *social network analysis*, especially if you've read popular books by Malcolm Gladwell (2002) or Albert-László Barabási (2003). Social network analysis (SNA) involves exploring direct, explicit connections among human beings, typically communication connections. (Network analysis could be applied to anything; social network analysis specifically takes human beings as nodes.) As the name implies, SNA is a sort of analysis rather than a description of a distinct phenomenon. SNA typically involves quantifying these connections; its data collection tends to focus on quantifiable data such as surveys (Burt 2010; Cross, Parker & Sasson 2003; Granovetter 1973; Small 2009), text analysis (Galbraith 2007; Nardi, Whittaker & Schwarz 2002; Quan-Haase & Wellman 2007), and case studies (Small 2009). SNA excels at finding weak and strong ties (Granovetter 1973; Krackhardt & Hansen 2003); detecting structural holes, or points at which people in a network don't directly connect (Burt 2010); and identifying brokers, people who serve to connect others across these structural holes (Burt 2010).

Notice that SNA does not describe a specific kind of organization. Any set of connections among people can be mapped as a social network. These links tend to be underdefined, often focusing on explicit communication (conversations, phone calls, e-mail) or the strength of relationships. In SNA, institutional hierarchies are considered networks, as are markets. SNA is also not well equipped to examine such connections in terms of rhetoric, argument, or persuasion, such as the stage management that we saw in chapter 3, since its basic analysis is quantitative rather than qualitative and focused on identifying connections rather than evaluating their qualitative impact.

ORGANIZATIONAL NETWORKS AREN'T SOCIOTECHNICAL NETWORKS

You may have also heard of networks in the context of *sociotechnical networks*, especially if you've read books by Bruno Latour (1999, 2013), John Law (1986), or others in science and technology studies (e.g., Callon, Lascoumes & Barthe 2009) or rhetoric (Jeff Rice 2012; Jenny Rice 2012; Spinuzzi 2008). Whereas SNA takes human beings as nodes, sociotechnical networks take other things as nodes as well: artifacts, activities, and beliefs. As the name implies, sociotechnical networks describe social and technical dimensions of a given activity. The implementation varies widely. For instance, in actor-network theory, humans and nonhumans are treated equally as heterogeneous nodes (Latour 1999). In activity theory, humans act (individually or collectively) as agents, mediated by artifacts (Kaptelinin & Nardi 2006); the entire object-oriented activity is the node.

Sociotechnical networks are analytical constructs that can be applied to any sociotechnical system: that is, like SNA, sociotechnical networks are a frame of analysis rather than a distinct phenomenon. But unlike SNA, sociotechnical networks rarely involve quantification. For instance, since anything can be an actor (node) in actor-network theory, no firm principle exists that could unambiguously ground a quantified analysis. Thus studies involving sociotechnical networks tend to involve qualitative data collection methods: observations, interviews, and text analyses that focus on persuasion, interpretation, mediation, and alliances.

Again, sociotechnical networks do not describe a specific kind of organization: Any observable set of connections among humans and nonhumans can be analyzed as a sociotechnical network. That being said, we'll return to the question of sociotechnical networks in chapter 6, relating them to organizational networks to deepen our understanding of the latter.

ORGANIZATIONAL NETWORKS ARE . . .

In contrast to the other sorts of networks I have discussed, organizational networks are phenomena. That is, the network is not a frame of analysis, but rather a distinct organizational form that we can contrast to other organizational forms such as hierarchies, markets, and clans (see chapter 8). Organizational networks are composed differently, they work differently, and they excel at addressing different sorts of problems.

Popular literature has examined organizational networks at work. Beyond Alvin Toffler's many books, we see discussions in books such as Ori Brafman and Rod A. Beckstrom's *The Starfish and the Spider* (2008). Alan Burton-Jones's management book *Knowledge Capitalism* (2001) also examines organizational networks, specifically from the perspective of outsourcing functions. Lee Rainie and Barry Wellman's *Networked* (2012) makes the case that networked individualism is beginning to characterize our dealings at work and elsewhere. And Manuel Castells's *The Internet Galaxy* (2003) applies the notion of the network society to e-firms.

One example that is often discussed is peer production. For instance, a case study in *The Starfish and the Spider* is that of the peer-produced open-source project Linux. Other popular books that discuss peer production include Howard Rheingold's *Smart Mobs* (2003), Clay Shirky's *Here Comes Everybody* (2008) and *Cognitive Surplus* (2011), Don Tapscott and Anthony D. Williams's *Wikinomics* (2006), Rachel Botsman and Roo Rogers's *What's Mine Is Yours* (2011), and Yochai Benkler's *The Penguin and the Leviathan* (2011).

So what are these organizational networks like? In this book, I focus on the four characteristics named at the beginning of this chapter:

- *Flat structure.* Team members in an organization can be connected in various ways. But in an organizational network or a cross-organizational network, they are connected nonhierarchically. That is, in an organizational network, no single node controls the rest of the network. Put simply, there's no permanent "boss," though one member might set the parameters and negotiate the schedule for the project. Since each member of the network has her own specialty, she tends to take the lead when focusing on that specialty, determining the time frame and resources she will need to complete a task. And during their time in the network, team members have to be trustworthy, especially since they have very little leverage over each other. In chapter 3, for instance, the nonemployer firms were able to direct but not control their subcontractors. In fact, they had little leverage over their subcontractors beyond the comparatively weak measures of withholding pay or giving bad reviews. Instead, they often recruited subcontractors with whom they have other trust relationships, such as affinities or friendships—although, as Ed found out, friendship was not always enough to bind a subcontractor network.

- *Changing composition.* Organizational networks tend to change composition frequently, bringing in specialists for particular phases and dropping them once their phase is finished. People circulate in and out of these networks, changing their composition and dynamic. And since networks change composition frequently, often their members are "part-timers," as in chapter 3: working on other projects at the same time. For instance, Sophie reported sometimes cutting a subcontractor out of a project, something that could happen much more easily than in an institutional hierarchy: "You don't even have to tell them why." Similarly, subcontractors could be brought into a project at any point, as Tom told me, if the nonemployer firm ran out of time or resources.

- *Flexibility.* Since organizational networks are often composed of "part-timer" specialists, the people who work in organizational networks tend to value flexibility and freedom over permanence. For instance, in chapter 3, we saw that Sophie wanted to preserve flextime so that she could spend time with her family; Bob and Tom wanted to preserve their freedom to work on the projects they preferred. This flexibility, however, also means instability. The nonemployer firms in chapter 3 were almost like pickup basketball games: contractors rounded out their teams with whichever trusted subcontractors were available. Internal relationships were loosely coupled, while external relationships were fluid. An outsider could easily become an insider—and vice versa.

- *Adaptivity.* Finally, because they are nonhierarchical, change in composition, and are built around flexibility, organizational networks are highly adaptive. If one team member can't complete a task, that member can be replaced with another specialist. If the network faces a new contingency—such as a new need that the client suddenly wants to add to the project—the network can pick up another team member to address that need. Problems might scale and change rapidly, and are often ill-defined, requiring networks to adapt quickly to handle them. For instance, when Benny coordinated his team via Skype and a spreadsheet, their synchronous communication allowed them to quickly and easily parcel out the parts of the project. If one of the team members dropped out, the adhocracy could pull in another with similar skills to finish the job.

These are the characteristics on which all-edge adhocracies are built. But not just them: our whole society is arguably transitioning to a network society (Castells 1996; Rainie & Wellman 2012), which is increasingly based on these characteristics. That means work, but also leisure, family, government, warfare, and on and on. In other words, all-edge adhocracies may be the way we organize much of our work in the future, but they may also be models for how we organize these other domains. (See chapter 8 for a more detailed discussion.) Let's take a deeper look at these characteristics, seeing how they manifested themselves in the subcontractor networks in chapter 3.

Flat Structure

As noted, in contrast to the other sorts of networks I have discussed, organizational networks are phenomena. That is, the network is not a frame of analysis but rather a distinct organizational form, identifiably different from other organizational forms such as hierarchies, markets, and clans (see chapter 8).

Why are networks ascendant at this point? In great part, it is because they can be. As we saw in chapters 2 and 3, for organizational networks to scale and work effectively, they require specialists (such as college-educated graphic designers, web developers, and copywriters) who can communicate quickly and easily (via Internet access and telecommunications), who own or have ready access to the infrastructure to complete their parts of the project quickly (such as laptops), and who can cheaply and quickly share the results of their work (in these cases, by e-mailing or otherwise electronically transporting them). And for those specialists to thrive in networks, they also require enough projects to sustain them and enough connections to find new projects. Organizational networks, as we'll see in chapter 8, have been around for a long time—but it's only recently that they have enjoyed conditions that would allow them to thrive.

Those conditions can be summarized in one term: *knowledge work*. Knowledge work is, simply put, work that involves thinking about, analyzing, and communicating things rather than growing or manufacturing things. It includes occupations such as graphic design, web development, and copywriting. It involves specialist work, it tends to be project oriented, and its products tend to be symbolic (designs, working websites, text) and thus electronically transportable, circulable through information and communication technologies. Knowledge work, in fact, tends to be fast changing and connective—that is, it needs what organizational networks can provide.

Another domain that is rapidly moving toward organizational networks is irregular warfare. As warfare theorist David Ronfeldt argues (2007), organizational networks do not necessarily displace older organizational forms such as hierarchies and markets; rather, they become layered over these other forms (as we'll see in chapter 8). For instance, an organization may retain an institutional structure and bureaucratic lines of authority but also develop organizational networks to flexibly address contingencies that change too rapidly for an institutional bureaucracy to effectively address (see chapter 7).

John Arquilla and David Ronfeldt (1997, p. 26) argue that

> the information revolution, in both its technological and non-technological aspects, sets in motion forces that challenge the design of many institutions. It disrupts and erodes the hierarchies around which institutions are normally designed. It diffuses and redistributes power, often to the benefit of what may be considered weaker, smaller actors. It crosses borders and redraws the boundaries of offices and responsibilities. It expands the spatial and temporal horizons that actors should take into account. And thus it generally compels closed systems to open up. But while this may make life difficult especially for large, bureaucratic, aging institutions, the institutional form per se is not becoming obsolete. Institutions of all types remain essential to the organization of society.

So institutional hierarchies aren't simply going away. We need them for certain things. But in many cases, they aren't the best fit—networks are. As Arquilla and Ronfeldt argue, "While institutions (large ones in particular) are traditionally built around hierarchies and aim to act on their own, multi-organizational networks consist of (often small) organizations or parts of institutions that have linked together to act jointly" (p. 27). And "the information revolution favors the growth of such networks by making it possible for diverse, dispersed actors to communicate, consult, coordinate, and operate together across greater distances and on the basis of more and better information than ever before" (p. 27).

One reason that networks are ascendant as an organizational form for some domains is that these domains (such as warfare) are increasingly reliant on "topsight," or an overall view of the domain space, leading to a deluge of information (see Gelernter 1991; Spinuzzi 2013). In an institutional bureaucracy, this glut of information can result in bottlenecking and information overload. Bureaucratic command-and-control breaks down, but adhocratic consultation-and-coordination can thrive under such circumstances (Arquilla & Ronfeldt 1997, p. 45).

FLAT ORGANIZATION: THE FRONT STAGE AND THE PROJECT

All this should sound familiar. The nonemployer firms (NEFs) in chapter 3 weren't stable teams—they represented individuals who chose to link together in a temporary multiorganizational network. In fact, that was their strength.

Each NEF could maintain low overhead and high flexibility by assembling a custom team for each project. But this strength was also a weakness, since the NEFs believed that they had to camouflage themselves as institutions, hiding the complexity of their subcontractor networks and presenting themselves to clients as a relatively stable team that has the capabilities, skill, and coordination necessary to deliver the client's product on time and with the appropriate specifications. Each firm had to bend its efforts toward meeting two distinct but interrelated objectives: its front-stage performance and the project that the nonemployer firm had been contracted to complete. Figure 4.1 shows how different organizational activities (the hexagons) link to two objectives, which involve different people, practices, and timescales; the box represents the back stage that the NEF applies to its network of subcontractors (figure 4.1).

The front-stage performance   The nonemployer firms were in it for the long term: Sophie, Albert, and the others created stable firms that their clients could rely on, firms that could garner repeat clients and referrals. So the front stage was also long term, lasting beyond a specific project. But behind the front stage, these NEFs organized temporary all-edge adhocracies of subcontractors, adhocracies that swarmed the short-term project. The nonemployer firm thus tended to avoid involving the subcontractors directly in front-stage work—although sometimes a few trusted subcontractors would be asked to help stage the performance when necessary (represented by the dotted arrow in figure 4.1).

The project   At the same time, the nonemployer firms and their subcontractor networks were organized around projects, like any adhocracy. The project gave shape and unity to the network, providing a temporary back stage. This specific and sharply delineated project that each nonemployer firm was hired to solve (the website, the brochure, the magazine redesign) was a second objective, more transient than the first one, lasting only for the duration of the engagement. To complete each project objective, a nonemployer firm had to assemble a network of subcontractors who shared this objective but saw different aspects of it: the copy to be written, the back-end website to be coded, the layout to be designed (cf. Adler 2007; Guile 2012; Yamazumi 2009). As figure 4.1 shows, this objective was mutual to the client, nonemployer firms, and subcontractors; all had a hand in transforming it (even if these parties were not aware of each other).

There's an underlying tension between these two objectives   Whereas a more stable organization maintains its front stage with a more or less permanent

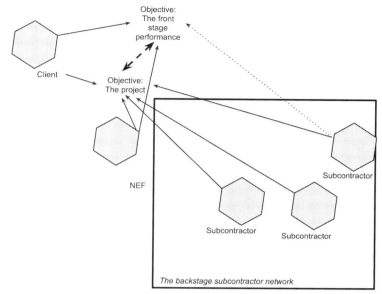

FIGURE 4.1. The front-stage performance versus the project. The network of subcontractors inside the box is "hidden" from the client.

cast, a nonemployer firm's performance is more like a play with a different cast every night, a play in which cast members can ad-lib and in which they have little stake in the success of the director. Each cast member—each subcontractor—has the potential to disrupt the performance. And that potential sometimes becomes actual, as Ed found to his regret when his friend-subcontractor let him down. Furthermore, bear in mind that figure 4.1 is actually an oversimplification, since each firm has multiple clients and thus multiple projects and front stages, all of which are daily threatened with disruption. As we've seen, these tensions are partially due to how mutable the network is. It constantly changes in composition.

The Changing Composition of Organizational Networks

The subcontractor networks in chapter 3 constantly changed in composition, adding and shedding different specialists; the all-edge adhocracy can flex to address different challenges and contingencies at different phases of the project. For instance, Sophie would sometimes drop underperforming subcontractors; Bob and Tom would add subcontractors if they foresaw running out of time or resources.

This flexing is characteristic of organizational networks. Indeed, as Castells argues, the circulation of people drives innovation in the network society (1996, p. 95), which is characterized by the "flexibility and instability of work, and the individualization of labor" (1997, p. 1). In particular, the network society demands more-flexible labor, which takes the form of part-time, temporary, and self-employed work—such as the subcontracting work we saw in chapter 3 (1997, p. 173). Flexible workers give up the stability and assurance of full-time employment, but they gain autonomy, which they pursue "not necessarily to increase monetary gains but to enjoy greater freedom, flex-time, or more opportunity to create" (Castells & Cardoso 2006, p. 10).

This decentralized structure of organizational networks is enabled in part by telecommunications and digital technologies, which have tended to encourage more work from remote locations, more cooperative work that is not collocated, and more work that is federated rather than permanent. In other words, the subcontractor network is built a bit like a mercenary group—or a terrorist cell. In fact, the parallels are strong and not coincidental.

In netwar, command may still be centralized, but operational control is pushed to the edges (e.g., Alberts & Hayes 2003). Such distributed networks tend to outperform hierarchies due to their rapid reaction (Edwards 2005), resilience (Ronfeldt, Arquilla, Fuller & Fuller 1999), ability to reach out to nonstate actors for political pressure (Ronfeldt et al. 1999), and ability to learn rapidly (Robb 2008). Netwar's primary tactic is swarming, "in which the scheme of maneuver involves the convergent attack of . . . semiautonomous (or autonomous) units on a targeted force in some particular place. 'Convergent' implies an attack from most of the points on the compass. . . . Swarming implies a convergent attack by many units as the primary maneuver from the start of the battle or campaign, not the convergent attacks that result as a matter of course when some unit becomes isolated and encircled because of some other maneuver" (Edwards 2005, p. 2).

Although swarming is described here as a battlefield tactic, it can also characterize nonviolent tactics. For instance, in their analysis of the Zapatista social netwar in Mexico, Ronfeldt et al. note that the Zapatistas were able to enroll "a multitude of civil society activists associated with a variety of nongovernmental organizations (NGOs) to 'swarm'—electronically as well as physically—from the United States, Canada, and elsewhere into Mexico City and Chiapas. There, they linked up with Mexican NGOs to voice solidarity with the EZLN's demands and to press for nonviolent change" (1999, p. xi).

What Ronfeldt et al. describe is an organizational network on a grand scale. But in kind, it is very similar to what the nonemployer firms did in chapter 3: they organized communication, coordination, and cooperation among autonomous actors with a temporary mutual orientation toward a shared, specific project. Swarming is projectification.

CHANGING COMPOSITION: THE CASTING CALL

In chapter 3, nonemployer firms reported having very little leverage over their flexible, autonomous subcontractors, all of whom pursue multiple income streams, all of whom may never work with the nonemployer firm again. This arrangement threatened both of the objectives we've seen so far: the front-stage performance and the project.

To protect both of these objectives, the nonemployer firm had to enlist specialists as allies, convincing them to support the firm's objectives. Finding the right specialists was tricky—as we've seen, even friends could let a nonemployer firm down—but they only had to make this arrangement work for the duration of the project (or just a phase of the project). Thus the firms had developed strategies for recruiting and building trust with subcontractors who could support them with yet another objective: collaboration.

As Adler and Heckscher (2007) argue, collaboration (in the broad sense of working together to achieve a goal) is a persistent objective in knowledge-work organizations. Even in these all-edge adhocracies, which have the lifespan of a mayfly, collaboration helped to align the front and back stages (see figure 4.2).

I mentioned earlier that swarming is projectification. In the third objective (the collaboration), projectification requires coordinating the swarm, ideally in a way that will address both the short-term project and the long-term front stage. This projectification requires mutual adjustment, which in turn requires high-volume information transactions for proper coordination—something that we are increasingly seeing in peer-to-peer crisis communications (Monroy-Hernández, Counts, Way & Wa 2013; Oh, Agrawal & Rao 2011; Potts, Seitzinger, Jones & Harrison 2011) as well as business (Dolan 2010).

Unfortunately, these three objectives (collaboration, the front stage, the project) don't always line up. Think of a literal net, made up of strands and knots. What gives the net its shape and strength is how it distributes tension across these strands and knots. And that's the case with organizational networks as well: the tensions among these objectives provide the network with its shape and—ideally—its coherence. As we'll see in chapter 6, these tensions can produce innovations, but they also produce disruptions and instabilities.

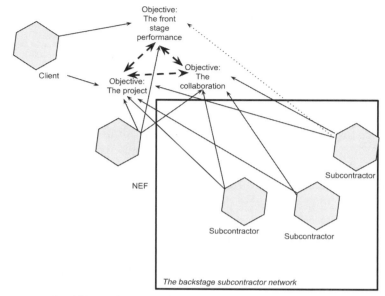

FIGURE 4.2. In addition to the project and the front-stage performance, the nonemployer firm and subcontractor network must also manage the collaboration.

The Flexibility of Organizational Networks

Because of these many potential tensions, organizational networks tend to be very flexible. For instance, if you were to hire Albert's company for two engagements, you would likely get two different teams, since Albert draws together a different temporary network to swarm each project. Not only are the networks different from project to project, they might even change from one phase of a project to another, expanding and contracting as needed.

Furthermore, Albert may have never even met some of these subcontractors. That's because Albert's work is knowledge work. He's not growing things or making things that must be physically transported; he's creating and shaping digital information, information that by its nature can be easily moved around the world. Couple the digital nature of Albert's work with contracting services such as oDesk (Albert's preferred service) and you get an exceptionally flexible workforce, one that can expand and contract rapidly to "right-size" a given project.

"In the networked information economy," Yochai Benkler says, "the physical capital required for production is broadly distributed through society" (2006, p. 6). The cost for distributing information drops to near zero, he adds, and the cost for producing it drops rapidly as well. Consequently, we see more distributed production strategies and production aimed at enacting public and liberal commitments rather than at recouping investment. Benkler believes that this development toward "an open, diverse, liberal equilibrium" (p. 22) will "lead to a substantial redistribution of power and money from the twentieth-century industrial producers of information, culture, and communications—like Hollywood, the recording industry, and perhaps the broadcasters and some of the telecommunications service giants—to a combination of widely diffuse populations around the globe, and the market actors that will build the tools that make this population better able to produce its own information environment rather than buying it ready-made" (p. 23). Benkler argues that the distributed costs of infrastructure allow sharing to come back from the periphery, and claims that social sharing—such as in open-source communities—is unlike sharing in markets or hierarchies (p. 121). The lower cost of information production results in a radical increase in producers and less focus on marketability or filtering (p. 166). A subcontractor with the right skills might be able to pick up jobs from Albert, whether she's in Boston, Bastrop, or Bangalore.

But along with this elevated flexibility, you also get an unstable workforce. Albert might be very happy with Subcontractor A, but he might not be able to enlist Subcontractor A next time. In fact, as we've seen, he has very little leverage over Subcontractor A. Networks are unstable for the same reason they are flexible and (for many) desirable: They are by consent among allies.

The Adaptivity of Organizational Networks

Finally, since networks are flexible, they are highly adaptable. They can easily pivot to meet new contingencies: adding or subtracting people, resources, skills, and objectives, as well as switching leadership. Today's contractor can become tomorrow's subcontractor.

Let's examine how this worked with chapter 3's all-edge adhocracies, which are built on temporary organizational networks. We might tend to imagine a "swarm" as a swarm of bees or flies—a cluster of relatively undifferentiated members. But all-edge adhocracies are composed of specialists who address different functions. If a project develops a new wrinkle, the all-edge adhocracy adds a new specialist to the swarm to address that wrinkle.

Thus, those who are assembling an all-edge adhocracy, such as Benny in chapter 3, can get a "right-sized" and "right-talented" team to address each project (ideally, anyway). They can assemble a team of specialists that can't be commanded and controlled but can be consulted and coordinated. As we saw in chapter 3, such a team does have drawbacks but also advantages. In particular, such teams are relatively autonomous (directing themselves within agreed-on parameters) and able to rapidly coordinate their labor via mutual adjustment (communicating and coordinating on the fly to address contingencies). For instance, when Benny wants to develop a bid for a client, he pulls a team of subcontractors into a Skype session, has them hammer out roles and timelines, and records these in a spreadsheet. Albert uses conference calls to coordinate local labor and oDesk to solicit distance labor. Sophie asks a subcontractor to sit down with her at the dining room table and discuss timelines. In all these cases, the independent specialists treat each other as allies, communicating copiously and rapidly to come to agreement.

Recruiting trustworthy collaborators is a necessary step but insufficient to ensure the collaboration's success. As we've seen, the subcontractor network must form a back stage so that it can effectively coordinate that collaboration, producing both the project and the front-stage performance. The tighter the coordination and the more trust shared, the more likely the nonemployer firm is to succeed at achieving—and aligning—its three objectives (the front stage, the back stage, and the collaboration).

To achieve that coordination, these nonemployer firms have developed rules (including tactics) and tools (including texts). In chapter 3, these rules and tools included portraying subcontractor work as the nonemployer firm's own, restricting client-subcontractor interactions, stage-managing subcontractors during conference calls, and using texts such as project management systems and spreadsheets to set and enforce deadlines. Many of these moves affect all three objectives simultaneously: improving the backstage collaboration itself, ensuring that the project will be done on time and with high quality, and minimizing threats to the nonemployer firm's long-term front-stage performance. And as I mentioned earlier, this alignment is quite complex: each nonemployer firm may be coordinating multiple sets of subcontractors as it works on multiple projects from multiple clients. Under such circumstances, it is remarkable that nonemployer firms manage to coherently control their self-presentation.

Four Characteristics in Search of a Home

In this chapter, we've looked at four characteristics of the ever-changing, loosely tied organizational networks on which all-edge adhocracies are built: flat structure; changing composition; flexibility; and adaptivity. Because of these characteristics, networks have very different strengths and weaknesses from institutional hierarchies. In particular, as I discussed in chapter 2, networks are well suited to unique projects that require innovation, flexibility, and creativity, particularly if these projects involve the inexpensive, rapid communication that is necessary for supporting constant mutual adjustment. But they're not well suited for projects that require repeatability, operating efficiency, or control; those requirements are better fulfilled by an institutional hierarchy.

Networks, as I said in chapter 2, are the foundation on which all-edge adhocracies are built. In particular, these networks span other, longer-term organizations such as nonemployer firms and small businesses; those networks allow people to contact a range of specialists to come together in their all-edge adhocracies. In these networked engagements, people can often achieve the flexibility, freedom, and creativity that they value, while rapidly building their temporary adhocracies with specialists from around the world. And since their work is knowledge work, as long as they have laptops, broadband access, and mobile phones, they can choose to work just about anywhere—home, coffee shops, hotel lobbies, libraries—and recruit other specialists who themselves can work from almost anywhere.

But these networks of specialists take a while to develop. As we saw in chapter 3, these people need opportunities to build out their network of contacts so that they can recruit team members who will be reliable, responsive, trustworthy, and expert. It's hard to do that from a home office or a coffee shop, or even through the friendships, referrals, and Craigslist ads that the nonemployer firms used in chapter 3. How do people network across specialties? How can they build trusting relationships with those contacts?

A new form of organization needs a new workplace, one that matches its characteristics. In the next chapter, we'll see one variation of an adhocratic workplace: coworking spaces.

5

Working Alone, Together: The Case of Coworking

Just as institutions developed a way of coordinating and managing themselves—the bureaucracy—organizational networks have developed their own way of coordinating and managing themselves: the all-edge adhocracy. As we saw in the previous chapter, in those organizational networks, specialists connect through various pathways to address problems. These networks change in composition as specialists circulate in and out of them, taking the lead on a part of the project, then fading away when their part is done. This always-changing, loosely organized nature of organizational networks means that adhocracies can rapidly adapt to new contingencies as they communicate, coordinate, and collaborate in temporary configurations.

But this strength is also a weakness. As we saw in chapter 3, in an adhocracy, people are relatively autonomous and thus they don't have much leverage over each other. A nonemployer firm (NEF), for instance, doesn't have any real authority or much leverage over a subcontractor. The NEF doesn't supply a steady paycheck, benefits, or a workspace to subcontractors. NEFs and subcontractors might not even share the same workspace—so they lack the sorts of serendipitous interactions that help to build trust in more traditional workplaces. Home offices generally don't have water coolers.

All of this suggests that all-edge adhocracies need something different from their workplaces. They need workplaces that support the independent work, autonomy, and rapid formation and dissolution of teams that characterize adhocracies. These workplaces also need to support the cross-specialty networking and trust building that are necessary preconditions for adhocracies—and to combat the social isolation that too often accompanies

This chapter is based on Spinuzzi (2012a).

autonomous work. Finally, they need to support the front-stage work that adhocracies often must perform when interfacing with more traditional bureaucracies. What would such workplaces look like? From 2008 to 2011, I studied one particular variation: *coworking spaces.*

Conjunctured

In April 2008 I came across the website of an Austin company called Conjunctured. It appeared to be a small web design and development agency. But its self-description sounded like nothing I had seen up to that point:

> We help organizations have conversations online.
>
> Conjunctured leverages the power of collaboration and community. We are inspired by the existing concept of coworking and call ourselves a "co-company"—it's a term we came up with that describes how the company is structured—we don't employ people. Instead, a team of independent free-lancers, all specialists in their own areas, come together to collaborate on the projects they feel most passionate about. (Conjunctured 2008a)

Interesting, I thought, and tossed the company's blog in my RSS reader, in-tending to check on it later.

"Later" was just a few weeks later. In early May, the company's blog announced that they had finally found a space (Conjunctured 2008b). Apparently the four principals—John Erik Metcalfe, Dusty Reagan, Cesar Torres, and David Walker—had visited several candidate spaces separately, tweeting about the locations to their potential members, and finally settled on a house in East Austin.

As I read this blog entry, I thought: What kind of company has "potential members"? For that matter, what kind of company goes into business first, *then* settles on a location? And what on earth was a "coworking company"?

After wondering for a few days, I decided to find out.

Flipping the Model

Conjunctured, it turns out, was a very loose brand, as Cesar explained to me a few weeks later at a coffee shop near the University of Texas campus. A dynamic twenty-four-year-old, Cesar explained that he had recently graduated from UT with a marketing degree. Throughout college, he had freelanced (over Craigslist) as well as interned at Apple. When he graduated, he had faced the prospect of working at Apple or at a conventional advertising firm.

But he preferred creative control. He had interned at advertising agencies, and he thought of them as a "big government" model: lots of overhead, layers between creative worker and customer. But technology replaces a lot of the overhead and infrastructure of the agency model: all the creative worker needs, he said, is a laptop and a mobile phone. So he decided to "flip the model"—joining John Erik, Dusty, and David under the Conjunctured brand.

Cesar, John Erik, Dusty, and David—all Gen-Y, all recent college grads—started Conjunctured in August 2007. They had begun working together in jelly meetings—open meetings at which unaffiliated freelancers would converge on a coffee shop and work in each other's presence—and at Austin's Social Media Club. Together, they worked on a model of individual work plus collaboration on projects that leveraged their unique skills. And whereas a conventional agency takes too big a cut due to infrastructure, Conjunctured allowed them to get freelancer wages.

Not only did they supply their own infrastructure (laptops, mobile phones) at low cost, they used free tools. Cesar described this approach as learning to "intertwine," learning to be efficient early adopters. The agency was an exercise in figuring out the value in social media and social connections.

How did Conjunctured work as an agency, since it was not a company in the traditional sense? Simple: the four principals worked as freelancers. When one received a contract, he would subcontract parts to the others, technically as consultants: he would send them 1099 tax forms, which would allow him to write them off as business expenses. And if they couldn't take on the work, he could turn to others in his subcontractor network, such as other people at jellies or in the Social Media Club. In practical terms, whoever brought in the contract led the project; Conjunctured had no permanent leaders, no defined roles, no hierarchy beyond the project. Every principal had a different line of expertise. That is, like the nonemployer firms in chapter 3, Conjunctured put together specialist teams to attack defined projects.

But at the point that I met Cesar, Conjunctured had decided to take the next step. That next step was not to become a full-fledged agency. No, it was to open a not-for-profit coworking space.

A coworking space is, roughly speaking, an open-plan office space in which unaffiliated professionals can lease a desk for a monthly fee. In June 2008, some other cities had coworking spaces—San Francisco had opened the first one, Spiral Muse, in 2005—but Conjunctured was to be Austin's first. It would give some of Austin's many small-business owners, freelancers, contractors and subcontractors, and remote workers a genuine workspace outside of their home offices and coffee shops. And it would give Cesar, John Erik, David, and Dusty an expanded subcontractor network under one roof:

a way to expand their subcontractor network, meet new potential subcontractors, facilitate rapid collaboration and swift trust.

Ideally, Cesar told me, the space would function as an incubator. He envisioned a recurring seven-minute period in which everyone would focus on one project to improve it. The space was a house, and Cesar said that wasn't accidental: Conjunctured, the coworking space, would be more like a family than a corporation.

When I talked to John Erik a week later, he used a different metaphor: In the Conjunctured model, coworkers were like white blood cells. When a hostile organism appears in the bloodstream, white blood cells swarm it. Similarly, Conjunctured's coworkers would swarm a project, parcel it out, complete it, then disperse until the next job.

As I said, Conjunctured was Austin's first coworking space—but not for long. They started popping up like mushrooms, all over Austin, faster than I could keep track of them.

Austin may be a leading city for coworking, but it's not unique. Coworking spaces have also spread globally, and for reasons that make a great deal of sense when we think of them in terms of adhocracies. According to the 2012 Global Coworking Survey at www.deskmag.com:

- About 53 percent of coworkers "are happy working mostly alone," while the rest work "in spontaneous, changing or fixed teams."
- Freelancers in coworking spaces "benefit the most from working in a collaborative workplace, with more than half (!) reporting a significant increase in income since joining."
- Freelancers in coworking spaces "find that both their social circle and business networks have increased (94% and 88% respectively). They are most often acquainted with new, helpful people (4.1 in two months) and experience the most marked increase in productivity."
- Freelancers have tried working from home before moving to a coworking space: "Prior to joining a coworking space, 64% of freelancers worked from home."
- Coworking is expanding: "36% of all coworking space operators who took part in the study said they plan to open at least one new location in the coming year."

In Austin during my study, coworking spaces charged about $250 a month to allow professionals to work there. These spaces differ radically in ambience, amenities, location, and clientele—and, just as importantly, their proprietors and the coworkers who work there differ radically in how they describe coworking in conversation and in a great variety of texts, including business documents, collateral, advertisements, websites, and social media.

In the two years after I first heard about coworking, I studied nine co-working spaces in Austin—interviewing coworkers and coworking-space proprietors; examining their business plans, websites, collateral, site reviews, and social media; and working in the spaces (see appendix). Along the way, I asked coworkers and proprietors how they defined coworking. I found out what sorts of people decided to cowork (in these spaces, during this period of time) and why.

The Problem with the Home Office

I mentioned in chapter 2 that Alvin Toffler got plenty of things wrong and a few things almost right. One of his near misses is the electronic cottage. In the 1980s book *The Third Wave,* Toffler predicted that personal computing would lead to the "electronic cottage," in which workers could do work at home. "Put the computer in people's homes, and they no longer need to huddle," he argued; "white-collar work . . . will not require 100 percent of the work force to be concentrated in the workshop" (1980, p. 199). Rather, people could create, analyze, and transform information in the comfort of their own homes—like Sophie and Bob and Tom did in chapter 3. Toffler saw the electronic cottage as a way to bring families back together.

But it turns out that working from home has severe drawbacks. Toffler's prediction of the electronic cottage has been repeatedly discussed in the telework/telecommuting literature (e.g., M. A. Clark 2000; De Jong & Mante-Meijer 2008; Ellison 2004; Ramsower 1985), particularly with regard to a drawback that became obvious in retrospect: working from home is potentially quite isolating and erodes the boundaries between home and work life (e.g., Gurstein 2001; Kjaerulff 2010; Kylin & Karlsson 2008). When you work at home, alone, you can't socialize or network. But that's exactly what people must do if they are to build all-edge adhocracies. They need networking and trust-building opportunities—and broader access to infrastructure, and at least some basic barriers between their personal and work lives. For instance, Jens Kjaerulff (2010) describes how teleworkers struggled to separate their work lives and home lives and sought other teleworkers with whom to socialize during weekly lunches. Similarly, Michael Antony Clark (2000) describes how rural teleworkers struggled with professional isolation and sought local networks of freelancers.

At the same time, even when people have an office where they can work, it's becoming increasingly harder to get there. Cities are becoming more and more immobile; commute times are lengthening. In fact, two industry analysts recently predicted that "the city will become more permeable, punctuated by a series of places to work" (Dixon & Ross 2011, p. 6; see also Lister & Harnish 2010). The Austin–Round Rock Metropolitan Area, which in 2009 was ranked fourth in the United States in terms of the lengthiest travel time for commuters (INRIX 2009, p. 12), seems to fit this profile well. At the same time, companies are beginning to see advantages of distributing their workforce. For instance, Austin employer Dell announced in 2013 that it intended to have half of its employees working remotely by 2020 (Calnan 2013).

To sum up, on the one hand, more people (nationally, but especially in Austin) can work anywhere—telecommuting, collaborating electronically, running their own businesses with mobile phones and laptops. On the other hand, their freedom to work anywhere often means isolation, inability to build trust and relationships with others, and sharply restricted opportunities for collaboration and networking. Although the ability to work anywhere can be celebrated as digital nomadism (Czarniawska 2013; Su & Mark 2008), it can also make the mobile workers feel like "vagabonds" working in meaningless "non-places" such as "airports, hotels and trains" (Costas 2013, p. 1474; see also Büscher 2014; Humphry 2013), non-places in which configurations are fleeting and stable relationships are not possible.

These drawbacks directly cut against all-edge adhocracies, which need exactly what isolation works against: sociality, trust, relationships, and collaboration. One emerging solution to these drawbacks is coworking spaces like Conjunctured. But it turns out that coworking is surprisingly difficult to characterize.

Coworking

In the United States, Brad Neuberg is generally credited with starting the coworking movement in 2005 when he organized Spiral Muse in San Francisco (Botsman & Rogers 2011; Hunt 2009; A. M. Jones 2013). By 2011, over seven hundred coworking sites had opened globally (Bonnet 2011), including thirteen in Austin. (By the end of 2013, Austin had sixteen coworking spaces.) A Google group and a wiki keep space proprietors in contact, as does an annual event held during the South by Southwest Interactive Conference.

But what *is* coworking? The Coworking Wiki (n.d.) defines it this way: "The idea is simple: that independent professionals and those with workplace flexibility work better together than they do alone. . . . Coworking spaces are built around the idea of community-building and sustainability. Coworking spaces agree to uphold the values set forth by those who developed the concept in the first place: collaboration, community, sustainability, openness, and accessibility." This definition is useful but imprecise. What kind of service is coworking? Beyond "independent professionals," who coworks? Why do they choose to cowork?

To find out, I interviewed people in the Austin coworking movement: proprietors of coworking spaces as well as coworkers at the three most populous spaces. I also worked in various coworking spaces; looked at coworking-space collateral such as brochures, membership agreements, websites, and Facebook pages; reviewed coworking-space reviews on Yelp and Google Places; looked at Gowalla and Foursquare check-ins; and, when available, read the coworking spaces' business plans. With all of these sources, I built a picture of coworking in Austin—one that seems surprisingly contradictory but that makes a lot of sense once we understand how all-edge adhocracies work.

Table 5.1 shows the coworking spaces and the people I interviewed. As I visited these sites and conducted these interviews, I tried to answer three key questions:

- What is coworking?
- Who coworks?
- Why do they cowork?

The answers were confusing at first: the proprietors and coworkers seemed to disagree at every point. But as I talked to them, coworking began to make a great deal of sense—for all-edge adhocracies.

TABLE 5.1. Austin coworking spaces, proprietors interviewed, and coworkers interviewed, 2008–2011

Site	Proprietors interviewed	Coworkers interviewed (pseudonyms)
Brainstorm	Martin Barrera	
Conjunctured	Jon Erik Metcalfe, Dusty Reagan, Cesar Torres, David Walker	Damon, Evan, Frank, Gerry, Helen
Cospace	Andrew Bushnell, Kirtus Dixon, Pat Ramsey	Isaac, Jason, Kerry, Logan, Matt
Cowork Austin	Blake Freeburg	
GoLab Austin	Steve Golab	
Link	Liz Elam	Nina, Odessa, Patricia, Quade, Rhonda, Sal, Tricia
Perch	Lisa McTiernan	
Soma Vida	Sonya Davis, Laura Shook	
Space12	Sam Lee, Paul Wang	

What Is Coworking?

When I talked to coworking proprietors and coworkers, they all described themselves as being part of "the" coworking community. But they seemed to be describing very different things:

- "It's a very cheap and easy way for me to work in an office space around people that are, I guess, very similar to me." (Damon, coworker)
- "A shared space to facilitate productive work for all the members." (Helen, coworker)
- "A kind of low-cost business platform with shared knowledge that amplifies your business opportunities." (Blake Freeburg, proprietor of Cowork Austin)
- "A place for people to find peace of mind, balance and community." (Facebook page for Soma Vida)

These definitions and metaphors were remarkably different, so different that sometimes it seemed like they weren't even talking about the same thing. But with a little work—and an understanding of all-edge adhocracies—we can make sense of them. We'll start with the coworking spaces themselves, as defined by their proprietors.

HOW PROPRIETORS DEFINED COWORKING

Even though they were all in the coworking business and they all described themselves as being part of the coworking community, proprietors gave me very different definitions of coworking. We can group these definitions—and these sites—into three basic categories: community workspaces, unoffices, and federated spaces.

The community workspace: Soma Vida and Space12   The proprietors of Soma Vida and Space12 considered their sites to be community workspaces and defined coworking in terms of serving their local communities—almost like privately owned community centers.

Soma Vida was a mixed-use center located in a recently gentrified neighborhood in East Austin. Its roomy interior was sectioned into various spaces, including spaces for child care, massage therapy, acupuncture, meetings, yoga, and coworking. Its Facebook page stated that Soma Vida was "a place for people to find peace of mind, balance and community." In the coworking space, individual desks sat in front of long padded benches. According to one of the proprietors, Sonya Davis, "cowork" is short for "community workspace," and she worried that people might think that "you have to actually sit down and collaborate with someone, like there's co-projects. But what we do is we work within a community, and that's what we're all doing as anchor tenants." Soma Vida's website and collateral media emphasized, "Our work space allows you to have dedicated time to concentrate and accomplish tasks." In fact, Soma Vida's policies handout stated that the coworking space was not for conversations: interactions between coworkers had to be confined to other areas, "which include our lounge area, kitchen, and outside garden areas" as well as a conference room. Rather than being a central focus, coworking was just one of many services that Soma Vida offered.

Space12 was also a mixed-use building. It had once been a notorious East Austin nightclub before a local church took over the site. The church now served the community in which the building is located. "It's kind of the opposite of a typical community center," codirector Sam Lee explained. "We . . . create a space so that people could use it to do their own community initiatives. . . . Instead of offering services, we're offering space." Space12 had a large open plan with a recreation area, shelves of books for a prison ministry, a stage area for concerts and church services, a small computer room for disadvantaged students, and a coworking space (figure 5.1). Its Facebook page

FIGURE 5.1. Space12's coworking area, one of the four quadrants of the open-plan space

reflected the wide variety of events held there, including concerts, church services, neighborhood barbecues and yard sales, and a swap-and-sew event, events that were reflected in people's Gowalla check-ins. Space12 did not have a dedicated conference room. Also like Soma Vida, Space12 had "quiet" rules, although they were restricted to "quiet" hours rather than a blanket policy: "You have a set quiet time between nine and three, probably, until the kids get out [of school]," explained codirector Paul Wang. Unlike the other coworking spaces in this study, Space12 did not charge coworkers, and its website's definition of coworking was minimal: "Co-Working Space at Space12 is a shared office space for people from all walks of life in our community."

The community workspaces defined themselves in terms of serving local communities; they expected coworkers to work alongside, but not with, others. Consequently, both had quiet policies in their spaces, a characteristic unique to this category of coworking space. Both also had mixed uses, in keeping with their larger community-oriented missions.

The unoffice: Brainstorm, Cowork Austin, Link, and Perch   In contrast, the proprietors of some coworking spaces saw their sites as providing office space for those who do not work in an office but miss the interactions and amenities of the office environment. The unoffice encouraged discussions; interaction between the coworkers was an essential feature of this coworking space. One proprietor, Liz Elam at Link, emphatically declared that if a space had a no-talking policy, "then it's not coworking"—that is, such a space provides a workspace, but not a collaboration or networking space.

Brainstorm, which was based in a Victorian house in East Austin next to the freeway, defined coworking on its website as "a style of work in which independent professionals share a working environment yet perform independent business activities. . . . Collaboration is common as a result of the social interaction that naturally occurs when talented and creative people share the same physical space." Brainstorm occupied the second floor of the house, upstairs from an architecture firm; it had two work rooms, a conference room, and a kitchen. Brainstorm sometimes rented out rooms for company retreats and other outsider meetings, and it hosted an Imagine Austin meeting.

Cowork Austin, on the third floor of a historical building in downtown Austin, defined coworking similarly. According to proprietor Blake Freeburg, coworking is "kind of a low-cost business platform with shared knowledge that amplifies your business opportunities. . . . And to a lot of the people out there, what is coworking to them? Oh, it's a cheap office. . . . But you get the bonus of community and shared knowledge and maybe avenues." Like Brainstorm, Cowork Austin saw interaction as natural but optional. Cowork Austin boasted three open-plan spaces, a kitchen, a conference room, and two private offices that could be leased. Blake confirmed that coworkers met clients in the conference room and also emphasized that Cowork Austin hosted various after-hours meetings for interest groups and organizations (e.g., a Women in Tech meeting, a Cassandra hackathon, an interface-design group, a tequila-tasting event).

At Link, a modernist space in North Austin that was renovated specifically for coworking, Liz Elam defined coworking as "a membership club that brings people together who share the need for a place to conduct their business in an interactive space." She likened it to a gym membership. In her business plan, she emphasized that "coworking not only provides a more desirable physical space [than a home office or coffee shop does] but promotes collaboration, networking and incubator-like sharing of ideas." But as she told me, "I am not here to form lah-di-dah, let's-all-sing-Kumbaya community. I want people paying me, and I'll provide a great space for you." In particular, Liz emphasized, Link was suitable for client meetings. It had a large open-plan room (figure 5.2), a kitchen, a conference room, and five small meeting rooms large enough to accommodate four people each. (Liz said she got the idea for the meeting rooms by observing business meetings

FIGURE 5.2. Link's open-plan space, showcasing its modernist design

at Starbucks.) Link also hosted networking lunches and after-hours events (e.g., Blogathon ATX, Rock a Charity, a book club, a summer concert series).

At Perch, another modernist space in a mixed-use development in East Austin, Lisa McTiernan defined coworking as "a nontraditional or part-time flex office space where [independent professionals] can truly get some serious work done, network with others" in an environment that is "affordable," "low-commitment," "flexible, and easy." Perch's Facebook page said, "Our space is designed to provide a wide variety of users with a creative, functional and affordable workplace community." Like Link, Perch emphasized that it provides a space for meeting clients in a professional environment and for networking. Perch offered an open-plan room for coworking and a conference room, which coworkers used for client meetings. Perch also hosted art shows and a regular yoga class.

Overall, the unoffice spaces defined themselves as flexible office spaces that allow workers to interact and to meet with clients. These spaces re-created characteristics of the traditional office environment that independent workers might miss. In particular, they emphasized that coworkers could exchange ideas and get feedback from other coworkers, and proprietors often stated that their meeting places were superior to the default meeting place for independents: the coffee shop. Two of these unoffice spaces, Cowork Austin and Link, had explicitly considered and rejected a third model: the federated workspace.

The federated workspace: Conjunctured, Cospace, GoLab Austin   Finally, some proprietors saw the mission of their coworking spaces as fostering more active connections between coworkers, connections that could lead to working relationships between businesses—contracts or referrals. Their focus was on entrepreneurship. Like unoffice spaces, federated workspaces strongly encouraged interaction, but they also encouraged formal collaboration.

I've already discussed Conjunctured, Austin's oldest coworking space, which was located in a large refurbished house in a gentrified area of East Austin (within walking distance of Perch and Soma Vida, in fact). Members who reviewed Conjunctured on Yelp tended to emphasize its proximity to popular restaurants and bars. When I interviewed them, Conjunctured's proprietors defined coworking as a "culture" and delineated between the culture of coworking ("people working together, collaborating, in the most general terms") and a coworking space ("a café-like environment/executive suite"). "Personally, I don't think it's about space at all," Dusty said. Similarly, Conjunctured's website defined coworking as "a global trend where freelancers, entrepreneurs, and other mobile workers come together to work in the same

FIGURE 5.3. Conjunctured's hall. Vending machines dispense candy and dog treats.

space. These mobile workers want to remain independent, but have hit a wall working in isolation at home. Coworking allows them to be part of a community of like-minded individuals with whom they can share ideas, trade business leads, foster business partnerships, and create friendships." That last point was emphasized on Conjunctured's Facebook page, where its entire self-description consisted of "Conjunctured loves you. Yup"—a sentiment that reflects Conjunctured's relaxed, playful atmosphere (see figure 5.3).

Conjunctured's proprietors said that they saw Conjunctured as a way to quickly form groups (i.e., all-edge adhocracies) of contractors in order to take on projects that were too large for individual contractors. As John Erik argued, "I've always thought of [taking on a project] as the white blood cells, right? So, everybody's kind of going along in their pipe. A project gets dropped in, we can swarm to kill it, disseminate, and keep flowing." Conjunctured could offer a brand that is larger than that of an individual contractor as well as a large stable of entrepreneurs who had gotten to know and trust each other. It could also offer referrals: if one coworker could not take on a job, that coworker could refer it to someone else in the space.

Conjunctured had a conference room, a kitchen, and three open-plan rooms. It also hosted frequent events and meetings of special-interest groups (e.g., CocoaCoder meetings, Bootstrap Interactive, Wordpress Meetup, and a poker game). These events were popular with coworkers, who described them frequently in their Gowalla check-ins.

Cospace was on the second floor of an office park in North Austin. Like Conjunctured, Cospace focused on entrepreneurs. And like Conjunctured's proprietors, Cospace's proprietors drew a distinction between coworking and a coworking space. "Coworking is an informal gathering of people who need to accomplish a task or a project or have some work to get done, but they want to work alongside others," coproprietor Kirtus Dixon offered, whereas a coworking space is "the more formal collection of all those people in one designated location, with the amenities . . . [including] access to resources, space, desk, WiFi, coffee." Coproprietor Pat Ramsey emphasized that independent workers need a "home base" where they can interact but not "a full time office where you sort of stovepipe yourself with a bunch of people, and you see the same people every day." Cospace's Facebook page stressed this aspect, describing the space as a "coworking, networking, and meeting space in North Austin."

Like Conjunctured, Cospace emphasized the federated aspect of the space. As coproprietor Andrew Bushnell put it, "It gives [the coworkers] a chance to form together into a group. . . . A group of fifty people is much more powerful than fifty individuals." Cospace had a large open-plan room, two conference rooms, a kitchen, and two offices that could be leased to groups. It also hosted frequent social events and meetings of interest groups (e.g., GeekAustin, Austin Drupal Users Meetup, WordPress Camp, Startup Weekend) as described in their coworkers' Gowalla check-ins.

GoLab Austin occupied excess space in the offices of FG Squared, an interactive marketing company. Unlike the other spaces, GoLab Austin focused specifically on the interactive media industry. Steve Golab, who owned FG Squared and was proprietor of GoLab Austin, defined coworking as "basically giving people the tools that they need to be effective in their work. Making sure that they are productive. . . . I think it's about helping facilitate relationships between one another and with people who are inside of the network." GoLab Austin's Facebook page made its federated model quite explicit, describing it as "more than just a shared office space" and promising facilitated interactions and referrals. At the time of the interview, GoLab Austin had not yet hosted events, though it planned to do so.

So the federated workspaces defined themselves in terms of fostering business relationships as well as personal ones; they wanted to facilitate collaboration with others in formal and informal relationships. That is, the proprietors saw these spaces as a place where individuals could meet and partner with others to attack specific projects. Although they emphasized this collaborative focus, the proprietors also saw their spaces as providing the benefits of interaction that the unoffice model provides.

So that's the proprietors' view. And if we took just this view, we could simply say that coworking spaces are workplaces where people work together. But when we talk to coworkers themselves, things get much more complicated.

HOW COWORKERS DEFINED COWORKING

To get the coworkers' perspective, I interviewed seventeen coworkers at the three most populated coworking spaces—Conjunctured, Cospace, and Link. (I also examined user-generated texts such as reviews on Yelp and Google Places and check-ins at Foursquare and Gowalla, but users did not define coworking in these texts.) Coworkers at these three spaces presented interesting differences in their definitions of coworking (see table 5.2). (Notice that in this section, I discuss how they defined coworking; in a later section, I discuss their motivations for coworking, which is a separate question.)

Coworking as space   Of these three most populated spaces, only Link was defined as an unoffice by its proprietor. But coworkers across all three spaces defined coworking as an alternative office space. For instance, at Conjunctured, Damon defined coworking as "a very cheap and easy way for me to work in an office space around people that are, I guess, very similar to me," whereas Frank defined it as "trying to re-create some parts of the office environment . . . the parts of the office hopefully that work better than working from home." Similarly, at Cospace, Isaac said that "just like in any office, you

TABLE 5.2. Characteristics in coworkers' definitions of coworking

Characteristics	Coworkers at Conjunctured	Coworkers at Cospace	Coworkers at Link
Space	Damon, Evan, Gerry, Helen	Isaac, Jason, Kerry, Matt	Nina, Odessa, Patricia, Quade, Sal, Tricia
Inexpensive office alternative	Damon, Evan	Matt	
Social hub	Frank	Isaac, Logan, Matt	Nina, Odessa, Quade, Rhonda, Tricia
Collaboration	Gerry		Nina, Odessa, Rhonda, Sal
Heterogeneous		Isaac	Quade, Rhonda
Homogeneous	Damon	Isaac	Odessa
Work/home separation	Evan		Tricia

know when Monday morning comes, what you're getting into," and Matt called it "an office opportunity. . . . It's a financial advantage to be able to have an office." Overall, seven of the seventeen coworkers explicitly defined coworking as analogous to the office, whereas fifteen of seventeen defined it as an office, space, or workplace.

Coworking as an inexpensive office alternative   Although coworking is dramatically less expensive than leasing an office space, only three coworkers (Damon, Evan, and Matt) mentioned that fact.

Coworking as a social hub   "I now have a water cooler," stated Rhonda. "I have a place where I can bounce ideas off of people." Like Rhonda, many coworkers across the sites emphasized interaction with other coworkers. For instance, Logan simply defined coworking as "social working. . . . It's a social environment to do your work." Similarly, Frank defined it as "combining social networking and working in a laid-back environment where the stress is gone." Overall, six of the seventeen coworkers used some variation of the phrase "bounce ideas off of people" (Rhonda), and nine of the seventeen coworkers defined coworking in terms of a social component.

Coworking as collaboration   Surprisingly, most coworkers did not define coworking as an opportunity to collaborate on federated projects (although more mentioned collaboration as a motivation, which I discuss later). For instance, Kerry, who worked in Cospace's federated space, defined it as people "working on different projects in the same shared space"—hardly the federated vision that Cospace's proprietors expressed in their interviews and texts. Overall, only five of the seventeen coworkers defined coworking in terms of collaborating on projects, four of whom worked at the unoffice rather than at one of the federated workspaces.

Coworking as heterogeneous and homogeneous   Proprietors and coworkers alike sometimes referred to homogeneous and heterogeneous populations. Websites and other collateral for Conjunctured, Perch, and GoLab Austin contained the phrase "like-minded," and proprietors of Perch and Soma Vida used that phrase in their interviews. Like the proprietors, three coworkers (one each at Conjunctured, Cospace, and Link) defined coworking in terms of working with people like themselves.

At the same time, three coworkers appreciated the heterogeneity of workers at the space. For instance, Rhonda emphasized, "I can get really different views because I have individuals across the spectrum in their jobs, and what they do. You can get a better idea of what people think outside of the industry that you're in." (Proprietors of Cospace, Perch, and Space12 all emphasized heterogeneity in their interviews, and Perch's Facebook page mentioned it.)

Coworking as work/home separation   Only two coworkers (Evan and Tricia) mentioned work/home separation as a component of coworking. (Others mentioned this component as a motivator for them, but not as part of the definition.)

WHAT IS COWORKING? SOME CONTRADICTORY DEFINITIONS

What is coworking, then? That is, what do people think they're doing at these coworking sites? As we have seen, answers vary. A coworking space is a place to get work done: specifically, knowledge or service work that originates outside the site in other intersecting activities. Although coworkers work together, they view that work as trying to reach different, contradictory objectives—such different objectives that it's easy to wonder whether coworking is a single thing at all.

For instance, the coworkers I interviewed tended to emphasize the unoffice model, particularly the combination of space and social interaction as they performed separate projects. Yet beyond saying that they worked in the presence of other people, they provided definitions that were far from unanimous.

That's a remarkable insight if you're a coworking proprietor. Proprietors structure, design, furnish, and run their sites on the basis of their understanding and model of coworking—and indeed they have considerable incentive to differentiate their sites from others. But the coworkers I interviewed seemed to base their understanding of coworking on one model: the unoffice. Coworkers were split on other characteristics of coworking, which meant that they came to their spaces with different expectations about the activity in general: Would they work in parallel or in collaboration? Would they socialize or find partners? Would they meet like-minded individuals or coworkers with different views and backgrounds? Across proprietors, across coworkers, even between the proprietors and their coworkers at a given space, people disagreed in their definitions of coworking.

We might expect that when people have such different expectations of a coworking space, some would leave dissatisfied. But in fact all three of the most populous coworking spaces continued to grow. And things become even more puzzling when we move to the next question: who coworks?

Who Coworks?

Who did coworking proprietors expect to work at their sites, and who actually did?

WHOM PROPRIETORS TARGETED

Proprietors targeted specific people—this we know from their interviews, from their websites and Facebook pages, from their collateral and business plans.

First, all proprietors, of course, identified individuals who could choose where to work. Those ideal coworkers had found home offices and coffee shops to be inadequate workspaces. (Coffee shops in particular are typically "non-places" in which configurations are temporary and stable relationships are very difficult to achieve; see Costas 2013.)

Second, interestingly, when proprietors envisioned their ideal coworkers, it was as if they looked in the mirror. Conjunctured's proprietors, who were experienced freelancers and entrepreneurs, sought freelancers who were used to working virtually. Cospace's proprietors, who had previously owned small businesses, sought small-business owners. Link's proprietor, a former global account manager for Dell, sought high-end Gen-X business travelers. Soma Vida's proprietors, who identified strongly as female entrepreneurs with children, sought "mamapreneurs" and "papapreneurs." Even Space12's proprietors, who targeted the most diverse set of coworkers, said that they wanted their church staff working there.

Third, proprietors identified people with specific characteristics, characteristics that differed from site to site. For instance, Conjunctured's proprietors specifically sought people seeking leads and business partnerships—in keeping with its orientation as a federated workspace—but also friendships. Cospace's proprietors specifically sought diversified small-business owners in North Austin needing a "home base" who can supply referrals to each other. Link's proprietor sought high-end independents who valued interaction with other coworkers but were more concerned with minimizing unwanted distractions and meeting clients.

So these proprietors sought specific types of coworkers for their sites. That didn't mean that they were turning away other types of coworkers—

far from it—just that they had set up their spaces with these specific types in mind.

WHO ACTUALLY COWORKED

But the actual coworkers often did not match the coworkers that proprietors expected. For instance, the coworkers I interviewed at Conjunctured, Cospace, and Link worked in various industries and capacities, but most of them were independent workers. Of the seventeen coworkers I interviewed,

- ten were small-business owners other than consultants (six of these were in one-person organizations);
- four were consultants (three of these were in one-person consultancies);
- one was a dependent contractor working remotely for a large business;
- one was an intern for a business in the coworking space;
- one was a permanent employee of a business in the coworking space; and
- twelve had an Internet or information technology component to their business (for instance, Evan worked in the apparel and fashion industry for a company that sold apparel exclusively online).

Notice that these follow roughly the same profile as the nonemployer firms in chapter 3.

There were differences too. At Conjunctured and Cospace, all of the coworkers I interviewed had an Internet or information technology component to their business. At Link, the coworkers I interviewed were diverse independent professionals, all of whom were small-business owners or consultants. Only two of the seven coworkers at Link had an Internet or information technology component to their business, and none of them fit the profile of business traveler. My survey of the member directories from these three coworking spaces suggests that this breakdown appears to reflect the membership at the three spaces as a whole.

WHO COWORKS? SOME CONTRADICTORY PROFILES

Who coworks? The proprietors had a clear idea about what made an ideal coworker, but the coworkers themselves often didn't fit these profiles very closely. (For instance, although Liz Elam set up Link with frequent business travelers in mind, none of the coworkers I interviewed fit that profile.) But these coworkers were similar in other ways: they tended to be involved in a wide variety of professional activities, activities that required different ties and relationships. Coworkers cowork, but freelancers freelance, consultants consult, entrepreneurs start and grow businesses, and small-business owners run small businesses. These are very different activities, particularly because they are exercised in different fields and disciplines and require different sorts of work and resources—and collaborations. Consequently, these coworkers expected very different things from their shared spaces—and had very different motivations, as we'll see below.

Why Do People Cowork?

What did coworkers expect to get from coworking? That is, what motivated them? To find out, I interviewed coworkers, but I also looked at Yelp and Google Places reviews and Foursquare and Gowalla check-ins.

All of the coworkers that I interviewed reported that they had tried working from home—like Sophie, Bob, and Tom in chapter 3—but found that the "electronic cottage" wasn't suitable for adhocracies. So fourteen of the seventeen had also tried working from coffee shops. As table 5.3 shows, participants were unhappy with these workspaces, reporting that they experienced distractions, self-motivation problems, and feelings of isolation. For instance, Isaac reported that when he worked at home, he would have to take conference calls in his parked car because "you never knew when [my dogs] were going to start barking. And it seemed like they would sadistically plan to bark when I was on a call." Rhonda found that when she worked from home, she would realize at noon that she was still in her pajamas, and she also found herself being distracted by domestic chores such as washing dishes and doing laundry. Kerry recounted, "I got really depressed [at home] because I

TABLE 5.3. Coworkers' experiences working from other spaces

Characteristics	Coworkers at Conjunctured	Coworkers at Cospace	Coworkers at Link
Had worked from home	Damon, Evan, Frank, Gerry, Helen	Isaac, Jason, Kerry, Logan, Matt	Nina, Odessa, Patricia, Quade, Rhonda, Sal, Tricia
Distractions	Damon, Gerry	Isaac, Kerry	Nina, Odessa, Quade, Rhonda
Self-motivation problems	Gerry	Isaac, Kerry	Nina
Isolation	Frank	Jason, Kerry, Logan	Odessa, Patricia, Tricia
Had worked at coffee shops	Frank, Gerry, Helen	Isaac, Jason, Kerry, Logan, Matt	Nina, Patricia, Quade, Rhonda, Sal, Tricia
Distractions	Gerry	Isaac	Quade

didn't talk to anybody all day long." And Frank described problems with coffee shops that many others had raised: "When you go to a coffee shop, you are obligated to buy something. You don't want to spend too much time there. It's not really conducive [as] a workspace because people are talking. People don't think of it as a workspace."

Given that the coworkers I interviewed were primarily small-business owners and consultants, such problems are critical: these professionals had to be highly motivated and focused because their livelihoods depended primarily or solely on their own initiative. Yelp reviews and a Gowalla check-in reflected how difficult coworkers found it to work in home offices and coffee shops and how these coworkers welcomed quieter, less distracting environs.

So coworkers had a good idea of what they wanted to avoid. They told me that they looked for several characteristics in a coworking space, and the various spaces provided key differentiators, according to their space, design, and professionalism; flexibility; and location and the benefits that coworkers tended to receive from each other.

SPACE, DESIGN, AND PROFESSIONALISM

Coworkers across the three sites specifically discussed furniture and space design—although they looked for different things. Gerry, for instance, told me that "if you're going to be sitting somewhere for three or four hours, the chair better be comfortable." Indeed, at Conjunctured and Cospace, coworkers included mostly entrepreneurs, freelancers, and consultants who seldom met their clients there, so these coworkers' focus was primarily on functionality and comfort. That is, the space design was inward facing, a comfortable place where people could get together, meet each other, and work on their projects informally, sometimes on the same project, sometimes on different ones. But an environment that is ideal for this sort of backstage work is not necessarily good for front-stage work such as a business meeting. Helen recalled one day that she met clients at Conjunctured: "That was the day that like three people showed up with their dogs. Like it was 4:00, and it was loud, and the dogs were barking and fighting. And they were laughing, and then somebody was like drinking beer." Gerry, also at Conjunctured, reported that he tended to meet clients at coffee shops instead.

In contrast, at Link, coworkers included mostly small-business owners who met with their clients face-to-face, so their focus was on image and professionalism. Six of the seven coworkers emphasized that they were proud to meet clients there. (The seventh coworker, an artist, did not have clients.) Patricia commented, "This place has a modern design, but it's organic and comfortable, and that's so hard to pull off. It's also clean, and there's no microwave-popcorn smell, and there's no worry about science experiments in the fridge. These things matter and especially if you want to bring in clients or friends or whatever." Link was designed to be outward facing, to facilitate professional contacts with outsiders, to impress rather than to comfort, to be a front stage. Sal, who had worked at both Conjunctured and Link, also mentioned how Link, as opposed to Conjunctured, had the "wow factor" for meeting clients.

Coworkers also mentioned how spaces supported events—a major function that was fulfilled by all three of the most populous sites, a function that was greatly valued by the coworkers since it gave them broader opportunities to network. For instance, in comparing Cospace to Conjunctured, Isaac claimed that Cospace had a greater ability to host conferences and meetings "because Conjunctured isn't quite as big as this place."

In social media, coworkers described the spaces approvingly, focusing on the unique characteristics of each space. For instance, Link was described on Google Places as a "high-end space" and in a Gowalla check-in as "such a beautiful space!" Soma Vida was described in a Foursquare check-in as "relaxing." And when a coworker checked in at Cowork Austin, she suggested that others "check out the patio and terrific conference room."

Going beyond specific space elements, coworkers at Cospace and Link, when comparing their sites to Conjunctured, often centered their comparisons on how the spaces allowed them to project professionalism. For instance, at Cospace, Jason claimed that Conjunctured represented an "artist-commune type" of coworking, compared to Cospace's "businessy" model; similarly, Matt said that Cospace was "a little bit more business minded" than Conjunctured. Coworkers at Cospace (Jason) and Link (Patricia, Sal) emphasized the age gap between themselves and the younger coworkers at Conjunctured, using terms that tied age to professional demeanor. For instance, Patricia said that Conjunctured "felt like college to me again. . . . I just wanted to have it be a place where I can turn on professional brain and stay focused and have the peer pressure to be Professional Lady."

At these two spaces, professionalism frequently came up in the interviews. Recall that in chapter 3, the nonemployer firms worried about how to control the front stage when subcontractors met clients. Coworkers at the three coworking spaces had a similar worry: when clients visited them, would the other coworkers help to construct a suitable front stage?

FLEXIBILITY

On the other hand, some people sought more time flexibility, particularly entrepreneurs and freelancers, who typically set their own hours and do not have to meet clients regularly. (As we saw in chapter 3, people often decide to work independently so that they can control their own time and work their own hours.) These people tended to frequent Conjunctured, which had extended hours and gave keys to trusted coworkers, more than Cospace, which charged extra for keyed access, and especially more than Link, which was open only during normal business hours.

LOCATION

Another differentiator was location. The coworkers sought coworking sites that were closer to their homes, clients, or desired amenities. The desired amenities differed from one coworker to another. For instance, Odessa and Patricia specifically cited Link's proximity to day care as one of its advantages for them. Conjunctured, on the other hand, was closer to downtown in a rapidly gentrifying area of East Austin. Using a Yelp review to rib people at other coworking spaces, one Conjunctured coworker wrote: "I seriously feel sorry for people that go to coworking spaces in North Austin or downtown," before describing Conjunctured's proximity to popular bars and restaurants. Different locations seemed to appeal to people in different life stages: Link's coworkers were mostly in their thirties and older, whereas Conjunctured's were mostly in their twenties. Finally, one coworker (Jason) argued that since Cospace was at the corner of a highway and major artery, it was more convenient for commuters coming from suburbs north of the city.

These differentiators, of course, sometimes conflicted with each other. Gerry articulated one such conflict: "The question is, is [coworking] going to be community based or proximity based? That, you know, 'do I come to this place because I like the people here or this happens to be the closest place, and the people don't piss me off?'" That is an important question because people also seek coworking sites to interact with others.

BENEFITS FROM OTHER COWORKERS

But it wasn't just about how the space was set up or where it was located. As we would expect from people working in all-edge adhocracies, the coworkers were just as interested in what they got from each other. They sought benefits

TABLE 5.4. Desired benefits from coworkers

Benefits	Coworkers at Conjunctured	Coworkers at Cospace	Coworkers at Link
Interaction	Frank	Isaac, Jason, Kerry, Logan	Nina, Odessa, Patricia, Quade, Rhonda, Tricia
Feedback	Damon, Evan, Frank, Helen	Isaac, Matt	Nina, Rhonda, Tricia
Trust	Damon, Gerry, Helen	Isaac	Odessa, Patricia, Quade, Rhonda, Sal, Tricia
Learning	Damon, Frank, Helen	Logan	Nina, Rhonda, Sal, Tricia
Partnerships	Damon, Frank, Gerry, Helen	Isaac, Jason, Kerry, Logan, Matt	Odessa, Patricia, Rhonda, Sal, Tricia
Encouragement	Damon, Helen		Quade, Tricia
Referrals	Helen	Matt	Sal

from each other such as interaction, feedback, trust, learning, partnerships, encouragement, and referrals (see table 5.4).

Interaction   Many of the coworkers across the sites told me that they chose to cowork because they wanted to interact or socialize with the other coworkers. For instance, Jason told me that "probably I am not going to work on jobs with these people, but I like to socialize with them and talk to them." This theme of interaction was common, especially in the Link and Cospace interviews but also in the Yelp and Google Places reviews; for example, one Cospace coworker enthused that "I get to see new people every day," a Conjunctured coworker described how "congenial" people were, and a Link coworker emphasized how much of a host the proprietor was. The spaces frequently held after-hours events that provided plenty of other opportunities to socialize and network, and those events were reflected particularly in some of the sites' Gowalla check-ins.

Interaction also took other forms. For instance, during his interview, Jason remarked that "for me, it is about just the casual relationships," and that he had a friendly rivalry with Logan on Foursquare: both competed to be mayor of Cospace. Later, Logan mentioned the same rivalry—then paused the interview so that he could check in. "He's not here," Logan told me, then added hopefully, "I might actually get the mayorship today."

Feedback   People across the sites also expressed their desire for feedback, although feedback had different meanings at different sites. For instance, at Conjunctured and Cospace, coworkers were generally in fields related to technology or the Internet, so they tended to seek feedback on problems from others in their field. In contrast, coworkers at Link generally worked in more diverse, customer-contact businesses, so they tended to seek feedback from coworkers in different fields. As Rhonda put it, "You can get a better idea of what people think outside of the industry that you're in."

Trust   We saw in chapter 3 that trust is vital for all-edge adhocracies. But trust looked different at the various coworking spaces. At Conjunctured, in accordance with its federated model, coworkers sought collaborators they could trust as partners. As Damon put it, "Do [subcontractors] have a handle on their time? Can they manage all the stuff that we need to get done?" Conjunctured provided an environment for developing such trust. Similarly, at Cospace, Isaac emphasized that "you like to do business with people you trust" and reported that "there are already trusting relationships being built here."

On the other hand, at Link, coworkers tended to work in parallel. These coworkers thought of trust in terms of personal possessions and in terms of sharing ideas with people with whom they were not partnered. For instance, Odessa told me, "I don't have to worry about my purse and my Mac. And at the same point, I feel like I've told [other coworkers] about my business plan. They're not going to go and tell my competition. I think they're going to keep it [to themselves]. I haven't sworn them to secrecy; I haven't made them sign a nondisclosure agreement." But she, and the other coworkers I interviewed at Link, had not partnered with coworkers on any projects.

Learning   As we've seen in the previous chapters, working in all-edge ad-hocracies means constantly learning about the work of other specialists and organizations—and wearing many hats during project-oriented collabora-tions. So I wasn't surprised that coworkers brought up learning often. Co-workers at the federated sites (Conjunctured and Cospace) often spoke about learning within their fields when tackling work problems. At Conjunctured, for instance, Frank said, "I feel comfortable to a point now where I know if I have difficult questions, I can ask people around here." Similarly, at Cospace, Logan anticipated learning from a "pool of talent." At Link, on the other hand, coworkers emphasized learning about business practices in general rather than about field-specific tools or processes. For instance, Tricia said she had sought guidance on outsourcing accounting and using billing prac-tices, whereas Rhonda had asked for guidance on a piece of collateral she had developed for her business, and Nina intended to seek help from someone who was "a brainiac on spreadsheets and budgets [since] I'm really bad about keeping my receipts."

Partnerships   The three sites also differed in their potential for forming business partnerships. As a federated workspace, Conjunctured had targeted entrepreneurs who could work virtually and who could seek business relationships within the space. The participants whom I interviewed generally fit this profile. At Conjunctured, all of the coworkers had an Internet component to their business, and three coworkers reported subcontracting others in the space. For instance, Damon said that Conjunctured was a good space to find subcontractors because people with a certain work ethic chose to work there. Damon, Gerry, and Helen all told me that working alongside coworkers helped them to assess whether those coworkers would be good subcontractors. As Helen put it, "I've seen them interact, you know, I've seen them make agreements and deliver or not deliver. . . . What better interview could you get?"

Helen also mentioned that at Conjunctured, subcontracting opportunities could be spontaneous: "One day we needed an editor, and I saw [a coworker] walk in . . . and I'm like, do you have three hours to edit something? She said yeah. So she took a left instead of going into the room, and came in here and edited this stuff that we had to deliver." Because Conjunctured was full of independent professionals within related industries, it gave coworkers a large set of potential subcontractors, providing the potential for the agile collaboration that all-edge adhocracies need.

At Cospace, although coworkers saw the potential for establishing business partnerships with each other, at the time of my interviews, they had not formed any. Jason and Logan expressed interest in establishing such relationships in the future. As Logan put it, "They're still getting started here, so there aren't really a lot of members yet. But, one of the cool things about coworking is that you meet other people that you could potentially work with at some point." Matt reported that he planned to refer web clients to a coworker.

Similarly, Link's coworkers had not yet established business relationships with each other. Four of the seven (Odessa, Patricia, Sal, and Tricia) expressed the hope of establishing such relationships, and Sal said that the promise of such relationships was "a big part of my choice to be involved in coworking originally." But these coworkers largely worked in very different customer-contact fields, so the business relationships that they envisioned tended to involve one-off services (e.g., buying a house, commissioning an interior-design session): they sought customers rather than partners.

WHY DO PEOPLE COWORK? SOME
CONTRADICTORY OUTCOMES

Why did these people cowork? Here, the answers were puzzlingly contradictory. All of these coworkers had worked at home, having tried out Toffler's "electronic cottage" and found it too distracting and isolating. Most had tried third-space alternatives such as coffee shops with similar results. But when they went to coworking sites, they sought different things. In fact, as we look across all of their motivations, we can see that they sought two different things.

Parallel work   Coworkers who expected to work in parallel wanted to interact with each other socially, sometimes gathering feedback from those in different fields, building a sort of neighborly trust so that they could leave their belongings unattended or discuss business dealings without having those details repeated. These coworkers often worked in sole proprietorships in customer-contact areas (e.g., interior design, real estate) and needed space to meet their customers as well as other amenities that would make them look more professional. They weren't collaborating on the same project. But they were working in the same front stage. And in that capacity, they communicated and coordinated quite frequently. They had to work at being good neighbors.

Cooperative work   Coworkers who expected to work in cooperation wanted to gather specific feedback and learning techniques from others in their own field, building a working trust that could lead to partnerships or subcontracting. Often these coworkers were freelancers or entrepreneurs who provided services to other businesses rather than individual customers, and sometimes they would never meet their clients face-to-face. As a result, these coworkers focused less on image and client meetings—explaining in part the extremely relaxed atmosphere at Conjunctured in comparison to the other coworking sites—than on generating cross talk and camaraderie that could lead to trusted partnerships. That is, they generally treated the coworking as a back stage, where they had to work at being good partners.

Parallel work and cooperative work—the front stage and the back stage—are very different outcomes. In fact, they involve two different sets of amenities and services. In this light, the coworking spaces seemed custom made for these two different outcomes. Conjunctured was arguably the place best suited for backstage work, with dog treats in the vending machines and beer in the fridge, while Link was arguably the place best suited for front-stage work, with its immaculate modern design, meeting rooms, and plentiful surface parking. Cospace was a blend of the two.

And yet people sought both parallel and cooperative work, both front and back stages, at all three sites. And given what we now know about how all-edge adhocracies work, we can certainly see why.

What Does It Mean?

Coworking is a little like a party. The host can send out the invitations, buy the drinks, and order the hors d'oeurves—but what makes the party a success is the guests who show up. Similarly, coworking is a service in which most of the value comes not from providing the space itself but from connecting people who can help each other out.

As we've seen, people can help each other out in at least two ways in coworking spaces: by being good neighbors and by being good partners (table 5.5). And although coworking spaces might be set up with one or the other in mind, coworkers are often looking for both—because as they work in all-edge adhocracies, they need both a back stage and a front stage. Backstage, they must be able to pull a team together from a pool of trusted partners, continue to build trust as they swarm projects, and coordinate this work through mutual adjustment. Front stage, they must be able to present themselves in an environment that clients will perceive as being more professional than a home office or coffee shop.

But at this point, coworking spaces have had trouble meeting both needs at the same time. It's this essential contradiction that I believe will continue to drive the development of coworking spaces and other workspaces that support all-edge adhocracies. To understand how, we need to learn more about the dynamic structure of all-edge adhocracies.

TABLE 5.5. Two configurations of coworking and their contradictions

	Good Neighbors	Good Partners
What is coworking (according to proprietors)?	Unoffice	Federated workspace
What is coworking (according to coworkers)?	Sociality (as neighbors); collaboration (as neighbors)	Sociality (as potential partners); collaboration (as partners)
Who coworks?	Small-business owners and consultants providing customer-contact services (front stage)	Entrepreneurs and freelancers providing services to businesses (back stage)
Why do they cowork?	Parallel work	Cooperative work

6

The Dynamic Structure of All-Edge Adhocracies: Activities

In chapter 5, coworking provides a uniquely adhocratic workplace that allows coworkers to build networks "backstage" while interfacing with clients "front stage." Unlike the workplaces you'll generally find in bureaucratic institutions, this workplace is separate from the organization. This new workplace supports at least two configurations: "good neighbors" and "good partners." And as those configurations suggest, this workplace is continuously being built by the coworkers themselves; it's a shared project in which they all participate as they communicate, coordinate, and collaborate with each other.

In the two cases I've examined, those of nonemployer firms and coworking spaces, we've seen that adhocracies tend to develop around projects. Such projects have defined beginning and ending points, and they involve assembling the right team of specialists. Every project can be different—but that doesn't mean that each is entirely novel. If all projects were novel, then these adhocratic workers would be perpetual amateurs, not professionals.

For instance, let's consider three people whom we met in chapter 5: Damon, who ran his Internet start-up from Conjunctured; Sal, who based his web design business at Link; and Helen, who ran a consulting business out of Conjunctured.

- Damon was developing an Internet service that he planned to soon roll out in a beta launch. Development on the site would happen in "waves," he told me: after launching the beta, he would concentrate first on developing functionality further toward a final product, then on attracting a large user base, then on acquiring a round of funding. His project was long-term, but with several stages, and at each stage, he planned to bring in different people, scaling the number of people up or down to match each stage. Some of those people were his fellow coworkers at Conjunctured. Sometimes they worked out; sometimes he had to let them go, which was awkward, since they continued to work alongside him in the coworking space. Still, he told me, "the people are definitely the perks" of working at Conjunctured—especially because some of the collaboration was through cross talk rather than formal arrangements: they tended to bounce ideas off of each other, give free advice, and suggest resources.

- Sal was a web developer at Link, working on a series of client projects, like the nonemployer firms in chapter 3. For him, each project was tightly bounded, with a specific beginning and ending point, and tended to involve different subcontractors. But the projects themselves were similar enough that he could establish a timeline, select appropriate tools, and subcontract appropriate people for each.

- Helen was a communication consultant, picking up both long- and short-term projects with various clients. Although she had employees working outside Conjunctured, she had also subcontracted with coworkers to complete tasks such as copywriting and photo editing. But as she told me, "The task is not the unifying attribute of the members at Conjunctured. It's simply not. A task done together is a byproduct of the relationship that you established while you were here."

Damon, Sal, and Helen were doing very different types of work, but their work shared attributes—not just with each other, but with most kinds of work:

- *It's stable, structured, and pulsing.* Each person's work focused on a specific project or set of projects, which had to be transformed in a predictable way, using specific processes and tools. For instance, Sal followed a similar process each time he took on a web design project, turning client specifications into a fully functional site. And as he repeated this process, he evolved it, figuring out how to avoid mistakes, do things more quickly, and organize his work more effectively. Each time he took on a project—each pulse of his work—he learned more and applied what he learned to the next pulse. Similarly, Damon's and Helen's work also pulsed, though Damon's project pulsed through different stages rather than different projects.

- *It's kinetic.* Even though work is stable, structured, and pulsing, work in adhocracies is what Alvin Toffler (1970) calls "kinetic." That is, these work activities come into contact with other dynamically structured activities, all of which may be developing at different rates and in different directions. For instance, every time Helen subcontracts work to someone from a different discipline, she has to understand enough of how that discipline fits into her project. Similarly, she has to understand enough of the client's business to be able to serve the client.

- *It's dynamic.* Finally, this work changes constantly because of tensions within and across these kinetic activities. These tensions can result in problems, disruptions, and strains, but they also result in innovations and adaptations; they're what drives Damon to improve his skills, broaden his network of contacts, and take on new challenges.

Damon's, Sal's, and Helen's work, like most people's, was in the middle of a perpetual tug-of-war between stability and change. The stability came from the activity's pulsing, structured nature. The change came from how they had to address the tensions within each project—such as the tensions between front and back stages that we saw in chapters 3 and 5.

How are these activities structured, how do they interact, and how do they develop? What characterizes an adhocratic activity? To understand the dynamic structure of all-edge adhocracies, we need a theory of human activity. That's what this chapter is about.

Understanding Work as Stable, Structured, and Pulsing: Activity Systems

Let's start with the stable, structured, pulsing aspects of activity. These are aspects that we might identify with institutional bureaucracies, which, as we saw in chapter 2, are set up to perform controlled work over and over. But even all-edge adhocracies have—and need—these aspects.

To understand these aspects, I start with a theory of human activity that developed in a place and era that was heavy with institutional bureaucracy— the Soviet Union. In particular, I apply the concept of the *activity system* (figure 6.1). (For more on activity theory, see Spinuzzi 2003, 2008.) The activity system describes the stable, structured, pulsing aspects of human activity, so it makes a good starting place for understanding the dynamic structure of all-edge adhocracies. But as we'll see, it's only a starting place.

An activity system is a way to examine an activity that forms around a specific, cyclically achieved object (Kaptelinin 2005)—which could be short term (say, Sal's web development project for a client) or long term (say, Damon's Internet start-up). Essentially, the activity system helps us to dissect the context of the recurring activity so we understand how it's put together. As figure 6.1 shows, it has the following components: object, outcome, tools, actors, rules, community stakeholders, and division of labor.

THE OBJECT: WHAT DOES THE WORK ACTIVITY TRANSFORM?

The object is that which the work transforms over and over as it pulses. For instance, farmers transform empty fields into full ones that can be harvested;

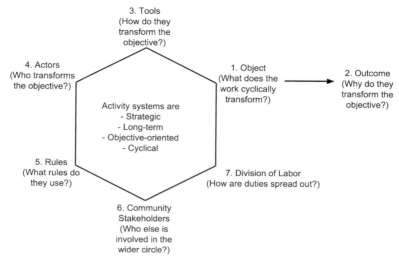

FIGURE 6.1. An activity system

factories transform raw materials into products; Sal transforms customer specifications into websites; Damon transforms his ideas into an Internet start-up. Everything else in the activity system—people, tools, rules, and so forth—is aligned to make sure that this transformation happens.

Each transformation is what I've been calling a *pulse* (Engeström, Engeström & Vähääho 1999). Work activity is dynamic: it pulses like a heart, with each pulse transforming the object. If your heart stopped pulsing, you'd be dead; similarly, if an activity stops pulsing, it's no longer an activity.

For instance, when Sal takes on a web development project, the project is the object: he has to take the client's specifications and turn them into a functioning site. Although he probably won't do this over and over for a specific client, he will turn many different clients' specifications into sites over the life of his firm, and he will tend to get better and better at it. Similarly, when Damon transforms his idea into a beta site, then a fully functional site, then to a site with many users, he is pulsing his object and learning more about successfully running a start-up.

In fact, sometimes we find that the same person or organization is involved in multiple objects. For instance, in chapter 3 we saw that the nonemployer firms (NEFs) had to achieve three objects: the front stage, the project object, and the collaboration. In chapter 5, we saw that coworkers had to manage these same objects. This multiple set of cross-organizational objects is inherent in all-edge adhocracies, since they bridge multiple organizations by their nature.

THE OUTCOME: WHY DO PEOPLE
TRANSFORM THE OBJECT?

The activity system forms around the object. But why do Damon, Sal, Helen, and the others keep pouring their efforts into transforming their objects? What's the intended outcome? When we talk about the outcome, we might think of it as the motivation—but motivation is an individual term. Activity systems—even activity systems describing small firms like Damon's, and even coworking spaces like Conjunctured's—are systems of people, tools, and rules. So what is the activity system itself set up to achieve?

To answer this question, let's look at the activity's strategic direction: motivations, desires, values. Understanding these helps us to understand why people like Damon, Sal, and Helen conduct their activity in a certain way. For instance, farmers may want to turn a profit—or maintain a family tradition. Factories may aim at higher short-term production—or a more stable business that supports long-term viability. Web developers may want to help convey a client's message—or generate strong pieces for their portfolios. And coworkers, as we saw in chapter 5, may give a range of reasons why they cowork.

Sometimes the activity's desired outcome is not what we might assume, and understanding that outcome is key to understanding why the activity is organized the way it is. For instance, in chapter 3, we saw that individuals chose to start nonemployer firms to maximize their freedom (as Albert did), to maximize their flexibility (as Sophie did), or to maximize their ability to select interesting creative projects (as Bob and Tom did). Or all three: Sometimes the activity attempts to achieve multiple outcomes based on the individuals' multiple perspectives on the object. That's not just true of all-edge adhocracies, but it seems especially true of them, since work is so interlinked across specialties.

TOOLS: HOW PEOPLE TRANSFORM THE OBJECT

When people like Damon, Sal, and Helen pulse their activities, they use (and often develop) tools to transform their objects. In fact, the typical activity uses many, many tools to get things done. For instance, in chapter 3, the nonemployer firms' tools included laptops, WiFi, mobile phones, software, spreadsheets, e-mail, printouts, and Skype. Many of these were shared: for example, web developers follow the same web design standards, while graphic designers tend to use the same software packages. At the same time, there's more than one way to skin a cat: chapter 3's NEFs could use different means to achieve the same thing, such as face-to-face meetings, conference calls, and Skype. The NEFs tended to have big "toolboxes," with interchangeable tools.

And they might need every tool in the box, since all-edge adhocracies rely so heavily on constant coordination and mutual adjustment.

ACTORS: WHO TRANSFORMS THE OBJECT?

Who's involved in the activity? Who is working, directly or indirectly, to achieve the object? In a stable team functioning in a bureaucratic hierarchy, the answer is fairly easy: you look at the organization chart or find the people at their desks. But in an all-edge adhocracy, the answer is harder, since the team changes composition from project to project and even from stage to stage. For instance, Tricia would act professionally when another coworker brought a client into the coworking space and, in so doing, became a minor actor in that coworker's activity. Similarly, Rhonda sometimes turned to other coworkers for advice in her business dealings, even though they didn't have a formal organizational or contract relationship to her. And when we ask who is an actor in the coworking space—or as I put it in chapter 5, who coworks?—the answer can include a range of different types of people. Who is an actor in a given activity? Whoever directly helps to achieve the object.

RULES: WHAT RULES DO THEY USE?

Rules are the ways people expect themselves and others to behave in the community or between communities. Think in terms of formal guidelines and protocols, but also dos and don'ts, unwritten rules, manners, and "the way things are done." For instance, when I talked with Bob and Tom (chapter 3) about how they conducted themselves with clients, Tom said, "There are some clients you can cuss with and some you can't." Bob followed up with an anecdote that is, unfortunately, unprintable. That's an example of an unwritten rule that the graphic designers had developed over time to deal with other communities with which they had to interact. Similarly, as Helen pointed out, Conjunctured had no rules against dogs or alcohol in the coworking space; Link most certainly did. Other rules are more formal. For instance, Soma Vida had a firm, printed rule against conversations in the coworking space, and all spaces had specific rules about access and rates.

COMMUNITY STAKEHOLDERS: WHO ELSE IS INVOLVED IN THE WIDER CIRCLE?

People don't just come from nowhere and start working on a project. We're all in different communities: broader, preexisting groups with shared ideas, values, or characteristics. In the workplace, obvious examples are fields, trades, and disciplines. And that goes doubly for all-edge adhocracies, which are inherently cross-disciplinary and cross-organizational. As Toffler (1970) points out, people working in adhocracies tend to feel more loyalty to their professions than to an organization. And that's critical, since we tend to get values, viewpoints, and ethical standards from our communities, including our professional organizations, families, and other affiliations. In the case of coworking, we don't have to look far to see what some of these communities looked like: for instance, Cospace regularly hosted events such as GeekAustin, the Austin Drupal Users Meetup, WordPress Camp, and Startup Weekend.

Those values don't have to be just about big things. For instance, in chapter 3, Bob and Tom told me that they didn't want to work with clients who expected them to wear khakis. And in chapter 5, when I asked coworking proprietors to describe the target customers for their spaces, each proprietor essentially described himself or herself!

DIVISION OF LABOR: WHAT ROLES DO THEY PLAY?

In all-edge adhocracies' projects, as in any other activity, people take on different roles: they decide who will pick up certain tasks, who will own phases of the work, who will interface with the client and who won't.

Sometimes divisions of labor are obvious—for example, when they're made on the basis of on job description or specialty. That's often the case in all-edge adhocracies, in which specialists come together to lend their unique skills to a project. For instance, if Helen seeks subcontractors for copywriting and photo editing, it's because she can't do those jobs herself. The problem object has different aspects, and Helen needs different specialists to address those different aspects.

But sometimes divisions of labor are less obvious. For instance, at Link, if someone brings a client to the space, everyone else who is working in the space knows that they have a job: to act professional. It's not a big job, but it's a job that they take seriously.

STABLE, STRUCTURED, PULSING—AND KINETIC

In a world full of institutional bureaucracies, like the 1970-era advertising agency in chapter 2, activity systems emphasize stability, control, and predictability. In fact, those characteristics are "baked into" activity theory, which was developed in the bureaucratic, industry-heavy environment of the

Soviet Union. So it is easy to think of activity systems as closed systems. But they're not.

As I said earlier, the activity system is a good springboard for understanding all-edge adhocracies, but it's only a starting place. That's because all-edge adhocracies require open systems. As Toffler (1970) puts it, adhocracies are "kinetic" organizations, interacting and colliding with others. To understand their dynamic structure, we have to examine those interactions and collisions. So I turn to a newer concept, also rooted in activity theory: activity networks.

Understanding Work as Kinetic: Activity Networks

Activity systems don't just float around like beach balls in the ocean; they connect to each other. They always have. But in an era of networks, those connections become denser and more overlaid. What's more, those connected activities are all changing, all at the same time, so the next pulse is never quite the same as the last.

Let's take a moment to distinguish activity networks from the organizational networks in chapter 4. As you recall, organizational networks are configurations of *people*: a kind of relationship distinct from other configurations such as hierarchies. When Helen subcontracts coworkers from Conjunctured to help her swarm her project, she's creating an organizational network. When we examine organizational networks, we're interested in how these individuals link up.

In contrast, activity networks are configurations of *activity systems* oriented toward a common object. When Helen's company attempts to pulse a familiar type of project, it needs to collaborate with other entities to pulse the object successfully. When we examine activity networks, we're interested in how clusters of actors, tools, rules, and practices interact to pulse their object.

Earlier I said that each activity system pulses its object. But with an all-edge adhocracy, a knot of interconnected activities (Engeström 2008) forms around the same project object, pulsing in unison as they collaboratively transform the object (see Heckscher 2007, p. 2)—once, perhaps twice, perhaps several times, depending on the engagement. Think of the temporary organization that Sal pulled together to accomplish a website project, or the different configurations of contractors that Damon planned to assemble during the phases of his project.

I call this knot of temporarily connected, simultaneously pulsing activity systems an *activity network* (Engeström 2008; Spinuzzi 2008). Other kinds of activity networks exist—for instance, a supply chain is a kind of activity network—but in the case of all-edge adhocracies, the activity network forms around and swarms the project object.

But because of the specialized nature of all-edge adhocracies, these activity systems are very different from each other: drawn from different specialist communities with different tools, different rules and expectations and values, different desired outcomes, and even competing objects that overlap the shared project object, to which they're temporarily synchronized so that they pulse together. With each pulse, they transform the project object in a way that no single activity system would or could. That's a remarkable feature— the primary feature that makes all-edge adhocracies so agile and effective— but it also creates problems that can only be mitigated through constant mutual adjustment, if then.

This sort of activity network is very different from the stable activities that we encounter in institutional bureaucracies. It's complex, since it draws from different specializations. It's complicated, since it is formed from alliances. It's often unstable—but the alliances only have to hold for the duration of the project. One pulse, maybe two, maybe more.

We can see why Toffler calls adhocracies "kinetic": they're always in motion. And sometimes that means social collisions: contradictions.

Understanding Work as Dynamic: Contradictions

Activity systems pulse. Activity networks pulse together. But these pulses aren't the only dynamic aspect of activities. Activities also develop basic systemic tensions: both internal tensions, within activity systems, and external tensions, across the activity systems in the network. These systemic tensions are called *contradictions*.

Whereas activity systems help us to understand the stable, structured, pulsing nature of work activity, and activity networks help us to understand how separate activity systems come together to transform a shared project object, contradictions help us to examine the tensions that inevitably develop in complex systems and networks of activity.

Like activities, contradictions take a bit of time to form and can take a long time to work themselves out. In institutions, which are relatively stable, contradictions tend to form slowly and simmer for a while before they have to be addressed. But in all-edge adhocracies, which form and dissipate rapidly, contradictions come to a rapid boil very quickly. That's partly because the networked activities have such large differences at so many points, with little time to reconcile them. And it's partly because each activity in the network is also connected to other, competing activities. As Damon told me: "Yeah, when working with contractors, they're trying to fit their bills, so they have to work with other people as well. The bigger question is, do they have a handle on their time? Can they manage all the stuff that we need to get done? I guarantee you, for every time that I'm staring down their eyes, saying 'We need to get this stuff done yesterday,' they're probably working for three other guys who are saying the exact same thing."

One basic contradiction that I discussed in both chapter 3 and chapter 5 was the contradiction between the front stage and the back stage. The back stage has to support the constant mutual adjustment that coordinates these all-edge adhocracies: the members of the adhocracy have to develop trusting relationships, address problems, discuss and recover from missteps, and settle their differences as they pull together their multiorganizational projects. Meanwhile, the front stage has to hide all of this complexity, presenting a much more controlled view of the firm to the client.

These two stages involve different actors, tools, rules, and divisions of labor; no wonder that they sometimes collide. The nonemployer firms I discussed went to great lengths to separate them—not always successfully. The coworking spaces I described had to accommodate both—again, not always successfully. This contradiction between front and back stages became a recurring problem for both sets of people, a strategic disturbance that affected them at each pulse.

But necessity is the mother of invention. Contradictions are not just strategic disturbances, they are also powerful sources of innovation (Cole & Engeström 1993). They are a vital part of the dynamic structure of all-edge adhocracies, driving them to develop rapidly with each pulse, and forcing them to become highly agile, flexible, and resilient. With that background, let's take another look at the coworking case in chapter 5.

Coworking's Contradictions

In chapter 5, I asked proprietors three questions that were meant to get at the activity of coworking. Let's look at these questions again, this time in terms of the activity system:

- *Object: What is coworking?* What were people trying to accomplish in the coworking space?
- *Actors: Who coworks?* Who decided to cowork? What were their characteristics and affiliations?
- *Outcome: Why cowork?* What did they expect to get out of coworking? What motivated them? What rewards did they expect from it?

As we saw in chapter 5, the answers were all over the map. They were contradictory. That is, they revealed contradictions: between proprietors and coworkers, among coworkers, across sites.

But coworking begins to make more sense if we examine it in activity theory terms, as "collaborations and engagements with a shared object in and for relationships of interaction between multiple activity systems" (Yamazumi 2009, p. 213; cf. Yamazumi 2013)—activity systems sharing collaborative objects that are "bounded hubs of concentrated coordination efforts" (Engeström 2009, p. 310). Doing so lets us connect some of the isolated contradictions we have noted in the objects, actors, and outcomes of coworking.

As Helen said in her quote at the beginning of this chapter, "The task is not the unifying attribute. . . . A task done together is a byproduct of the relationship that you established while you were here." Coworking wasn't a task, it was a broader ongoing object that people reached largely through their relationships. But the coworkers did not agree on what that object was; many seemed to be internally conflicted. Should coworking be about working with good neighbors or good partners? Let's think of these as two competing configurations.

THE GOOD-NEIGHBORS CONFIGURATION: HELP ME WITH MY FRONT STAGE

One coworking configuration can be described as the good-neighbors configuration (see figure 6.2). In this configuration, coworkers (whose activities are represented by hexagons) regularly meet with customers face-to-face. These coworkers bring their work into the coworking space (the circle) and work on it in parallel. For them, coworking means sustaining their neighborly relationships so that the coworking space can best support everyone's parallel work. That especially means helping each other provide a front stage of professionalism that is appropriate for meeting with customers.

In these coworking spaces, this good-neighbors configuration was reflected in several areas. Proprietors modeled their spaces on the unoffice. Coworkers looked for ways to be social with each other. They wanted to meet with customers face-to-face, so they wanted to work in a professional space where they could meet and impress customers. Most importantly, coworkers were willing to play the part for other coworkers, making sure to act professionally when their neighbor brought in a customer.

When we look at those puzzling, contradictory answers that coworkers gave, we can start to make sense of them when we understand the good-neighbors configuration as a nexus of otherwise unlinked external activities.

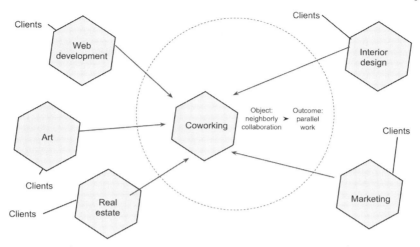

FIGURE 6.2. The good-neighbors configuration

That is, they were working on their own projects, but shared one common object: a front stage. Like neighbors, these coworkers were entirely unconnected in their work lives but were committed to sharing and improving a communal space.

THE GOOD-PARTNERS CONFIGURATION: HELP ME WITH MY BACK STAGE

In contrast, in the good-partners configuration (figure 6.3), independent, unaffiliated specialists (whose activities are represented by hexagons) can link up inside the coworking space (represented by the circle) to attack shared work problems. These shared problems are the project objects of their momentary collaborations, the problems that individuals from the space are recruited to swarm; the more enduring object, however, is the networking that facilitates these fast-forming all-edge adhocracies. One such transient team is illustrated in figure 6.3: experts in web development, search engine optimization, web services, and copywriting have temporarily linked up to solve a problem posed by an external business client. (The graphic designer and retailer have been left out of this particular collaboration but could be picked up on future jobs.) The good-partners configuration supports not a front stage of professionalism but a back stage in which coworkers can coordinate and mutually adjust as they swarm the project. This good-partners configuration is reflected in the coworking spaces in several areas: the proprietors' federated workspace model, coworkers' focus on collaboration and

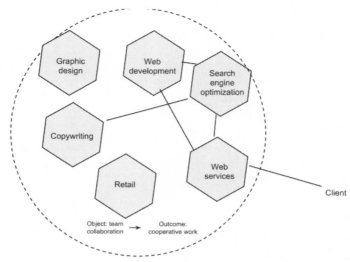

FIGURE 6.3. The good-partners configuration

sociality, coworkers' business-services orientation, and coworkers' desire for a back stage in which they can make these projects happen. These aspects of the object, actors, and outcomes make sense when we understand the good-partners configuration as a nexus of transient work teams composed of specialists. As partners, these coworkers forged connections through their work lives as well as their social lives, and they treated the coworking space as the back stage for making these connections happen.

THE SUPERIMPOSED CONFIGURATIONS: HELP ME WITH BOTH STAGES

So these are two configurations of coworking, two distinct ways in which a coworking space can function as a nexus of networked activities. Obviously other configurations are possible, and other activities can interfere with these patterns. For instance, coworkers preferred certain locations because they were closer to certain amenities, suggesting that other activities (e.g., parenting) also influenced coworking. Similarly, a detailed study of a coworking space founded on the community workspace model might well turn up another configuration in which other activities are networked.

Once we get this big picture, we can start to understand the contradictions we saw in the object (what is coworking?), the actors (who coworks?), and the outcomes (why cowork?). The two configurations are oriented to two different objects—the front stage and the back stage. But they are *superim-*

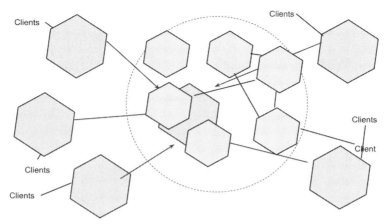

FIGURE 6.4. The two configurations superimposed

posed in each space (figure 6.4). They interfere. Even though one coworking space may cater to one or the other of these configurations, both happen in each space, and contradictions manifest every time the activities pulse.

What's Next for Coworking?

But as I mentioned earlier, contradictions aren't just disturbances, they're points of innovation. Coworking continued to evolve after I finished my visits with Austin's coworking sites, yielding new models and new variations. These include Center 61, which focuses on small nonprofits and social entrepreneurs; Plug & Play, which offers on-site child care; Vuka Co-op, a cooperative for entrepreneurs and digital artists; and Capital Factory, a city-run incubator and coworking space. We can expect further, rapid differentiation as these and other spaces address the quickly forming contradictions that make all-edge adhocracies so dynamic.

When we understand all-edge adhocracies as interlinked, structured activities, we can get a better sense of why they're organized the way they are. The view may seem chaotic, as these all-edge adhocracies rapidly form, pulse, and dissipate. But sometimes we see all-edge adhocracies forming under much more stable conditions. To see how this happens, I move away from independents and look at one final case, this time set inside a larger organization.

Lone Wolves: The Case of Search Engine Optimization

Up to this point, I've been discussing all-edge adhocracies as they form among relatively independent workers. But adhocracies can form wherever work is organized within networks and around projects—including hierarchies with organizational charts and payrolls. Yes, bureaucratic hierarchies and adhocracies are very different things, optimized for very different outcomes, but they aren't necessarily antithetical: networks can overlay and interact with hierarchies. When they do, we see some interesting interactions.

That's certainly true in this case. When I first began studying the work at Semoptco in fall 2008, I expected to learn about how it managed projects. But what I found in this study, which spanned 2008–2009, was adhocracies— adhocracies that crystallized around specific projects, involved collaboration among specialists with a high degree of autonomy, and were built on networks of activity. Those adhocracies overlaid a bureaucratic hierarchy and were anchored by common texts and tools. And although the adhocracies were mostly along the lines of the institutional adhocracies I discussed in chapter 2, every once in a while they pulled in people from other organizations to swarm projects, becoming all-edge adhocracies. But I'm getting ahead of myself. Let's back up and talk about what Semoptco does and why it needs adhocracies to do it.

Semoptco's Business: SEO

WHAT SEO IS

In 2009, Republican Kay Bailey Hutchison announced her intention to leave the US Senate and seek a prize closer to home: governor of Texas. Unfortu-

This chapter is based on Spinuzzi (2010).

nately for her, Texas already had a sitting Republican governor, Rick Perry. So Hutchison decided to challenge him in the Republican primaries.

Perry was vulnerable along some fronts, including an unsubstantiated but persistent rumor that this socially conservative governor of a socially conservative state was secretly gay. Consequently, some Texans apparently performed Internet searches for phrases such as "rick perry gay." And since Hutchison's website vendor had included a script to secretly incorporate common search keywords into her site—a common "black hat" technique for attracting Internet traffic—her site soon incorporated that phrase along with about 2,200 others (Anderson 2009; Selby 2009). Since the website contained that exact set of keywords, soon it ranked high in the search results of anyone searching for "rick perry gay."

That is, until Google yanked the site from its search index—the death penalty for a website. After that, no matter what people searched for, Google wouldn't return the site. Google didn't pull the plug because the phrase was offensive—it pulled the plug because the phrase was irrelevant to the content of the site. Hutchison's campaign site didn't actually supply relevant information for "rick perry gay" or "texas grape growers" or "orthodox synagogue" or most of the 2,200 hidden keywords in the site.

What Hutchison's vendor did was "black hat SEO": that is, an unethical, ham-handed attempt at search engine optimization (SEO). SEO is simply an effort to make a site rank high in the search results for a specific set of keywords. Whether you're selling a product, a service, or a political candidate, you want your site to show up in the first couple of screens of search results. (Unfortunately, people usually don't click past the first couple of screens.) The higher your site ranks, the more likely people are to see it. And that's critical, since people increasingly search for results rather than finding them in other ways.

Black hat SEO, as we've seen, comes with several dangers. One is that it might attract click-throughs but not genuine engagement, since it isn't necessarily relevant to the site: when someone searches for "rick perry gay" or "britney spears pics," he or she will likely not be engaged by irrelevant content. Another is that search engine providers don't want to serve irrelevant results—it threatens their own business model—and will take steps such as delisting sites that violate their guidelines. Vendors who provide black hat SEO, like the vendor who provided Hutchison's site, generally know this. But they sell black hat SEO because it's easy to provide.

White hat SEO, in contrast, is SEO done right. It involves identifying relevant keywords, building appropriate content on the client's site that incorporates those keywords, keeping the content fresh, building genuine links, monitoring click-throughs and engagement each month, adjusting to other influences such as news events that might depress the client's search rankings, and keeping on top of the nearly constant changes to search engine algorithms. (Yes, Google and the other search engines frequently tweak their algorithms, and these tweaks have a significant effect on the search results.) It's hard work, requiring experts with an ethical code.

White hat SEO was the business of Semoptco, an Internet marketing firm that I studied in fall 2008. In my interview with Stan, Semoptco's director of product development, he explained that Semoptco offered "a very data-centric approach":

> Even our SEO team, which is very content-driven, they still spend a lot of time looking at data to go make decisions and then figure out what happened. I mean, Google changed their ranking algorithm about a month and a half ago. And we collect data every day for somewhere between five and fifty keywords for our clients to say "how are you ranking?" We saw about three quarters of them go up over two days. In some cases, it was a spot or two. In some cases, it was ten, fifteen, thirty spots. . . . We've changed a lot of techniques we're using . . . over the last nine months, and it was great to see that . . . completely objective proof point that those things had kind of, had done the addition.

He characterized this replicable, evidence-based analytical approach as Semoptco's "secret sauce": something genuine and reliable and measurable, something that Semoptco could communicate clearly to clients through monthly reports. Therefore those monthly reports included "report cards" that specified the methods Semoptco used and their results over the entire campaign's history. Semoptco could be trusted because it had turned SEO into a methodical, well-managed, data-driven business. Semoptco's workers were intensely aware that they had to build trust and authority in this complex, contingent, ever-changing business, primarily through the monthly reports.

Of course, finding the right workers was a problem. In 2008, there was no college education to prepare people for working in SEO. That's partly why Stan was talking with me in the first place.

LEARNING SEO

When I visited Semoptco in 2008 (see appendix), it employed about forty account managers and specialists, six of whom were SEO (or "natural search") specialists. Semoptco's objective was to drive up conversions, visits to their clients' sites that turned into transactions.

Semoptco offered four basic services: SEO, paid search, display advertising, and website effectiveness strategy and consulting. But in this chapter, I focus on SEO, in which specialists select the right keywords to reach the customer, then optimize for those keywords; their measures include (*a*) analyzing keyword performance, (*b*) advising the client on website revisions and additions, and (*c*) building links that point to the client's site.

Since no reputable college offered an SEO degree at that point, Semoptco's specialists had obtained degrees in a variety of fields, then learned SEO on the job. To find out more about how they worked, I visited, observed, and interviewed three of the six SEO specialists as well as their manager and one of the three account managers.

- Stan, the director of product services, had been at Semoptco for about a year at the beginning of the study. He had worked for similar companies. Stan had a master's degree in information architecture.
- Daria, a senior specialist in natural search, had worked at Semoptco for just over a year. This was her second job after graduating with a liberal arts degree and a master's degree in information.
- Luis, a senior specialist in natural search, had worked at Semoptco for two years, initially as an intern while he finished his bachelor's degree in advertising. He had been promoted to senior specialist just before our first interview.
- Carl, a specialist in natural search, had worked for Semoptco for six months at the time of the first interview. He had apprenticed with Luis during this time. Before then, he had graduated with a history degree from a liberal arts college, then worked a series of jobs, including one with AmeriCorps and another in quality assurance at a videogame developer.
- Stacy, an account manager, had worked at Semoptco for seven months at the time of the first interview. She had held similar positions at PR agencies, where she "did tech PR," but had not worked at a search marketing firm before Semoptco. She had a bachelor's degree in public relations.

At first glance, SEO might seem like a job for a bureaucratic hierarchy. After all, nothing sounds as bureaucratic as a monthly report, driven by data-centric analysis, generating metrics that are presented in "report cards." These sorts of predictable outcomes require solid, controlled processes. And no organizational structure does controlled processes and predictable outcomes better than a bureaucratic hierarchy (see chapter 2).

But at the same time, these specialists also needed the strengths of a networked adhocracy. Even though the process was the same each month—they had to pulse the objective of improving clients' search results—the work itself was constantly changing because SEO was full of contingencies to which they had to adapt. These contingencies included constant customization to collaboratively address the unique constraints of each client's industry and the new tools and analytics available for SEO; constant boundary crossing to better analyze each client's industry, its target audiences, and what keywords would draw them; and constant trust building through results demonstrating that Semoptco's specialists were competent, honest, and accurate.

And since these contingencies were constant, so were the learning opportunities. In each monthly cycle, specialists had to learn new techniques, new tools, new capabilities. For each client, they had to learn a little about the client's industry and the background of the customers that the client wanted to attract. Since everything in this fluid industry was changing at once, the specialists had to teach themselves and each other how to perform SEO.

When we look at it this way, SEO requires constant innovation and learning, constant boundary crossing, constant contingency handling, and constant coordination among specialists. And no organizational structure does these things better than an adhocracy (see chapter 2).

Should Semoptco be a bureaucracy? Or an adhocracy? Simple: It became both. Semoptco managed to create a hybrid structure that drew on the strengths of both forms. And the advantages of this hybrid structure were most visible in the reports that Semoptco's specialists produced every month, reports that could only happen because of the strengths of both forms.

REPORTING SEO

Every month, each of the six SEO specialists wrote an eighteen- to twenty-page report for each client he or she handled. A lot rested on each report: Semoptco wanted to retain and upsell clients, and clients in turn wanted to drive more people to their sites. Remarkably, each SEO specialist produced ten to twelve such reports within the first ten business days of each month. That's a lot of reports, especially since the specialists were not trained writers, nor did they consider themselves to be writers per se.

After writing the reports, the specialists used the rest of the month to keep up with the fast-changing SEO landscape, build links to their customers' sites, analyze keyword performance, inspect clients' sites for flaws and opportunities, learn new tools and techniques, and communicate new findings to others. This work was all in addition to the research- and writing-heavy work of launching new clients' campaigns.

The reports varied in content and complexity. On one end, tier 3 clients received a "report card," a set of simple data tables showing how well each keyword was driving traffic to their site, along with action items for the clients and Semoptco to take to improve keyword performance. On the other, tier 1 clients received monthly meetings with the specialist and additional sections in the reports: an executive summary; a campaign overview; detailed action items including opportunities; short- and long-term goals and objectives; and deep analysis including comparisons of keyword performance for the three major search engines. These reports and meetings demonstrated how well Semoptco was serving the client: how much traffic was being driven to the site and from what referring sites, how much of this traffic was being converted into sales (if applicable), how close keyword performance was to its stated goals. Together, they demonstrated how well Semoptco was serving the client, justifying further actions to improve SEO.

Since SEO was working within a relatively new and highly customized industry with a rapidly changing landscape, specialists often encountered unprecedented issues. That meant that even in routine monthly reports, they sometimes had to invent and explain innovative analyses and argue for innovative courses of action.

How did they do all of this work with little formal training to speak of? There's the interesting part. And as you might have guessed, it has to do with how they put together their bureaucracy and their adhocracies. More on that in a moment.

PERFORMING SEO

As I explained in chapter 6, work activities tend to be cyclical; they have a rhythm, a pulse. In Semoptco's case, it had to first launch clients, which involved defining clients' goals and developing a plan of action to meet them. Then it had to maintain those clients, continuing to make progress on long-term goals, adjusting those goals when necessary, and reporting progress via monthly reports. Both phases involved extended sets of texts, some of which were shared across phases. And both were loosely coordinated, giving each specialist quite a bit of autonomy to perform work. Let's briefly look at each phase.

Launch mode   Launching a client looked somewhat like traditional project management (Duncan 1996), and it involved some of the heavily coordinative texts that are associated with project management. When a client first comes to Semoptco, Stan told me, it might have a history with "snake oil" SEOs that makes it more cautious. Semoptco typically extracted the client's verbal commitment to stick with Semoptco for at least six months, since that's how long it usually takes for an SEO campaign to show results. Similarly, if a client paused or terminated its SEO campaign, results degraded over time.

At Semoptco, the CEO selected a project team for each client, pairing an account manager with an SEO specialist. The project team then produced texts associated with the launch. Initially, it would present the client with a launch plan, built from a standard template, showing a few milestones for the client and the project team to accomplish by launch. Milestones included "client research," "non keyword specific link building," "web analysis," "recommended SEO keywords," "keyword specific link building," "on page recommendations," and "competitive analysis." The launch process typically took four weeks, and milestones were relatively fixed.

Maintenance mode   Once the campaign was launched, it went into maintenance mode. Specialists worked toward long-term objectives related to performance metrics but without fixed milestones. Instead, they maintained campaigns according to weekly, monthly, and sometimes yearly cycles (or pulses, as I called them in chapter 6). But even though maintenance mode was routine, it wasn't on autopilot: every month, the specialists had to actively problem solve to improve each campaign. As one specialist told me, they acted as "lone wolves"—specialists had remarkable discretion over their work, as long as they delivered and as long as they kept within ethical boundaries.

For the specialists, maintenance mode involved three main tasks: writing monthly reports for clients, meeting with clients (either in person or in conference calls) to report results, and building links. In my initial observations in early October, reporting and meetings took the first two weeks of the month, with link building taking the second two weeks. But by late October, Luis told me, "the first ten days are getting shorter due to business tools" such as BRILLIANCE, a system developed in-house to automatically track analytics, metrics, and notes on clients' websites. Carl confirmed that at this point, "that first third of the month is reporting, the middle third is meetings with the clients about those reports . . . that last third is even more 'do whatever you need to do.'"

Luis clarified that the first three days of reporting were dedicated to tier 1 clients. But beyond monthly deadlines, individual specialists structured their own time. As Daria told me, "For the most part, even just with client stuff, it's kind of expected—okay, here's what you need to have done by the end of the month. You've got your timeline, you know this client's done with launching, so here's how much we need to spend on links, here's how many of these types of links we need to build." So SEO specialists, like the others we've seen in adhocracies, were quite autonomous compared to workers in a bureaucratic hierarchy: they mostly managed their own time, identified their own tasks, and communicated their own accomplishments to clients.

For the account manager, the monthly cycle meant ensuring that clients received reports and monitoring progress. As Stacy told me, "Once a client gets in maintenance mode, it's less contact and more—every few weeks, try to touch base on things." She not only had to check the status of the specialists' work but also the clients': for instance, after I observed her prodding one client via e-mail for feedback, she said, "The marcomm [marketing communication] managers aren't superinvolved, and so they will, like, forget that we exist for weeks and months at a time." She had to actively involve those outside managers in the "pulse" of the activity.

Account managers sometimes needed to frame monthly reports as well, explaining Semoptco's services and their value. In one observation, Stacy received a specialist's report that recommended increasing the budget for buying links. Stacy drafted an e-mail to the client arguing for increasing the link-buying budget as well as increasing the management fee—something that would result in more Semoptco revenue, yes, but also in better SEO.

Beyond framing the reports, account managers also vetted the reports for clients. As Stacy explained after one observation, specialists sometimes wrote these reports to the client, sometimes to the account manager, "so they each need a different amount of editing." Specialists sometimes used technical language that the account manager had to translate for clients. But account managers also had to look for unusual variations in the reports. When reading one report, for instance, Stacy noted language that "didn't look right," so she consulted with more-experienced account managers.

In the launch process, then, project management was quite minimal, and in maintenance mode, it was nonexistent. That doesn't make sense from the standpoint of a bureaucracy, but it makes perfect sense from the perspective of an adhocracy, in which workers are relatively autonomous specialists who mutually adjust to handle contingencies creatively. SEO was full of contingencies that a static bureaucracy would not be flexible enough to handle. Yet clients also wanted a stable, proven approach to SEO with a stable, predictable interface: the monthly report and its "report card." Such regular outcomes are best handled by bureaucracy. In other words, we're back to the contradiction between the back stage and the front stage—the contingent, inventive SEO work and the reliable, predictable report.

Semoptco handled the contradiction with a hybrid that could draw on the strengths of both structures. On the SEO side, it pushed autonomy and discretion to the level of the individual specialists and set up multiple ways for specialists to mutually adjust, coordinate, learn, experiment, and share results on the fly. On the reporting side, it set up an automated system (BRILLIANCE) to reliably generate "report cards" and templates into which specialists could input their results. Between these two was a standing set of transformations (Spinuzzi 2008), a flexible process for bridging the two kinds of work by moving them through a set of representations. Let's take a look at this standing set of transformations and how it bridged these two sides of the work.

Specialists spread out their work by using sets of information sources, strung together to steadily transform different pieces of information into reports— and adhocratic innovations into bureaucratic results. They assembled reports, to some extent automatically, from information they entered into BRILLIANCE. But that oversimplifies the many acts of reading and writing involved.

For instance, Luis heavily highlighted and annotated the previous month's report, then entered notes from it into BRILLIANCE; these notes would become sections of the current month's report. He also gathered text from client e-mails, instant messages and face-to-face conversations with Carl, a spreadsheet he used to track his own projects, the WikiAnswers site, and an autogenerated draft of the current month's report (see left side of figure 7.1). Like other specialists, Luis didn't consider himself a writer, and from his perspective, he wasn't "writing" a twenty-page report: he was analyzing website traffic, making notes, and double-checking e-mails. Nevertheless, these actions generated reports that connected clients' goals, Semoptco's actions, keyword results, and other information into a complex document that provided an appropriately bureaucratic interface.

As the right half of figure 7.1 shows, the completed report was then e-mailed to the account manager for that client, who sometimes had to edit it. Here, Stacy had to review a report, ask other account managers if they had seen similar language, tweak the wording so that her client could understand it, then e-mail the report to the client with some explanatory text. Finally, as figure 7.1 indicates, top-tier clients also received a meeting. And then the document would become the previous report for use in the next cycle.

Figure 7.1 depicts the standing set of transformations that Luis and Stacy used. Each information source flowed to the next, contributing information that was transformed as it was transferred into the next information source. For instance, when Luis asked Carl a question over instant messaging, he summarized the answer in the BRILLIANCE notes; when he generated the draft report, those notes were pulled into the report; when he sent the report to Stacy, she edited it for clarity. Some of these transformations were automated

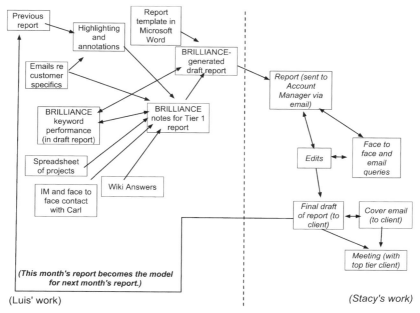

FIGURE 7.1. Generating a monthly report at Semoptco

or heavily regulated (such as keyword performance tables), some regularized (such as highlighting and annotations), some coordinative (such as the projects spreadsheet), some specific to that project and cycle (such as e-mails and IMs). Some were innovated in a given cycle, then instantiated in the resulting report—after all, each month's report became the model for the next month's report, meaning that the report evolved constantly to address SEO changes.

Although I've separated launch and maintenance modes here, specialists and account managers had to attend to both modes simultaneously: each could be involved with multiple launches and multiple maintenance projects at the same time. Sometimes these cycles collided, with maintenance meetings, launch deliverables, and link building happening at the same time.

FIGURING OUT SEO

So SEO at Semoptco was a two-sided affair, balancing the client's need for reliable, comparable results with the practice of SEO, which had to change constantly for at least three reasons:

- First, the business of SEO was audience analysis (cf. Killoran 2009). What people already come to the client's site, and what people should come

there? Which keywords will bring the right people to the right site, connect the right customers to the right services?

- But as with any form of audience analysis, this business was inherently full
  of contingencies. What Google gives, Google can also take away: search
  engines often tweaked their algorithms, changing the rankings to combat
  the "snake oil" techniques that characterize black hat SEO. Other SEO
  companies were also at work, optimizing their clients' sites and perturbing
  the rankings. News items could unpredictably crowd the rankings, pushing down results. The clients themselves were unpredictable: sometimes
  slow or negligent in implementing Semoptco's recommendations on their
  own sites.

- These and other contingencies, from multiple directions, made Semoptco's business inherently complex, inherently fast moving, requiring
  rapid response and a high degree of autonomy from its SEO specialists.
  They had to collaborate and plan effectively, demonstrating contingencies and their effective responses through monthly reports. These reports,
  then, had to be structurally and rhetorically complex.

Beyond all that, the specialists had to be quick. These reports were due every
month.

So what challenges did Semoptco face as it marshaled all of these textual
resources to generate its analytical reports? At least three emerged: constant
customization, constant boundary crossing, and constant trust building.
These are, of course, challenges for which adhocracies are uniquely suited.

Semoptco's Flexibility: Constant Customization

"Do you think campaigns usually go in the same track," I asked Stacy during one visit, "or is each one a unique situation?" Without hesitation, she
responded, "They're all very different." This point was repeated, with many
examples, by Daria, Luis, and Carl. Each campaign, each client, each launch,
and each iteration of the monthly maintenance cycle was considered unique.
For some, specialists and account managers developed innovations. But what
made these situations unique? How did Semoptco's specialists and account
managers collaboratively address them and produce reports?

THE CHALLENGES OF CUSTOMIZATION

Semoptco had established firm launch timelines, three tiers of reports, and
templates for its monthly reports and other deliverables—all of which are
bureaucratic moves, moves that we might expect would lead to greater stan-

dardization and inflexibility, not greater flexibility. In fact, Daria stated in her pre-observation interview that when she began training new hires, her goal was

> to make it a really structured process with lots of documents. And I have documents. But . . . *you're never sure what you're going to be doing the next day*. So the structure . . . just hasn't been able to happen as much as I would like it to. So really, it's been a lot of—at first, learning, reading, looking at examples of the documents, looking at examples of our deliverables. And then—pretty much mentoring, *letting people just do it* and help them as they go and let them get practice at it. (my emphasis)

Luis, who had worked at Semoptco longer, found this structure to be a starting place: "We like follow the template, and then . . . *customize it according to the client*, which we do very often" (my emphasis). The template was bureaucratic, but the customization, which required innovation and flexibility, was a job for adhocracies.

Customization for specific clients   This turned out to be a major contingency driving innovation at work. For instance, clients' contingencies motivated both Daria and Luis to innovate new documents or new variations of documents. At one point, Luis was working on the competitive analysis for a client whose campaign was about to launch. As Luis reviewed the competitors the client had named, he concluded that these were not the best online competitors to target. He identified better competitors, then developed a table to demonstrate that this set was superior. Later, he explained, "I didn't have planned to create this other extra document to show the client, why are we picking up these competitors. Uh, sometimes . . . they understand pretty easy, it's not required. But this time *the client really doesn't understand why*. So we have to show him, like, another kind of deliverable to make him understand why" (my emphasis).

Similarly, while examining analytics for one client, Daria was trying to determine whether the client's monthly e-mail blasts were causing traffic surges. She spent about half an hour pasting numbers into a spreadsheet from different sources, then generating graphs with titles such as "Daily SEO Revenue vs. Email Blast Dates." Later, she told me that these graphs were innovations responding to a unique situation. She would improvise such graphs "probably only for big important clients."

"You pay for bigger customization," Luis told me, and indeed tier 1 clients received more customized solutions. For instance, Daria reported that one of the biggest clients received annual reports as well as monthly ones: "If they want it, they'll get it." Similarly, Stacy developed a spreadsheet for keeping track of contacts at a large client, and Carl tracked additional analytics for a client who requested them.

Customization in response to search engine changes   This was less frequent but exceedingly important: even small algorithm changes can strongly affect search engine results. Semoptco had to detect these changes and adjust accordingly, keeping clients informed. For instance, in one report, Luis wrote that "[Semoptco] noticed negative fluctuations for targeted keywords within MSN rankings" and discussed how to address them. Constant search engine changes led Semoptco to hire more flexible, self-motivated specialists: "Google . . . starts evolving and you have to evolve with it," Daria explained.

Customization by offloading problem solving   On the other hand, once a specialist solved a recurring problem, she or he didn't have to solve it over again. Specialists constantly developed routines and tools to encapsulate their solutions so that they could move on to the next problem. Today's innovations became tomorrow's regulated, automated solutions and templates. By examining and offloading their processes, workers freed up more time to conduct work they couldn't offload, such as in-depth analysis.

At Semoptco, this constant offloading took at least three forms:

- *Internally refining and automating resources.* Semoptco's workers refined internal resources. For instance, Semoptco had recently tracked links with "a lot of spreadsheets with macros pulling into other spreadsheets," but "a lot of that has migrated to BRILLIANCE, so we don't have to mess with that anymore," Daria reported. BRILLIANCE also autogathered information on specified links and tracked client expenses; it became a rolling context for any given project, context shared by specialists and account managers. Daria even used BRILLIANCE's data on paid search (a separate service) to generate ideas about selecting proper keywords. Another part of BRILLIANCE's work was to autogenerate key components of the templated reports. Eventually, Luis told me, Semoptco planned to serve reports directly to clients through BRILLIANCE rather than e-mailing documents. Beyond BRILLIANCE, Semoptco's templates offloaded the work of developing deliverables from scratch.
- *Internally developing new resources.* Semoptco's development team also created internal tools for automating work. During one observation, specialists talked excitedly about a tool under development that would let them post to several social bookmarking sites simultaneously, using multiple login names, and simultaneously update BRILLIANCE. "The interns will love this!" one specialist enthused (interns usually had to do

this task). But specialists would still need to use discretion: if too many links were submitted at once, "it pops up on the link graph" and could negatively affect search results.

- *Scouting for new resources.* Workers also sought external tools. As Daria said, "Sometimes the SEO team will find a new tool or process that will help us streamline things or just find new info so they'll talk about it and offer it. You just have to look for that stuff on your own and then present it to the team." Like Daria, Carl and Luis scouted such tools. As operationally autonomous agents, specialists ranged independently and brought valuable external resources back to their teams.

That's a lot of customization and innovation. To do it well, Semoptco had to provide a flexible organizational structure that would allow a high degree of operational autonomy but still enable constant communication among workers, keep projects on track, and foster constant innovation.

FLEXIBILITY THROUGH NETWORK STRUCTURE: MAINTAINING TEAM COHESION IN CONTINGENCY-LADEN WORK

To get it done, Semoptco established an overlapping set of at least six teams—organizational networks (table 7.1). These teams were held together through constant mutual adjustment as well as self-regulative tools and practices. Semoptco was not an entirely "flat" organization, but below the upper-management layer, workers enjoyed considerable autonomy, organized in networks where they played multiple roles and established multiple relations.

Note that not all of these organizational networks qualified as all-edge adhocracies: they weren't all interorganizational or temporary. In fact, they mostly resembled the 1990s-era institutional adhocracies that we encountered in chapter 2. But as we'll see, they sometimes reached outside the organization to temporarily pull in others with specialized knowledge.

Here's the thing: Specialists served on all these teams simultaneously. Each team had a well-defined scope; most were small; all focused on pulsing specific objectives beyond the monthly report. Stan explained that Semoptco desired "a lot of small nimble teams tackling specific problems: they could be internal problems, they could be client-focused problems."

As is common with adhocracies, most teams did not have strongly defined leadership roles. For instance, although account managers nominally managed project teams, that management consisted of conveying reminders about the timetable and vetting reports for the clients. Similarly, although I had initially thought that support teams constituted a nascent middle-management

TABLE 7.1. Teams functioning as networks at Semoptco

Team (network)	Description	Objective	Composition	Mutual adjustment venues
Project	Teams that launched and maintained campaigns. Team members were in separate physical spaces.	The account.	Account manager, one to two specialists. Assigned by CEO.	Instant messaging, e-mail, meetings, conference calls, drop-in visits, generic and specialized project management texts.
Apprenticeship	Colocated buddy/mentoring teams. In SEO, these gave way to support teams during the study.	The apprentice.	The three account managers formed an apprenticeship team in their shared office; pairs of specialists formed teams in shared cubicles.	Informal conversations in workspace, instant messaging.
Support	Colocated, formal three-person teams that rapidly developed to determine load and status of accounts. Framed as mentoring, not a middle-management layer.	Oversight and awareness of current service for clients.	Senior specialist and two less experienced specialists.	Drop-in visits, instant messaging, e-mail, BRILLIANCE notes, meetings.
Functional	Teams encompassing entire departments: SEO, paid search, etc.	The department's function.	All department members.	Reporting parties, brown-bag lunches, instant messaging, e-mail, internal blog, internal wiki.
Values	Cross-boundary teams, initiated during the study, that worked on enacting core values (leadership, accountability, cooperation).	The cultural value, made concrete through actions such as reorganizing the documents on the server (accountability) and volunteering with local charities (leadership).	Self-chosen from across the company.	Meetings, e-mail.
Taco club	Pairs who shared breakfast tacos on Wednesday mornings.	The cross-departmental social network.	Self-chosen pairs of workers from different functional teams.	Meetings, e-mail.

layer, Daria and Carl indicated that her leadership role was support, not close management. As Daria put it, "The goal, especially with the reorganization, was to have . . . more oversight and awareness of what's going on with clients." This structure matches Manuel Castells's description of the "e-firm" as "based on a flat hierarchy, a teamwork system, and open, easy interaction between workers and managers" (2003, p. 91); such e-firms "give workers as much initiative as they can handle, under conditions defined and organized by management" (p. 233)—conditions that include team composition, timelines, and templates.

These teams, then, functioned as adhocracies: project oriented, agile, innovative, allied, decentralized, and autonomous. Each adhocratic team had its own objective; each contributed to the problem solving that culminated in the monthly reports; in aggregation, the teams reached the objectives of Semoptco. Consequently, workers knew what relations they could draw on when working on a specific project, but they also established relationships and mutual adjustment across the entire company.

One important tool for maintaining mutual adjustment was Semoptco's use of instant messaging. Every worker had an instant messaging client running, listing every worker of the company who was logged in. Workers would log into the service as soon as they arrived, and they used it to determine whether other workers had arrived. That is, the instant messaging program functioned as a task support tool (see Pazos, Chung & Micari 2012; Quan-Haase & Wellman 2007) that also provided virtual copresence (Subramaniam, Nandhakumar & Baptista John 2013). According to Stacy, IMs had essentially replaced phone calls within Semoptco.

In some cases, IMs replaced even more-familiar forms of contact. For instance, in one observation, Luis wanted to ask a question of Carl, who shared his cubicle. He glanced at Carl, but Carl was wearing headphones. Rather than interrupting, Luis turned back to his screen and sent Carl an IM.

This incident illustrates how important IMs were at Semoptco, but it also illustrates how autonomously specialists worked. I called this the "lone wolf" model in interviews with Daria and Carl, and they agreed, describing their work in memorable phrases such as "every man for himself" (Daria) and "do whatever you need to do" (Carl). Carl described specialists' isolation in this way: "For a new hire, just imagine, it's like you came in and you're on an island. And I don't necessarily dislike that." Similarly, Daria said that "there's no one saying 'do this, you have to do something like this.'" Specialists developed their own routines, schedules, and time-management procedures within the framework of monthly work cycles and launch milestones; diverged widely in how they spent their time; and exercised considerable autonomy in selecting their tools, conducting individualized analyses, and customizing reports for clients. For instance, Daria, Luis, and Carl used a range of idiosyncratic checklists and highlighting schemes. Not just anyone could take on this sort of role: understandably, Stan and Daria both said that they looked for "self-starters" when hiring.

But these autonomous specialists also scouted new tools and information, continually adopting or inventing new ways to encapsulate innovative solutions in tools. They developed ways to circulate their knowledge across apprenticeship, support, and functional teams, including shared documents, templates, copies of previous reports, checklists in Google Docs, internal and external blogs, and meetings. This scouting model had problems, but it let Semoptco balance operational autonomy with the need to stabilize work. Ultimately, Semoptco's networks provided enough flexibility to conduct audience analysis and build trust.

As I noted earlier, although Semoptco was clearly using adhocracies, what I've described so far are not all-edge adhocracies: adhocracies that span organizations, swarm a common project objective, then disperse at the end. Yet all-edge adhocracies did have a place at Semoptco, as we'll see in the next section.

Semoptco's Audience Analysis: "Is Anyone's Dad a Doctor?"

Audience analysis is the main product of SEO (Killoran 2009), and monthly reports described progress in analyzing audiences. But it's a complicated sort of multistakeholder audience analysis, one that simultaneously involves (*a*) analyzing the client, (*b*) analyzing the client's prospective customers, and (*c*) convincing the client that the customer analysis is correct. And it's even more complicated in that the specialists will probably never meet the client's customers, who may reside anywhere on the globe and who may not even know they are looking for the client's product, service, or information. So SEO's audiences must be balanced against each other: as with other texts that are realized via digital information and communication technologies (Geisler et al. 2001; J. Jones 2014; Pennell 2007; Sherlock 2009; Walton 2013), these texts must speak to multiple audiences simultaneously.

Semoptco had to address four wildly different audiences:

- *Clients.* With the content in mind, what customer behaviors should the client desire, and how can Semoptco guide and educate clients in selecting desired behaviors so that it can best connect client and customer?
- *Intended website customers.* Who is the intended customer audience for the website, and what behavior does the client desire from them?

- *Current website customers.* Who is the current customer audience for the website—people who are finding it already? What currently draws them? Which segments exhibit the behavior the client desires?
- *Search engines.* What practices are most likely to raise rankings for specific search engines and across search engines? Which are least likely to result in flagging content?

Workers analyzed audiences in many ways, resulting partially in monthly reports: both explicitly (in goals) and implicitly (in selected keywords and recommendations such as developing specific kinds of site content to draw visitors). Let's see how they pulled together different texts, resources, and connections to coordinate audience analysis, then fed that audience analysis into the monthly report.

Part of what makes Semoptco's work so complicated is that this process is multidirectional: the four audiences define each other. For instance, the client may have unrealistic expectations about what customer behavior to desire, given the site content and the ability to encourage and monitor the behavior. The intended web customers may not exhibit that behavior even if they come to the site. And the current web customers may exhibit different behaviors, some of which could redefine what should be considered desirable. The search engines, finally, can be fickle in how they apply algorithms. Let's take one incident to illustrate this multidirectional audience analysis— and to see how all-edge adhocracies sometimes formed briefly to address these complex problems.

THE CHALLENGES OF AUDIENCE ANALYSIS: DEFINING STAKEHOLDERS FOR A MEDICAL SITE

During one observation, Daria joined an account manager and two paid-search specialists for a conference call, talking with a representative of one of Semoptco's biggest clients. The client had several websites, including an informational website on medical issues. According to the client's internal analytics, this site was underperforming, partly because SEO efforts had focused on patients rather than doctors. Worse, the representative told them that the client was facing internal dissention about the web strategy. So the representative needed Semoptco to rethink its SEO strategy.

After the conference call, the three specialists and the account manager soberly discussed how to shape this site. The account manager explained that this client's sites were hard to monetize. The only way to show value was through a feature to help patients find doctors. Semoptco's specialists had provided several ideas about showing results, she added, but none had stuck. One way to measure results, the one favored by the client, was through conversions. But as Daria pointed out, "Info stuff is just different." It was unclear whether this information really led people to seek a doctor. Daria asked whether the site should project authority and credibility instead. They discussed whether to conceive of the site in terms of branding.

Then a paid-search specialist asked the rest of the team: "Is anyone's dad a doctor? Can we get the inside scoop that way?" The question hung in the air as people went on to other discussions.

They discussed insurance companies as a possible audience. But, as Daria pointed out, "I just don't think this site is set up for conversions." The mismatch between customer expectations and the site's content reminded them of another customer who was obsessed with bounce rate. All chuckled as they remembered this client, simultaneously viewing the site's analytics on their individual laptops. "I don't know what I'll do about this situation," the account manager sighed. Stymied, they brainstormed how to learn more about the audience that was already using the site. One asked: "Can we track who views videos to the end?" Meanwhile, Daria copied down *pacemaker* and other popular keywords from the analytics into her notebook.

Afterward, Daria told me:

> This professional site . . . has been really difficult. Because the other ones are all aimed at just consumers. So, you know, *we can figure that stuff out really easily*. But when you're talking about, okay, we want doctors to get here? *Well, we're not doctors!* We don't know, do the doctors search for this or do they search for the product name or do they search for the brand name or do they even search for it at all, do they look for it? So, yeah, and we don't know the process—so it's definitely been more difficult. (my emphasis)

To gain insight, Daria reached out through her personal networks, just as the paid-search specialist had suggested: "I've got friends in med school, and I've talked to them before."

Two weeks later, I observed Daria discussing this situation in a support-team meeting with Carl, who had inherited this account. "People are searching for ICD even when they type in 'pacemaker,'" she told him. She suggested looking for professional resources for doctors: developing suitable keywords would be hard, since they would have to figure out what doctors search for.

In this incident, three audiences collided. The client described an *intended website customer* who leads to conversions—a customer who will contact doctors that the client represents. But that desired behavior wasn't supported by this informational site, and anyway, how do you measure that behavior?

Clients, who sometimes become obsessed with irrelevant analytics, are not necessarily the best judges; they must be guided to realistic goals for desired customer behavior. So the project team discussed what desired behaviors—and intended customers—the site could support. Branding is an obvious function for an informational site, but it's hard to measure or monetize directly. They returned to the analytics: what *current website customers* are finding their way to the site, and how can we figure out what they're doing? Clues came from keyword analysis and from video analytics, but the project team also drew on personal connections and professional resources.

That is, project teams could temporarily pull in people from outside the organization to help solve the problems. These people weren't just contractors (though Semoptco used them too), but also "friends in medical school" and even employees of the clients. Briefly, but critically, all-edge adhocracies formed to swarm particular points of the project, lending expertise that the specialists didn't have, supplying insights that the specialists could not.

I saw similar incidents throughout my visits. But each incident had different contingencies, requiring customized border crossing, specialized audience analysis techniques, and therefore custom adhocracies.

THE TECHNIQUES OF AUDIENCE ANALYSIS

Audience analysis was multidimensional and complex at Semoptco. The SEO specialists reached out in several direction for partners: personal networks, contractors, even employees of the clients themselves. They deployed several audience analysis techniques, including the following:

Soliciting ideas from the client   Specialists solicited ideas from the client at launch, starting with the kickoff meeting, where they learned about the client's industry and solicited keyword suggestions. "Usually they can give us at least some ideas," Daria explained. "Like 'In your industry do they call it this or this?' 'Well, they call it this.' 'Okay, good enough.'" They also gathered client collateral, including offline sales and marketing materials, "so you know if *they're pushing essentially a keyword offline*, then obviously you want to optimize it online," Carl explained (my emphasis). After generating a suggested keyword list, the specialists elicited more feedback from clients.

Generating ideas from competition   Specialists also generated ideas by examining competitors' sites and analytics during the competitor analysis. Usually this meant examining the sites of competitors identified by the client, finding out what keywords drew customers for whom the client was competing, as well as keywords that competitors had missed. Occasionally, as Luis mentioned, this also meant identifying more-suitable competitors.

Generating ideas from analytics   Specialists also examined analytics for the client's site, both during the launch process and during maintenance. Analytics provided better understanding of current customers as well as a sense of how well the site was drawing intended customers. But beyond that, analytics gave clues about productive variations that specialists might not have contemplated. For instance, in one observation, Carl examined the analytics of a site that was intended for a UK audience. He discovered common misspellings of keywords as well as British spellings and terms (e.g., *medi* instead of *medical*). He used these to "try to optimize for the, the lingo. As much as possible."

Assessing clients' knowledge of web development and analytics   Since SEO results depended in part on how well clients implemented Semoptco's recommendations, specialists assessed how well clients understood web development, and they worked hard to find contacts with whom they could work, sometimes as de facto members of an all-edge adhocracy. For instance, Luis recounted that one client's web developer "understands everything" but the CEO "understands nothing"—so he worked backstage with the trusted web developer to improve results. Carl said he liked to make contacts with clients' web developers during the launch process to assess what they knew, and he stayed in contact with them throughout the project (as we'll see below). Sometimes assessments were negative: in another instance, Daria told an account manager over instant messaging how relieved she was that their client's incompetent web developer had been fired. As Stacy explained, unlike paid search, SEO involves educating the customer; specialists had to assess customers' current knowledge and ability to assimilate new knowledge.

Drawing on personal networks   As I noted above, specialists looked past the strong ties in their organization, also drawing on weak ties (Granovetter 1973) in their personal networks to understand sites that were not consumer facing.

Multidimensional audience analysis isn't unique to SEO; but here, audiences were consciously being defined through traces such as misspelled keywords, traces that became incorporated into standing sets of transformations (e.g., by monitoring performance for these keywords). Specialists faced situations in which their potential audience could include nonhuman search engines and anyone who might use a search engine. To cut down the possibilities, they drew on personal networks and analytics to establish relations among potential team members beyond the organization. Once they did so, they learned more about audiences through keyword analysis, guesswork, and personal networks. This networking was never quite done, given changes in search engines, objectives, keyword performance, and even clients' websites. Consequently, Semoptco's specialists constantly engaged in border-crossing activities involving reciprocal changes to reports and the standing sets of transformations that produced them. Audience analysis also helped Semoptco build its authority and trustworthiness.

Semoptco's Results: Constant Trust Building

"Hey Jeannie," Stacy called to a more experienced account manager, "have you seen anything like this in a report?" She read from a draft monthly report stating that the customer's keyword results had dropped in response to the economy. "I have *not* seen anything like that," Jeannie responded. Together, they discovered that some keywords were related to lending, and on the morning of November 12, 2008, lending had been a big news topic due to the financial crisis. The client's rankings were unaffected relative to others in the same business, but news had taken up "shelf space," crowding the client's results from the first few pages of search results. "With a lot of news about those kinds of words, then they're just, like, taking up space in Google. So my client doesn't [have] as high rankings," Stacy explained later. This was rather unusual. Semoptco had to explain it in the monthly report and outline a response. So Stacy edited the monthly report, changing one passage to "articles about the economy taking shelf space in Google," then making other changes.

This situation was unusual, but trust building was an everyday activity at Semoptco, as it usually is in adhocracies. In an industry characterized by "snake oil," Semoptco had to convince clients that it was not cheating them or being unscrupulous, that its results were measurable and verifiable, and that it had a higher degree of knowledge and experience of SEO than the clients themselves. These arguments were sometimes significant challenges, challenges that were addressed in the monthly reports and meetings, but also in framing texts such as e-mails that account managers and specialists sometimes sent to clients. Although Semoptco certainly worked on building trust with other audiences, particularly search engines, let's examine trust work aimed at paying clients.

THE CHALLENGES OF TRUST:
THREATS TO SEMOPTCO'S REPUTATION

In this contingency-laden sector, building trust was not easy. Beyond "snake oil," Semoptco had to anticipate and coherently explain the contingencies that perturbed its results, and it also had to manage clients' own (potentially damaging) actions.

The threat of contingencies   Although contingencies such as algorithm changes and news topics might affect rankings unpredictably, Semoptco had to demonstrate that its work generally helped clients to raise their rankings sustainably and predictably over the medium to long term.

The threat of clients   Of course, confidence was a two-way street. Clients themselves represented a contingency: after all, they owned and controlled the websites that Semoptco was trying to optimize. When Semoptco took on a client, part of the launch process involved evaluating the client's current website. Had the website been well constructed? Or had well-meaning webmasters or previous SEO firms built the site in ways that raised red flags for search engines? Did clients think they knew more than they actually did, and would they fight Semoptco's recommendations, question Semoptco's choice of analytics, and make changes without informing Semoptco? Semoptco met those threats with specific trust-building techniques.

THE TECHNIQUES OF TRUST BUILDING:
FRAMING RESULTS

Semoptco applied several techniques that involved anchored, stable reporting as well as flexibly enacted updating and customization.

"Report cards"   As Stan mentioned, Semoptco generated "report cards": measurable, verifiable, reliable summaries of how its SEO was performing relative to targets set during the launch process. These "report cards," Semoptco's most bureaucratic genre, appeared in monthly reports under the heading "Analysis of Natural Search Campaign Performance," and contained tables describing campaign rankings, the rankings summary, traffic, the conversion rate, and visitors. At the time of my data collection, Semoptco was considering making the "report cards" available online via BRILLIANCE. These data-driven results allowed Semoptco to show precisely where keywords were performing well, where they were not, and what trends the key-

words were following. But the report cards also allowed clients and SEO specialists alike to see what progress had been made on the stated goals. In the first- and second-tier reports, specialists also spelled out this progress with analytical sections. As Semoptco's collateral warned, results could take months to show; the monthly "report cards" helped both parties to detect these results.

Standard monthly reports   The "report cards" were part of the monthly reports, which also included methods, action items, and short- and long-term strategies. These reports allowed Semoptco to surface its methods in the analysis sections and to establish long-term framing in the goals and objectives section, reminding customers that SEO takes time. Like "report cards," reports were increasingly automated through BRILLIANCE, templated in Microsoft Word, then vetted by SEO specialists and account managers. Reports included an executive summary, campaign overview, action items, goals and objectives, analysis, budget status, and campaign history.

Customized analysis   As discussed earlier, Luis and Daria both produced supplemental, customized analyses in specific situations, incorporated into reports and corresponding client meetings. Both indicated in interviews that such customized analyses were not usual, but they were not rare either; most applied to tier 1 clients with special situations. As Castells notes, layering customization on top of an automated product—such as a customized analysis attached to a templated, largely autogenerated report—is "the key to the new form of conducting business" (2003, p. 77; cf. Engeström 2008). Semoptco had developed a balance between automated BRILLIANCE reports and customized analysis (i.e., between regulated, bureaucratic solutions and loosely regularized, adhocratic innovations).

Relationships   Beyond these documents, specialists maintained relationships with clients, both through formal meetings and through less formal ongoing contact. They individually maintained these relationships, generally at the specialists' discretion.

For instance, Luis and Carl stressed how important it was to assess the client and the client's website. Sometimes "clients will make changes without telling us" or perhaps the client's site is "hiding some stuff" because "they are building it for robots, not for the users," Luis argued. Or perhaps the site uses "cloaking" (showing different content to humans and to search engines), Carl added. Other factors included frames, Flash, titles, and ALT text for figures. But these technical issues signaled relational ones. Would the client change the site without telling Semoptco? How had the client previously constructed the site? Did the client's site actually hurt it at present, creating a hole from which Semoptco had to dig it out?

Consequently, specialists sought to form ongoing collaborative relationships with clients. After one meeting, Carl explained: "Social media is a big part of what we do. . . . [It is] very much about the user; you need to get out there and interact with them. So anytime a client is willing and able to do that, it's like [claps] *yes!*" During that day's observation, Carl read a *Wired* article that related to a client, so he e-mailed the client representatives the article's web address and a short explanation. Such contacts were highly individualized. These contacts were important in part because they allowed specialists to negotiate the level of trust with the client. Luis, for instance, discussed how he sometimes approached clients when he wanted to test new techniques on their website. Clients were naturally worried that an untested technique might hurt their brand, so Luis deployed trust-building arguments to overcome these fears.

As the specialists developed their individual relationships with clients, they were able to build trust in this uncertain environment, and that trust helped them to implement further-ranging reforms, generating better measurable results. Trust, negotiated between the monthly reports, led to changes in direction that were then instantiated in subsequent reports' goals, methods, and keyword analyses.

In sum, Semoptco's approach to trust building involved (*a*) generating a stable set of reporting measures through automation and (*b*) customizing that base product through innovations, specifically actions that individual specialists took largely of their own volition. Together, these two moves generated trust—an ongoing accomplishment of trust optimized for Semoptco's network. Yet this combination yields divergent practices, so Semoptco periodically overhauled its automated systems and templates, constantly turning regularized innovations into regulated genres, thus cyclically stabilizing its practices.

Optimizing Semoptco

How did Semoptco handle the competing needs of SEO, some of which played to the strengths of a bureaucratic hierarchy, some of which required the flexibility and innovation of an adhocracy? As we saw in this chapter, the company established a hybrid structure that could meet both goals during the monthly pulse.

Bureaucratic hierarchy   Semoptco was able to produce predictable, regular outcomes via a well-defined process, an automated system, and templating.

Institutional adhocracy   Semoptco was also able to flexibly generate innovative solutions in a fast-changing, contingent space via multiple overlapping networks. In these networks, discretion and autonomy were pushed down to the level of individual specialists, specialists could share innovations and information through constant mutual adjustment, and those innovations could then become part of a shared, regular process.

All-edge adhocracies   Finally, Semoptco could also reach beyond its organization when it needed specialized knowledge and expertise. These all-edge adhocracies formed briefly and pulsed irregularly, but they gave Semoptco abilities that it could not develop on its own.

This hybrid structure allowed Semoptco to leverage the strengths of each form. But these forms are very different: not just in structure, but in purposes, values, and assumptions. And those differences could also create tensions within Semoptco and other hybrid organizations.

To understand these tensions better, in chapter 8, I use Semoptco as an example as we look at how different forms of organization develop, combine, and interact. And in chapter 9, I examine how this interplay creates new kinds of work.

8

The Configurations of All-Edge Adhocracies: Hierarchies, Markets, Clans, and Networks

In chapter 6, we saw that we could analyze an organization as an activity system working within a network of interrelated activities. But at Semoptco, people have to pulse different types of objectives to reach different types of outcomes—simultaneously. These different objectives and outcomes in turn require different capabilities, structures, logics, relations, and tools to empower Semoptco's employees to communicate, coordinate, and collaborate.

For instance, in chapter 7, Semoptco's object was search engine optimization (SEO). But SEO had several aspects:

- *The report.* SEO had to be a controlled, predictable object. Semoptco had to efficiently measure results and reliability in SEO so that it could compare regularly produced results to judge progress. Semoptco represented SEO to itself and clients through metrics that it defined, including the monthly report's "report card."
- *The budget.* SEO had to be an explicitly defined object of exchange. Semoptco had to keep SEO under budget and cost-effective, and that meant that it had to shift resources cost-effectively so that it could fulfill its contracts with its clients—clients who did not necessarily trust it. That's why Semoptco sometimes contracted out SEO work.
- *The relationship.* As a continually changing form of knowledge work, SEO had to be an internal relationship object. Semoptco employees had to cultivate and maintain internal, interdependent relationships and a common identity so that they could trust each other's work and share information effectively inside Semoptco. That's why they generally worked together very closely in trusted teams to achieve SEO and to interpret its complex, emergent aspects.

This chapter is based on Spinuzzi (forthcoming).

- *The cross-organizational collaboration.* Finally, SEO had to be a cross-disciplinary and frequently cross-organizational collaborative object. Semoptco employees had to network with others outside the organization to produce SEO in an agile, customized fashion that leveraged different specialties in an ever-changing space.

As we saw in chapter 2, different conditions imply different organizational forms—institutions and networks—which excel at different things. But organizations with any level of complexity must pulse different kinds of objects—as Semoptco did—and thus require a range of capabilities. That is, they tend to be hybrid organizations. And these hybrids, since they must pulse different objects and reach different outcomes simultaneously, embed contradictions. How can we conceptualize these? How can we analyze them and see how they interact?

To an extent, these deep differences should not be surprising: an activity is defined by its object (Kaptelinin 2005), an object that it attempts to cyclically pulse (Engeström 2008; Engeström, Engeström & Vähääho 1999). Essentially, the rest of the activity unfolds around the object, configuring itself to effectively pulse that object.

But as I demonstrated in chapter 7, organizations are complicated, and their objects are often shared across the activity network. Moreover, the objects are construed and pulsed in different ways by different parts of the network, and require different configurations. These configurations often work together, but their differences—in rules, tools, actors, stakeholders, and divisions of labor—sometimes interfere with each other, causing tensions.

We saw some examples of these configurational tensions in chapter 4 and chapter 6. But here, in chapter 8, I examine how different ideal types of configurations (including objects, actors, tools, rules, communities, and divisions of labor) form and how their linking results in predictable patterns of tensions. Even in the same organization, different objects and outcomes require different divisions of labor and tools, imply different rules and values, and necessitate different kinds of communication. But they're all happening at the same time, in the same networked organization. Tensions—contradictions, in the sense I discussed in chapter 6—are inevitable.

Understanding Different Configurations
of Organizations: Some Background

In chapters 2 and 7, I discussed institutional adhocracies—the adhocracies that Alvin Toffler, Henry Mintzberg, Warren Bennis and Philip Slater, and others saw appearing within, and overlaying, institutions. These, as I said in chapter 2, were built on the "chassis" of the institutional hierarchy but were taking on the characteristics of the organizational networks that had begun to develop within institutions.

Such hybrids are everywhere. For instance, in his study of video game development, Fabienne Autier (2001) describes how an adhocracy—a team focused on developing a specific game—lost coherence, then reverted to a bureaucracy. In her study of a humanitarian aid organization, Elizabeth Cullen Dunn (2012) describes how its bureaucracy had to take on characteristics of an adhocracy, relying on rules of thumb, guesswork, and "satisficing" while acting as if it were meeting the bureaucratic goals of control and efficiency. And in my own study of a telecommunications company, I show that even though the company had a well-defined hierarchy, it still relied on informal networks to get things done (Spinuzzi 2008).

But hierarchies and networks aren't the only ways to organize work. Several people have described different forms of organization. For instance, in his book *The Third Wave*, Toffler (1980) argues that we have undergone three fundamental waves of change: agricultural work, industrial work, and knowledge work. Each is associated with different organizational configurations. RAND researcher David Ronfeldt (1996, 2007; Ronfeldt, Arquilla, Fuller & Fuller 1999) presents a similar framework, TIMN, named after the four forms of organization it represents: tribes, institutions, markets, and networks. Robert E. Quinn and his associates (Cameron & Quinn 2011; O'Neil & Quinn 1993; Quinn & Rorbaugh 1981, 1983) describe four types of organizational values: clans, bureaucracies, markets, and adhocracies. Max Boisot, Markus Nordberg, Saïd Yami, and Bertrand Nicquevert (2011) use Boisot's I-space framework to describe institutional structures such as clans, fiefs, bureaucracies, and markets, with adhocracies described as structures that are more diffused versions of clans. David J. Snowden and his collaborators (Snowden 2005; Snowden & Boone 2007) describe organizations as working within and adapting to four different types of environments: simple, complicated, complex, and chaotic.

These frameworks are quite different from each other, but they point to certain common distinctions in how people organize themselves:

- Sometimes people need to organize their work on the basis of the *authority* of a leader controlling a *dependent* group, achieving *control*—as when Semoptco's CEO assigned specialists to teams.
- Sometimes people need to organize their work on the basis of *competition* among *independent* agents, achieving *flexibility*—as when Daria outsourced link-building work to a contractor.

- Sometimes people need to organize their work on the basis of their *identity* as part of an *interdependent* group, achieving *belonging*—like Carl and Luis's close-knit team.
- And sometimes people need to organize their work on the basis of *trust* in each other as part of an expansive *interdependent* group, achieving *knowledge growth and innovation*—as when Semoptco's "lone wolves" brought new techniques and tools back to their many teams.

We can see this push-pull in the Semoptco case in chapter 7: the organization is not a pure network but rather a hybrid of different ideal types, each with its own values (see Cameron & Quinn 2011; Heckscher 2007). In fact, most organizations are. And sometimes—often—these hybrids encounter internal contradictions (in the sense discussed in chapter 6) due to the different organizational types and the values embedded in them.

The frameworks above have one other thing in common. To put it colloquially, they slice the pizza in different ways, typically by using two aspects of organizations as axes for a matrix. The resulting typologies tend to produce rough equivalencies in organizational types (table 8.1). Each framework is complex, representing a substantial amount of thought and theorization, and I don't do justice to them with this brief characterization. They also look at different aspects of organizations: epochs, structural configurations, situational expectations and constraints, efficiency criteria, responses to environmental complexity, coordination mechanisms, and societal organization. And unfortunately, none are well suited for characterizing types of activities in the activity-theoretical sense: they do not characterize specific objects, which are crucial for identifying activities.

Yet, as table 8.1 suggests, these frameworks do tend to provide rough congruencies. In all of these frameworks, we see discussions of constrained, authority-based hierarchies; low-trust, highly codified markets; and high-trust clans with shared values. In most, we see discussions of cross-specialized networks characterized by swift trust and distributed or rotating leadership. Each type of organization has its own tendencies; typing them allows the frameworks to generalize findings across similar organizations.

- *Hierarchies*, as we saw in chapter 2, excel at controlled, ordered, and predictable tasks that are explicitly and internally defined.
- *Markets* excel at flexible tasks that are explicitly and externally defined.
- *Clans* excel at value- and culture-oriented tasks that are tacitly and internally defined.
- *Networks* excel at interdisciplinary and interorganizational emergent tasks that are tacitly and externally defined. They take advantage of new

TABLE 8.1. A partial comparison of frameworks for describing organizational forms, with loose equivalencies

Adler, Kwon & Heckscher's (2008) collaborative communities, describing *organizational principles*	Ronfeldt's (1996, 2007) TIMN, describing *forms of organization*	Cameron & Quinn's (2011) competing values framework, describing *values of organizations*	Ouchi's (1980) typology of organizational forms describing organizational efficiency	Boisot et al.'s (2011) I-Space, describing *cultures and institutional structures of organizations*
Hierarchy: authority, dependence, control	*Institutions:* organized by authority to achieve control	*Hierarchies:* highly stabilized and controlled, with high internal focus and integration	*Bureaucracies:* respond to conditions of moderately high performance ambiguity, moderately high goal incongruence	*Bureaucracies,* with undiffused information, structured information, hierarchical control and coordination
Market: competition, independence, flexibility	*Markets:* organized by competition to achieve flexibility, especially in low-trust environments	*Markets:* highly stabilized and controlled, competitive, with high external focus and differentiation	*Markets:* respond to conditions of low performance ambiguity, high goal incongruence	*Markets,* with diffused information, structured information, horizontal coordination via self-regulation
Community: trust, interdependence, innovation	*Tribes:* organized by identity to achieve belonging	*Clans:* collaborative, with high flexibility and discretion, high internal focus and integration	*Clans:* respond to conditions of high performance ambiguity, low goal incongruence	*Fiefs,* with undiffused information, unstructured information, face-to-face coordination, hierarchical control and coordination
				Clans, with diffused information, unstructured information, face-to-face coordination, horizontal control via negotiation rather than hierarchy
Collaborative community: a hybrid of the other forms, with collaborative independence and a focus on contribution	*Networks:* organized by trust to achieve knowledge growth and innovation.	*Adhocracies:* highly flexible, with high discretion, high external focus and differentiation		*Adhocracies,* as a variation on clans, but more diffused, more geographically dispersed, more loosely coupled, without necessary face-to-face interaction (p. 74)

communication capabilities to generate new possibilities of interaction—
and in the process, they make all-edge adhocracies possible.

Networks entail a metalevel collaborative focus. That is, networks—like
the ones underlying the all-edge adhocracies in chapters 3, 5, and 7—join together collaborators with different focal objects, different desired outcomes,
different specializations and sets of expertise, and frequently different values. As an activity network pulses (in the sense I used in chapter 6), it often
generates emerging values. And it often develops embedded contradictions
when those differences collide. To understand these collisions, let's go back
to activity theory. Specifically, I look at ways to characterize the objects of
activities.

Understanding the Objects of Activities

As discussed above, activity systems are identified by the object they try to
cyclically transform or pulse. Different objects require different configurations from their activities and imply different pulses. To develop an adequate
typology of activities, then, we must characterize these objects.

For simplicity, I use a two-dimensional matrix inspired by those of Quinn
(Cameron and Quinn 2011; Quinn & Rohrbaugh 1981, 1983) and Boisot
(Boisot and Child 1996, 1999; Boisot, MacMillan & Han 2001; Boisot et al.
2011). But this matrix is focused on the activity's object itself, characterized
along these dimensions:

- *How is the object defined?* Is it defined explicitly and deductively, or tacitly
  and inductively?
- *Where is the object defined?* Is it defined within the activity's division of
  labor, or outside it?

The matrix allows us to characterize activities in four quadrants (figure 8.1).

THE VERTICAL AXIS: HOW THE OBJECT IS DEFINED

The vertical axis represents *how* the object is defined. At the top of the axis,
the object is *tacitly* defined (Polanyi 2009) and reached *inductively*. This work
is often unique, involving initially loose tolerances and specifications. Examples include exploratory and creative work, workplace culture, wicked problems, and emerging collaborations. At the bottom of the scale, the object is
explicitly defined (Polanyi 2009) and reached *deductively*. This work involves
strict tolerances and specifications, and often tends to be repeated.

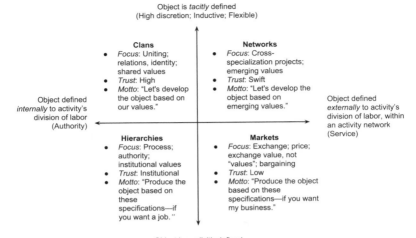

FIGURE 8.1. A typology of activities

THE HORIZONTAL AXIS: WHERE THE OBJECT IS DEFINED

The horizontal axis represents *where* the object is defined. At the left of this axis are objects that are defined *internal* to the activity's division of labor (i.e., by the actors who pulse the object). Examples might include manufacturing, in which the manufacturer internally develops specifications and ensures that it can produce goods based on those specifications, and internal governance, in which an organization decides how best to run its own affairs. At the right of the axis are objects that are defined *external* to the activity's division of labor. (e.g., by stakeholders in other networked activities who will receive or also pulse the object). That is, the actors who pulse the object produce it according to someone else's definition. One example is contract work, in which a contractor receives specifications from an organization and produces work according to those specifications.

Now that I have defined the typology, I discuss the quadrants and how they can help us better understand the configurations of different types of activities—bear in mind that since the objects of activity systems are multiperspectival (Spinuzzi 2011), these configurations will often overlap. In this chapter, I discuss each configuration, then examine how it created interference patterns that Semoptco had to mitigate.

THE STEADY PULSE: HIERARCHIES

To understand hierarchies, let's return to something Stan, Semoptco's director of product development, told us in chapter 7. Stan explained that Semoptco offered "a very data-centric approach":

> Even our SEO team, which is very content driven, they still spend a lot of time looking at data to go make decisions and then figure out what happened. I mean, Google changed their ranking algorithm about a month and a half ago. And we collect data every day for somewhere between five and fifty keywords for our clients to say "how are you ranking?" We saw about three-quarters of them go up over two days. In some cases, it was a spot or two. In some cases, it was ten, fifteen, thirty spots. . . . We've changed a lot of techniques we're using . . . over the last nine months, and it was great to see that . . . completely objective proof point that those things had kind of, had done the addition.

These meticulous statistics were presented in a "report card," a section of the monthly SEO report that the in-house system BRILLIANCE generated. By including the "report card" in its monthly reports to clients, Semoptco could provide clear metrics that allowed it and its clients to measure progress reliably and steadily. These metrics are internally and explicitly defined: Semoptco itself has developed them and regularly collects data to generate them.

Such objects—defined internally and explicitly, produced at regular intervals, conforming to tight specifications—are typically produced by hierarchies. As we saw in chapter 2, hierarchies have their drawbacks. They tend to be inflexible at dealing with change and bad at innovation (Galbraith 1983; Mintzberg 1979; Cameron & Quinn 2011; Ronfeldt et al. 1999; Weber 1978). But for certain purposes, they are ideal. In particular, they tend to have a steady pulse: steady like an assembly line.

That steadiness is what allows hierarchies to be efficient at doing things repeatedly and within explicit specifications (Mintzberg 1979)—such as engineering (Adler 2007; Haas & Witte 2001), law (Schuster & Propen 2001; Engeström, Brown, Christopher & Gregory 1997), or education (Russell 1997; Schryer 2003). In fact, as the typology shows, they excel at pulsing objects that are explicitly and internally defined—like Semoptco's metrics.

In fact, metrics are classic objects of hierarchies. They represent predictable, uniform outcomes (i.e., they result from processes that can be applied to any of Semoptco's projects). To produce such outcomes, the hierarchy tends to be rigid and slow to change, involves broad promulgation and well-defined genres and procedures, and follows a well-defined, hierarchical division of labor. Let's look at the characteristics of a hierarchical activity more closely.

Object and outcome   Hierarchies excel at pulsing explicitly and internally defined objects, producing highly predictable outcomes. Think in terms of objects that are mass-produced, highly controlled, and consistently processed to reach outcomes that are controlled, ordered, and predictable (often in terms of criteria such as quality, cost, and time; Adler & Heckscher 2007; Bennis and Slater 1998; Cameron & Quinn 2011; Ronfeldt 1996, 2007; Ronfeldt et al. 1999). We can see that impulse toward control, efficiency, and predictability in Semoptco's data-centric approach, particularly the automated "report cards," which (as Stan pointed out) yielded predictable, efficient outcomes. But we can also see it in Semoptco's organization. Although they had considerable discretion at Semoptco, Carl, Luis, and the others still worked in an institutional hierarchy. As we saw, these specialists were assigned to each client by someone higher in the hierarchy; they had to follow rules laid down by others in the hierarchy; they were hired and they could be fired.

Tools and rules   Hierarchies tend to use well-defined tools and rules to keep the pulse steady, the object explicitly defined, and the outcome predictable. Information tools such as databases tend to demand structured, explicit information (Boisot et al. 2001; cf. Weber 1978, p. 973). Knowledge about this information tends to be explicit and formalized rather than tacit (Polanyi 2009). The object is pulsed according to specific, explicit rules (Ouchi 1980), rules that are developed and promulgated by an authority (Cameron & Quinn 2011; Ronfeldt 1996, 2007; Ronfeldt et al. 1999). For instance, Semoptco's report cards were autogenerated by BRILLIANCE, which gathered specific metrics, processed them via specific rules, and output them in a predictable form.

Actors and community stakeholders   Hierarchies require a great deal of internal trust; they are trust intensive (Adler & Heckscher 2007). They tend to focus internally (Cameron & Quinn 2011) and to define the outcome in terms determined by the actors who pulse the object, not by the community stakeholders who receive it—for instance, by the company that owns the assembly line, not by the customers who receive the products. Certainly that's the case at Semoptco, where the "report cards" are generated by internal processes informed by the expertise of SEO analysts.

Division of labor   This internal focus, paired with the explicit nature of the object, tends to result in departments that establish clear specialties and delineations of responsibility. Hierarchies demand control. So the division of labor involves clear lines of authority (Boisot et al. 2011; Cameron & Quinn 2011; Mintzberg 1979; Ronfeldt 1996, 2007; Ronfeldt et al. 1999). Relationships among actors tend to be dependent—with those lower in the hierarchy depending on those above them—and trust intensive (Adler & Heckscher 2007). At first glance, Semoptco doesn't seem to follow this pattern—as we saw in chapter 7, Semoptco's analysts often worked in a relatively flat manner. But when it came to producing "report cards," those dependencies do show up: analysts were assigned to specific projects and were required to use BRILLIANCE to produce "report cards."

As discussed above, activities pulse their objects. And in hierarchies, the pulse tends to be steady, predictable, and repeated. Semoptco had to treat each client according to the same procedures, metrics, and guidelines, which produced predictable outcomes. But as we look outward to how hierarchies interact with external activities, we see a different kind of pulse.

THE QUICKENING PULSE: MARKETS

To understand metrics, let's look at something Luis said in chapter 7. As Luis was working on the competitive analysis for a client whose campaign was about to launch, he concluded that the clients had targeted the wrong competitors. He identified better competitors, then developed a table to demonstrate that this set was superior. As he told me: "I didn't have planned to create this other extra document to show the client, why are we picking up these competitors. Uh, sometimes . . . they understand pretty easy, it's not required. But this time *the client really doesn't understand why*. So we have to show him, like, another kind of deliverable to make him understand why" (my emphasis).

We saw earlier that one aspect of Semoptco's object, the "report card," is defined internally and explicitly; the client doesn't get to tell Semoptco what metrics to use or how to produce them. But clients do define the goal of SEO. They all want their search results to rank more highly. And they select what they want the results to rise against. That involves selecting the right keywords so that they can rise against specific competitors. It also involves deciding on a budget—an agreement that covers how many keywords Semoptco will optimize, how detailed Semoptco's reports will be, how much additional service the client can expect (e.g., in-person briefings), and what other options Semoptco has (e.g., paid search). These parameters are defined explicitly (in contracts) and externally (by each client rather than by Semoptco). In Luis's case above, he can argue that the client is targeting the wrong competition, but ultimately the client gets to decide whether to accept his argument.

That is, Semoptco's SEO service has a market aspect. Markets, like hierarchies, demand explicitly defined objects. But the objects are externally defined—that is, defined by stakeholders external to the activity's division of labor. And this combination means that markets excel at some things that hierarchies don't.

Markets provide alternatives to internal capacity. Indeed, over the last several decades, companies have increasingly turned to the market to do things that they once did internally, because the market can often produce these things more cheaply, flexibly, and effectively (Burton-Jones 2001). So turning to a market solution means that an organization doesn't have to build capacity and therefore can react more quickly to changes. Luis's client doesn't have to hire an SEO specialist, for instance; when it discovers that it needs SEO, it can approach Semoptco or another SEO provider and sign a temporary contract.

Market activities include sales (Kallio 2010; Ludvigsen, Havnes & Lahn 2003), entrepreneurship (Holt 2008; Miettinen 2008), and grant writing and proposal writing (Ding 2008; Hart-Davidson, Spinuzzi & Zachry 2007). Markets allow people to interact in low-trust, high-velocity transactions—think in terms of an actual market, where you examine the merchandise, perhaps even haggle over it, and pay a mutually acceptable price to a stranger. Markets flourish whenever human activity needs to be related at arm's length, in a competitive milieu. Markets allow individuals to meet their personal interests through free, flexible interactions, interactions that link them with trade partners who are otherwise unaffiliated with them. That is, markets are atomized competitive exchanges (Ronfeldt 1996, p. 8), with no necessary permanent relations. At their best, markets promote efficient and rapid economic exchanges, providing a mechanism for individuals to make exchanges in low-trust relationships, and yielding fair exchanges at competitive prices. At their worst, markets can be ruthlessly exploitative.

Semoptco's market relationships were closer to "best" than "worst"— both for their clients and their contractors. In terms of clients, as we saw above, Luis genuinely wanted them to select the competitors that would best support their goals. In terms of contractors, when Daria's unit hired a contractor to build links, it was because the contractor could do the work for a price that was more competitive than Semoptco could manage internally. Daria had only to specify the types of links to build, the guidelines, and the time frame. She didn't need to know (or even meet) the contractor. But she did have to check his work before Semoptco paid him, just as Semoptco had to demonstrate every month that it was living up to its own clients' contracts.

Object and outcome   Markets are good at pulsing objects that are explicitly defined and that are differentiated (i.e, competing with other objects; Cameron & Quinn 2011). The outcomes tend to be externally defined (i.e., defined by the community stakeholders outside an activity); an organization must give up control to seek market solutions (Mintzberg 1979). But in return, the organization gains the outcomes of competitiveness and flexibility. In Semoptco's case, the client defined the object (sometimes with Semoptco's help) and Semoptco made it happen—just as Semoptco defined the contractor's work and the contractor made it happen.

Tools and rules   For market solutions to work, inputs and outputs have to be explicitly specified and often standardized. Tools must include highly structured communication, including exchange price—a high level of abstraction and codification (Boisot and Child 1999; Boisot et al. 2001), so that the market can perform the job competently and efficiently without too much supervision. Rules are spelled out in formal contracts, like Semoptco's, and (in the best cases) enforced via reciprocal self-regulation: the market determines the price (Boisot et al. 2001; Ouchi 1980). In Semoptco's case, it supplied contracts and demanded a price that, although premium compared to smaller SEO shops, was commensurate to the results it provided.

Actors and community stakeholders   In a market, the object is—broadly speaking—defined not by the people who pulse the object but by people in other activities who purchase it. (To use an obvious example, Hasbro produces toys on the basis of market research, not what its toy designers want to play with—even if some of its toy designers do like to play with toys in their off-hours.) Relationships among actors and community stakeholders are not necessarily steady from exchange to exchange, pulse to pulse (Adler & Heckscher 2007; Cameron & Quinn 2011). In a pure market, trust between buyer and seller is low (Adler & Heckscher 2007), since the market involves making exchanges between two otherwise unrelated activities, activities that may interact for just a single transaction. Often, though, buyers and sellers develop relationships. Semoptco, for instance, sought repeat transactions that allowed it to develop a relationship and to raise trust through trust-building measures (such as the monthly reports and regular contact with specialists and account managers).

Division of labor   Relations among activities in a market are independent
and formal; they are based on the exchange for goods and services (Adler &
Heckscher 2007). The labor is coordinated horizontally via self-regulation
(Boisot et al. 2001); that is, buyers and sellers coordinate via highly structured but contextually shallow information such as price and specifications
(in Semoptco's case, both specified in the initial contract).

From the point of view of the market, the activity looks like a swap or
exchange: money for goods and services. Each pulse is an exchange, but not
necessarily between the same two organizations each time. Although some
exchanges can be time delimited, such as six-month contracts, others are
not. In some markets, more competition can quicken the pulse. Markets are
optimized for low-information, high-velocity transactions, so the pulse—
the transformation of the object—tends to quicken, to transform the object
more quickly. But other sorts of objects and pulses exist.

THE VARIABLE PULSE: CLANS

To understand clans, let's examine something I noticed the first time I first
visited Carl and Luis's cubicle at Semoptco. An object balanced atop the low
wall of their cubicle: a mannequin head in a black-and-orange Halloween
hat and novelty glasses. At the last departmental meeting, they had won the
monthly prize for teamwork, and the mannequin head was their trophy,
serving to identify them as a high-performing team (figure 8.2). The trophy was a source of considerable pride for them. It demonstrated that they
worked extremely well as a team, distinguishing them sharply from the other
mentor teams in their department. No wonder they displayed it high on the
cubicle wall.

This pride in a mutual identity is a characteristic of what, for a better
word, I call *clans*. Clans, like hierarchies and unlike markets, are internally
focused: The actors who pulse the object define the outcome. But in this
case, the object itself is defined tacitly rather than explicitly: it is the internal
culture of teams. Clans characterize close-knit work such as craftwork, but
also team-building and identity-building, as in professional identity formation (Schryer & Spoel 2005) or internal culture formation in an organization
(Artemeva & Freedman 2001).

Clans particularly characterize internal culture. One often-cited example
is that of Apple: as Kim Cameron and Robert Quinn (2011) tell it, during his
first term as CEO, Steve Jobs encouraged the Macintosh development team
members to consider themselves "pirates"; they defined themselves against

FIGURE 8.2. Carl and Luis's trophy

the rest of Apple and even hoisted the Jolly Roger over their building (see Hansen 2009). The mannequin head wasn't exactly a Jolly Roger, but it did help to define Carl and Luis against other specialists in adjacent cubicles.

Clans provide identity, which allows teams to achieve strong internal solidarity on the basis of similarity and alignment (mechanical solidarity, in Durkheim's [1933] terms). This closed relationship sharply distinguishes insiders from outsiders. Clan members share stories, develop rituals of membership, and incur mutual obligations. And clans are often segmentary: members have heavily overlapping skill sets. They are egalitarian and frequently leaderless. And they tend to have different sets of rules for insiders and outsiders (see Durkheim 1933; Ronfeldt 2007).

For instance, though Luis was technically senior to Carl, the two worked in an egalitarian fashion, asking each other for advice and mentoring each other in various ways. They shared the same space comfortably. And when I visited them for the first time, they did something that I have rarely encountered in my many workplace studies: they insisted on being interviewed together.

Object and outcome   Clans work well for addressing customized objects, such as craft objects (Cameron & Quinn 2001). The objects themselves are defined tacitly rather than explicitly, and often inductively rather than deductively. They are also internally defined, typically leading to outcomes of team identity or belonging (Adler & Heckscher 2007; Cameron & Quinn 2001; Ronfeldt 2007). Outcomes are often customized as well. In the case of internal culture (such as Luis and Carl's team), clans inductively develop their own internal values and characteristics over time on the basis of their internal needs and experiences. But clans do not just focus on internal culture; they also tend to focus on other emerging objects that the team produces internally. In the Apple example, the Macintosh team was working on a machine unlike anything the company had produced. At Semoptco, Carl and Luis often focused on underdefined aspects of SEO—tricks, interpretations, and value judgments that fell outside the explicitly defined metrics handled by Semoptco's hierarchy.

Tools and rules   Since clans' objects are defined tacitly and internally, they often lead to tools that are unstructured and diffused. Face-to-face coordination is common (Boisot et al. 2001), especially in terms of mutual adjustment—that is, "the coordination of work by the simple process of informal communication" (Mintzberg 1979, p. 3). In this context, rules tend to be commonly held traditions, values, and beliefs within the tight-knit group of actors (Ouchi 1980; Ronfeldt 2007; cf. Weiner 2013). In Carl and Luis's case, the two frequently coordinated via mutual adjustment, by asking each other questions; in one incident I mentioned in chapter 7, Luis glanced at Carl as if to ask a question, noticed that Carl was wearing headphones, and instead elected to send Carl an IM.

Actors and stakeholders   Actors in clans are especially tight-knit as they pulse the object. They sometimes become very clannish, defining themselves against others in the same organization. As noted above, Steve Jobs placed the Macintosh team in a separate building on the Apple campus and told its members, "Let's be pirates" (Hansen 2009). Like the Macintosh team, clans tend to focus on belonging and integration (Cameron & Quinn 2001; Ronfeldt 2007). Similarly, Luis and Carl identified strongly as a team, both in observations and interviews. Clans confer identity on a group—such as the identity of kinship, family, and brotherhood (Ronfeldt 2007, p. 22). Such groups obviously started small; in fact, some evidence suggests that the human brain's neocortical processing capacity limits the number of people with whom we can maintain stable interpersonal relationships to one hundred to two hundred.

Division of labor   Since they are so tight-knit, clans tend to have a very flexible division of labor, coordinating horizontally via negotiation (Boisot et al. 2001). They are interdependent—that is, dependent on each other as they coordinate to pulse the object (Adler & Heckscher 2007). Consequently, they must develop and maintain high levels of trust (Adler & Heckscher 2007), partly via shared values (Cameron & Quinn 2011; Ouchi 1980). We can see this level of trust in the fact that when Luis and Carl coordinated, they were not just sharing information; they were asking each other's advice about difficult questions.

From the point of view of the clan, the object is an expression of the clan's internal values. The clan often takes the activity as an aspect of internal human development and participation (Cameron & Quinn 2011). The pulse is variable, due to the internal, tacit definition of the object. Up to this point, I have discussed the steady pulse of hierarchies, the quickening pulse of markets, and the variable pulse of clans. In the next subsection, I discuss the opportunistic pulse of networks.

THE OPPORTUNISTIC PULSE: NETWORKS

To understand networks, let's go back to another event discussed in chapter 7. At one point, SEO and paid-search specialists were trying to figure out how to retool SEO strategy for a particularly demanding client in the medical industry. This client wanted to focus on doctors rather than patients. But the specialists didn't know much about doctors. One paid-search specialist asked the rest of the team: "Is anyone's dad a doctor? Can we get the inside scoop that way?" Later, Daria reached out through her personal networks: "I've got friends in med school, and I've talked to them before."

Networks, like clans, deal with tacitly rather than explicitly defined objects: problems to be solved rather than specifications to be filled. But unlike clans and like markets, networks define their objects externally to the division of labor: the object is defined across a network of activities rather than within the division of labor of a single activity. To achieve these pulses, actors with different specialties tend to link up temporarily to swarm the object, dispersing at the end of the engagement (cf. Arquilla & Ronfeldt 2000; Edwards 2005; Ronfeldt et al. 1999). That is, these networks are adhocratic.

Networks require relations based on shared interests and projects (Ronfeldt 2007, p. 22), as we've seen in previous chapters. When freelancers assemble their teams-for-today (chapter 3), they don't and can't rely solely on market exchanges; they don't have the leverage. When coworkers provide the front stage for each other's clients (chapter 5), they don't do this because the coworking proprietor has the ability to order them around. And when SEO specialists reach out to contacts both inside and outside their organization (chapter 7), including family, friends, and colleagues, they are not relying solely on kinship. Those other relationships can shade these new, networked relationships, but they don't explain those relationships. Rather, those relationships are allied, connecting dispersed organizations, groups, and individuals (Ronfeldt 1996, p. 13; Ronfeldt & Varda 2008, p. 26). They are collaborative and interdependent (Adler, Kwon & Heckscher 2008; Heckscher 2007, p. 238), with high flexibility and discretion and a high external focus (Cameron & Quinn 2011), geographically dispersed and loosely coupled (Boisot et al 2011, p. 74).

At their best, then, networks promote trusting, collaborative relationships, allowing people to preserve their autonomy while pursuing interdependent agendas (Ronfeldt 2007, p. 15; cf. Adler, Kwan & Heckscher 2008; Castells 1997). For these reasons, David Ronfeldt and Danielle Varda (2008, p. 26) suggest that networks may come to dominate in civil society, providing ways for otherwise unrelated people to join and address large-scale problems; one example is that of the Zapatista social netwar, in which the Zapatista army networked with nongovernmental organizations to press for civil rather than military solutions to their grievances (Ronfeldt et al. 1999).

At their worst, networks can allow bad agents to betray that trust (Ronfeldt 2007, pp. 19–21), as we saw in chapter 3; can fail to solidify adequate alliances, allowing projects to fall apart; and can overload individuals with too much information. After all, networks are information intensive, requiring constant mutual adjustment across a rotating set of specializations—as we saw in chapter 7.

Whereas the other organizational forms matured in the past, Ronfeldt (2007, pp. 1–2) argues, networks are maturing today—partly, as we'll see, because the information technologies that would allow them to broadly flourish were not generally available until the mid-twentieth century. Paul Adler, Seok-Woo Kwon, and Charles Heckscher (2008, p. 361) characterize their parallel concept of collaborative community as a "profound mutation."

Although they are maturing now, networks (like the other organizational forms) have been around for ages. As we saw in chapter 4, for instance, John Arquilla (2011) argues that they have long characterized irregular warfare, while Sean Edwards (2005) examines case studies of swarming, a tactic of networked warfare, in historical conflicts as far back as 329 BCE.

But networks, as we saw in chapter 2, require continual communication. That's because they are flat, spanning boundaries, connecting many different types of actors: actors from different organizations, spaces, and specializations; actors who are already embedded in existing tribes, institutions, and markets. And since networks value equity among these participants, and preserve autonomy among these actors with their interdependent agendas, they rely on mutual adjustment (Mintzberg 1979)—just as clans do, but across boundaries and distances rather than internally. The lines of communication must be constantly open, requiring cheap and robust means of communication. And that, as we'll see below, required the information age. "What is distinctive about information-age networks is that people who are far removed from each other can connect, coordinate, and act conjointly across barriers and distances," Ronfeldt (2007, p. 22) argues. That is, the information age lifted the caps on scaling networks. According to Ronfeldt, "This form is suited to enabling people to address modern, complex policy issues that may require efforts from many directions at the same time, such as health management and disaster recovery. These networks offer new designs for mutual collaboration that cannot be characterized as tribal, hierarchical, or market in nature" (p. 22). And those networks tend toward the multiorganizational (Ronfeldt & Varda 2008, p. 26).

Object and outcome   Adhocratic networks pulse objects that require various types of expertise, particularly objects that require collaboration across specialties (and thus activities). Such objects are defined tacitly at first; for the cross-specialty collaboration to be fruitful, each specialization must naturally contribute to the definition, which develops inductively. In fact, one could argue that the cross-specialty collaboration itself is always an aspect of the object (Adler & Heckscher 2007). This object is externally defined (i.e., defined by stakeholders in the intersecting activities). This configuration is especially well positioned for producing innovative outcomes, outcomes that cannot be achieved by individual specialties (Adler & Heckscher 2007; Cameron & Quinn 2011; Mintzberg 1978; cf. Castells 2003, p. 67; Guile 2012). For instance, when SEO specialists had to deal with SEO in an unfamiliar specialty, their SEO knowledge by itself was inadequate; they had to reach out through their personal networks to draft others (in this case, friends in medical school). With the help of these additional actors, they could develop SEO solutions that would otherwise be impossible.

Tools and rules   The tools used by adhocratic networks can be, and often are, unstructured, diffused, and loosely coupled (Boisot et al. 2001). They are pulled together across specialties to attack unique problems, so they are often cobbled together for a unique engagement. Rules are emergent and tend to develop over the life of the collaboration, as they must be when a unique combination of specialists attacks a unique problem (Adler & Heckscher 2007). We saw examples across Semoptco in chapter 7: specialists constantly sought new tools and adopted new rules to keep up with the fast-changing, contingency-ridden SEO space.

Although networks have been around throughout history, their high communication burden meant that they could not scale well until rapid long-distance information technologies began to spread in the mid-twentieth century: first the telephone and telegraph, then faxes, e-mails, mobile phones, and instant messaging. And in the twenty-first century, more digital technologies have proliferated: texting, WiFi, social media, videoconferencing, content management systems (McCarthy, Grabill, Hart-Davidson & McLeod 2011), activity streams (Hart-Davidson, Zachry & Spinuzzi 2012), and publicly available online services (Divine, Hall, Ferro & Zachry 2011).

In particular, rapid asynchronous electronic communication has made a large impact on how networks operate. As Shoshana Zuboff (1988) has documented, in the late twentieth century, digital technologies began to introduce new opportunities for workers to share information laterally, including through e-mail and discussion boards. Even more recently, social networking has begun to function as an additional communication layer within and across organizations (e.g., Divine et al. 2011). These are enabled through cheaper, more mobile devices. As one set of authors noted in 2007, "Wireless communication networks are diffusing around the world faster than any other communication technology to date" (Castells, Fernández-Ardèvol, Linchuan Qiu & Sey 2007, p. 1). A more recent industry report noted that "43 percent of mobile workers store their smartphone within arm's reach when they sleep at night. Those that do this are 60 percent more likely than average to wake during the night to check their smartphone" (iPass 2011, p. 3). And another industry report tells us that as of 2012, 63 percent of mobile phones are smartphones (Ghemawat & Altman 2012, p. 55).

Such technologies have allowed us to do something that we couldn't do before: share copious amounts of information, laterally, in mutual adjustment across organizational and geographic boundaries. This ability opened the way for networked innovations such as peer production, in which loosely organized communities generate large-scale innovations with positive economic impacts (e.g., Benkler 2006; Mueller 2010; Spinuzzi 2009). But it's also opened the way for the all-edge adhocracies I've discussed in this book: adhocracies build on the new workplace networks that, for the first time, can easily span organizations.

Actors and community stakeholders   In networks, actors can be internal to an organization (as in traditional adhocracies) or cross-organizational (in all-edge adhocracies; e.g., Bilton 1999; Dolan 2010; Ronfeldt et al. 1999). Like actors in clans, actors in adhocratic networks tend to be interdependent: specialists need each other's contributions if they are to complete the project (Adler & Heckscher 2007). They are collaborative, attempting to reach outcomes that will mutually benefit people in their separate, networked activities. As Adler, Kwon, and Heckscher put it, "Collaborative community is distinctive especially in its reliance on interactive social character and *interdependent self-construals*: rather than orienting to a single source of morality and authority, the personality must reconcile multiple conflicting identities and construct a sense of wholeness from competing attachments and interactions." (2008, p. 17; original emphasis). Networks characterize the organizations we have seen throughout this book, but they are also beginning to characterize various movements in the social sphere, from the Tea Party to Occupy to the Arab Spring. Such movements are (famously) connected through relatively new information and communication technologies, which allow networks to scale beyond their traditional boundaries. In this particular case, most of the SEO work is done by Semoptco's specialists themselves, and as we saw in chapter 7, those specialists are connected to several overlapping networks within Semoptco. But in addition, parts of the SEO work are done via contractors, friends, and, to some extent, even client contacts.

Division of labor   Adhocratic networks do not have a necessary center of control; typically they are horizontally controlled via the emerging collaboration (Boisot et al. 2001; Mintzberg 1979). They tend to establish interdependent relations and they must develop swift trust in order to work well (Adler & Heckscher 2007). Networks establish connections among entities, connections that are not as lasting as those in clans or as structured as those in hierarchies, but that are more durable than those in markets. These connections are characterized less by command-and-control and more by consult-and-coordinate. Internally, these are loosely coupled (like the connections of the "lone wolves" in Semoptco). Externally, these ties are fluid and open, with people willing to reach across different networks and organizations when necessary. In networks, the pulse is opportunistic: the focus is on the opportunities that might be inductively defined at the meeting point of separate activity systems.

I have discussed the four forms, seeing how they play out at Semoptco. Now let's compare them. Table 8.2 outlines significant differences among these in terms of key purposes, key values, structure, information technologies, and limitations. Yet they aren't completely separate. Organizations are complex, and they draw on multiple forms—which are good for different things (Cameron & Quinn 2011). Modern organizations have to address needs such as accounting and regulations (hierarchy), retention (clan), competition (market), and innovation (network).

As I illustrated above, Semoptco manifests various characteristics associated with different forms. That's typical of hybrid organizations. Overlapping these different forms yields considerable flexibility for meeting different challenges. But it also yields contradictions in the sense I discussed in chapter 6: fundamental tensions in the purpose, value, structure, and internal and external ties of the organization. As Ronfeldt tells us, "All the forms are contradictory, but they are not incompatible" (2007, p. 66). Such contradictions can disrupt organizations, but they are also sources of innovations, as Michael Cole and Yrjö Engeström (1993) told us in chapter 6. Let's take a look at three of these contradictions and how Semoptco handled them.

TABLE 8.2. The forms compared

	Hierarchy	Market	Clan	Network
Coordinating mechanism	Authority	Price	Trust (in shared value orientation within a group)	Trust (as common object across groups)
Values	Stability, order, risk aversion	Competition, responsiveness, individualism	Shared goals, cohesion, teamwork	Adaptivity, creativity, flexibility
Benefits	Control	Flexibility	Interdependent contributions (within a group)	Generating and sharing knowledge (across groups)
Structure	Vertical dependence	Horizontal independence	Enabling interdependence (within a group)	Enabling inter-dependence (across groups)
External ties	Local, closed	Global, open	Local, open	Global/local, open

Sources: Adler & Heckscher (2007); Boisot et al. (2011); Cameron & Quinn (2011); Heckscher (2007); Ronfeldt (2007).

Contradictions across Configurations

Up to this point, I have described activities as fitting comfortably within the presented typology. Yet they often do not—especially as we shift to the right of the matrix, in which multiple stakeholders collaboratively define the object.

In a complex collective activity, different stakeholders may have different motives (Hyysalo 2005, p. 22; Nardi 2005, p. 40) and different perspectives on the shared object (Christiansen 1996; Engeström 1999; Foot 2002; Holland & Reeves 1996). In any collective activity, an object is "multifaceted, evolving," and even "dialogical" (Foot 2002, pp. 132, 138). That is, the object is understood, transformed, and enacted differently by different participants at different points. Activities become polycontextual (Engeström, Engeström & Karkkainen 1995, p. 331) and polymotivated (Kaptelinin 2005, p. 13; Nardi 2005); stakeholders become more heterogeneous (Miettinen 1998). This pattern is common in knowledge work and has led activity theorists such as Engeström (2009) to propose a shift from the current third generation of activity theory to a fourth generation: "Third-generation activity theory still treats activity systems as reasonably well-bounded, although interlocking and networked, structured units. What goes on between activity systems is processes, such as the flow of rules from management to workers. [But] in social production and peer production, the boundaries and structures of activity systems seem to fade away. Processes become simultaneous, multidirectional, and often reciprocal. The density and crisscrossing of processes makes the distinction between processes and structure somewhat obsolete. The movements of information create textures that are constantly changing but not arbitrary or momentary" (Engeström 2009, p. 309; see also Spinuzzi 2012b).

Yet even in well-bounded activity systems, we can detect some hybridization across different configurations. For instance, people who work in a hierarchy may also develop clannish relationships within their departments (Artemeva & Freedman 2001); people in a hierarchically organized research group with its own internal agenda might also adopt goals held by external granting agencies (Ding 2008); people who buy a service in the marketplace might also form adhocratic networks with others buying that same service (Sherlock 2009). In these cases, objects become multiperspectival, with different aspects perceived and emphasized by different stakeholders and at different points of the pulse.

As noted earlier, organizational typologies generally acknowledge that organizations tend to be hybrids, not ideal types. Similarly, we can understand activities as hybrids of different types. And those hybrids have differences in tools, rules, actors, stakeholders, divisions of labor, and pulse. They exhibit patterns of contradictions.

Authority is the purpose of institutions, while their value is order and control. How were the purpose and value of institutions balanced with the purpose and value of networks at Semoptco? Let's look at one example.

Semoptco's SEO specialists all used social bookmarking services such as delicious.com or StumbleUpon to create bookmarks pointing to their clients' sites. They had considerable latitude in using these services: they could decide which bookmarking service(s) they wanted to use and how to write and tag bookmark descriptions; and they could even individually try out various tools that post bookmarks to several services at once. But that freedom was not absolute—and that was a good thing. One day, Carl noted excitedly that Semoptco developers were developing an automated bookmarking tool for all SEO specialists at Semoptco. "The interns will love this!" he exclaimed. After all, since social bookmarking was relatively low-skill work, specialists farmed it out to interns whenever possible.

This incident reminds us of a basic cycle I discussed in chapter 7: when specialists solved a problem, they usually tried to offload it to a tool so that they could solve other sorts of problems. In this case, they had already begun offloading the solution's implementation to less experienced people (interns) who could follow directions and who wouldn't be expected to show the same level of discretion as the specialists. But an automated tool went a step further, turning the work into code that would get this work done even more quickly—and leaving even less discretion for the interns.

In this case, networks provided flexibility, allowing specialists to develop innovative new solutions. But as we've seen, networked adhocracies are much better at innovation and creativity than they are at repeated, controlled, predictable outcomes. So naturally the specialists tended to find ways to institutionalize their solutions as quickly as possible. After all, they would rather give the tedious work to someone or something else (an intern, an automated system, a report template) so that they could get back to the interesting work of creating innovative solutions.

Carl and the other SEO specialists recognized the need for institutional solutions. But they also recognized that their real expertise as networked specialists was in innovation and creativity. By establishing a cycle to turn new innovations into generic, institutional solutions (see Spinuzzi 2012a), they could balance the values of both institutional and network forms.

MARKET VERSUS NETWORK: "YOU NEED TO GET OUT THERE AND INTERACT WITH THEM"

Wealth or capital is the purpose of markets and their value is competition. How were the purpose and value of markets balanced with the purpose and value of networks at Semoptco?

Let's go back to two instances I discussed earlier. In one, Daria described how her unit had contracted out link building to an external entity. In another, Daria and her team considered their personal networks as they tried to gain more insight into what their clients' customers might need from a website.

In the case of the contractor, Semoptco had already identified a clearly defined need: it needed specific sorts of links built on certain kinds of websites, and its budget was a fixed dollar amount. The contractor was given clear instructions, although she or he had discretion over how to perform the task. And payment was contingent on success. In other words, this was an external, low-trust contract relationship with highly structured explicit information. Finally, it was competitive: the better the contractor did on this task, the more likely she or he was to be hired for the next task.

But in the case of the personal networks, Semoptco had an ill-defined need; the team really didn't know what it was looking for. So it didn't have clear instructions to give the contractor, nor did it have a clear idea of what success would mean. So even though this case also involved external relationships, these had to be high-trust relationships with relatively unstructured, tacit information to be developed inductively. Finally, they were cooperative: Semoptco's specialists weren't running a competition; they were looking for help from trusted sources.

These trusted relationships were also cultivated with clients' representatives and employees. For instance, after one meeting, Carl explained, "Social media is a big part of what we do. . . . [It is] very much about the user; you need to get out there and interact with them. So anytime a client is willing and able to do that, it's like [claps] *yes!*" During that day's observation, Carl read a *Wired* article that related to a client, so he e-mailed the client representatives the article's web address and a short explanation. Such contacts were highly individualized—and selective. For instance, Luis said that he was careful to support an ally working at a particular client, the web developer, because that web developer "understands everything" while the company's owner "understands nothing."

Identity is the purpose of clans and their focal value is belonging. But innovation is the purpose of networks and their focal value is trust and equity. How are these two purposes and value sets balanced at Semoptco? Let's look at a final instance.

One day, about a month after I first noticed Carl and Luis's trophy, I showed up to observe and interview Luis. But he was no longer in the cubicle he had shared with Carl—he had been replaced by another specialist. Carl told me where to find Luis: in another cubicle down the hall.

"What happened?" I asked Luis.

He shrugged. "They just move me around," he said. "I'm paired with Nessa now."

As I settled in for the interview, I noticed a sticky note on Luis's side of the cubicle. It read: "Bye Luis! We will miss you!— Carl and Macy."

Carl and Luis had felt pride in being associated as a team. But at Semoptco, where people had to perform well in agile networks, it wasn't a good idea to let teams become too close, too internally focused, too tribal. Networked teams meant breaking down interiors—and breaking up teams. Clannish pride and identity had to give way to networked trust and equity.

EASING INTERFERENCE PATTERNS IN ORGANIZATIONS

In each of the cases above, we see interference patterns between different kinds of activities seeking to pulse the same object: SEO. Semoptco eased the contradictions among competing organizational forms by "translating" from one set of values, purposes, and strengths to another. In the social bookmarking example, networked innovation could hand off solutions to institutional control. In the contractor case, low-trust, explicit transactions were handled competitively while high-trust, tacit transactions were handled cooperatively. And in the trophy instance, clannish solidarity gave way to networked coordination. Semoptco was able to combine forms through these little acts of translation.

In fact, multiform organizations must be able to combine forms while easing their contradictions. Each form has different strengths, useful for different things:

- *Hierarchies* provide order, control, and authority, which are essential for providing efficiency at predictable, explicitly defined tasks within a group.
- *Markets* provide efficiency and structure in low-trust environments with explicitly defined tasks across groups.
- *Clans* provide identity and solidarity, which are essential for trusted collaborations on tacitly defined tasks within a group.
- *Networks* provide innovation and creativity, which are essential for collaboration on tacitly defined tasks across groups.

Blending these is a challenge. Indeed, as work gets more complex, with different hybrids of organizational forms, specialists will need to find different ways to integrate their efforts within complex systems. What kinds of ways? Three integrations are going on right now in networked organizations. In the next chapter, we'll see what they are.

9

The Work of All-Edge Adhocracies:
The Three Integrations

In chapter 8, we saw how different kinds of objects require differently configured activities to pulse them. And I argued that complex organizations' objects tend to be multiperspectival, with different aspects that require them to be pulsed in different ways simultaneously. The tensions among these differently configured activities cause interference patterns that threaten to tear the objects—and their activities—apart.

Such tensions have long been part of organizations but are greatly exacerbated when networks are involved. That happens for two reasons, which are related to the two axes discussed in chapter 8.

How the object is defined Unlike markets, networks deal with objects that are tacitly defined and inductively reached. In markets, stakeholders haggle over low-context, highly structured, standardized information such as price and specifications. But in networks, stakeholders and actors must collaboratively determine what they want the object's qualities to be; they seek creativity and innovation. That means that they must develop shared values as well as specifications, and they must manage this process during the collaboration rather than determine it beforehand. For instance, when the search engine optimization (SEO) specialists in chapter 7 agree to improve SEO for their clients, they know that SEO will be affected by unpredictable events such as news events, competitors' SEO, and search engines' algorithm changes. Consequently, they can't guarantee a specific ranking or a specific rate of improvement. Each month they have to innovate to keep up with the SEO space.

Where the object is defined Unlike hierarchies and clans, networks draw in stakeholders from outside activities, increasing the number of perspectives on the object. Rather than being defined just by the people who transform it, the object is (also) defined by other stakeholders with their own standards, values, agendas, and desired outcomes. When the freelancers in chapter 3 assemble specialists from different fields, when the coworkers in chapter 5 develop a back stage that can support the work of all coworkers in the space, and when the SEO specialists in chapter 7 struggle to understand the content they're supposed to optimize, they must manage the different perspectives and the specialties in which those perspectives are grounded.

Consequently, networks greatly complicate the organizations in which they are a part. Particularly when the networks serve as a base for all-edge adhocracies. Yet that is the challenge we face, due to the increasing prevalence of networks and all-edge adhocracies that connect across organizations to do things that individual organizations can't. As a result, organizations face increasing stresses, stress patterns, and instability. They face the danger of disintegration.

Complexity and the Threat of Disintegration

We can think of this threat of disintegration as a tug-of-war between standardization and innovation. To understand the difference between the two, let's examine the difference in terms of two scholars, Max Boisot and Manuel Castells.

CODIFICATION, ABSTRACTION, AND DIFFUSION

Boisot and his collaborators argue that "how far knowledge gets articulated determines how speedily and extensively it can be shared" (Boisot, MacMillan & Han 2001, p. 109). They argue that we can understand information in three dimensions:

- *Codification.* Information can range from very uncodified to very codified. "Codification is indexed by the amount of data-processing required to distinguish between categories and to assign events to these" (Boisot, Nordberg, Yami & Nicquevert 2011, p. 33). Codification involves descriptive complexity (Boisot et al. 2001, p. 155). For instance, if you're conducting a poll, the people you poll may find it easier to answer your questions if you provide them with closed-end questions (yes/no, Likert scales, multiple choice) than if you ask open-ended questions. They'll also tend to provide more-uniform answers—"yes" or "no" rather than many different shades of agreement.
- *Abstraction.* Information can vary from very concrete to very abstract. "Abstraction is indexed by the number of categories required to perform

a given categorical assignment." (Boisot et al. 2011, p. 33). Abstraction involves computational complexity (Boisot et al. 2001, p. 155). In the poll example, the closed-ended questions limit the kind of answers people can give, making the criteria for each answer clearer and more restricted. Abstraction also makes it much easier for you, the pollster, to compare answers across a broad data set: rather than compare qualitative statements with many variations, you can count the yeses and nos for each question.

- *Diffusion.* Information can range from very concentrated to very diffuse. Here, I'm talking about the degree to which information can be diffused over time. "The greater the degree of codification and abstraction achieved for a given message, the larger the population of agents that can be reached by diffusion per unit of time" (Boisot et al. 2011, p. 34). Diffusion involves relational complexity (Boisot et al. 2001, p. 155). In the poll example, diffusion might involve the number and breadth of people you poll, but it also might involve how broadly you circulate the results of the poll. The more broadly information is diffused, the greater the number of activities that can work with it.

The more that information is codified and abstracted, the easier it is to diffuse—but in codifying and abstracting information, we face data losses (Boisot et al. 2001, p. 131). For instance, if I conduct a poll with open-ended questions, I must spend considerable time figuring out how to relate and interpret the results, perhaps reading each individual's answers. Even though I'll have a more rich, nuanced set of data, I won't be able to poll a large number of people—I simply won't have the time and resources to scale the poll beyond a certain limit. But if I use closed-ended questions, I can handle a much larger set of respondents.

We can think of codification and abstraction under the umbrella term *standardization.* The more standardized information is, the more easily it can be diffused. At one end, embodied knowledge—which tends to be tacit, habitual, craft knowledge—is concrete and uncodified, and therefore difficult to diffuse (p. 131); we tend to transfer this sort of information one-on-one, through apprenticeships and coaching. At the other end, abstract symbolic knowledge—which tends to be highly categorized or quantified—is highly abstract and codified, and therefore easy to diffuse (p. 131); think in terms of prices, stock market information, or numerical poll results.

Boisot and his colleagues argue that these characteristics of information have had a big impact on how we organize work. For instance, they argue that bureaucracies evolved from local, personalized structures to large, ubiquitous, impersonal ones due to an information and communication technology (ICT): the printing press, which provided information storage and diffusion

(Boisot et al. 2001, p. 148; Weber 1978, p. 957). Similarly, modern ICTs might favor organizations other than bureaucratic hierarchies and competitive markets—in particular, Boisot says, clan-like networks (Boisot et al. 2001, p. 150; Boisot et al. 2011, p. 51).

This should be a familiar assertion: as we saw in chapter 2, these ICTs affect the ways that we can organize our work. By making it cheaper and faster to communicate, coordinate, and collaborate across distances, ICTs such as telephony, videoconferencing, e-mail, and social networks "shift the curve" (Boisot et al. 2001, p. 161; Boisot et al. 2011, pp. 50–51), allowing us to diffuse information more broadly with less codification. This impact, Boisot and his colleagues argue, comes from two effects of new ICTs:

- *The diffusion effect.* "At any given level of codification and abstraction, more information will reach more people per unit along the diffusion scale than hitherto" (Boisot et al. 2001, p. 160). That is, it's simply easier to move all kinds of information around—across organizations, across distances, across time—with new ICTs. We can converse, text, send photos and graphics, and "like" each other's statuses; most forms of information can be digitized (in text, audio, video) and shared very quickly to a very large number of people. And that brings us to the second effect.
- *The bandwidth effect.* "Any given proportion of the population located at some point along the diffusion scale can be reached at a lower level of codification and abstraction—that is, at a higher bandwidth—than hitherto" (Boisot et al. 2001, p. 160). That is, even information that resists codification and abstraction, such as embodied knowledge, can be digitized and broadly diffused. Think of YouTube videos that demonstrate hard-to-describe skills, skills that until recently could only be demonstrated one-on-one in an apprenticeship or coaching situation.

Because ICTs have shifted the curve, people find it easier to share less-standardized information, including the tacitly defined objects I discussed in chapter 8. These ICTs allow organizations to worry less about the dictates of the bureaucracy (control, order, and predict) and focus more efficiently and pervasively on the ethos of the adhocracy (acknowledge, create, and empower). They make possible the characteristics of all-edge adhocracies, the same characteristics that allow these adhocracies to creatively swarm complex and tacitly defined problems: a weak division of labor, teams of specialists crossing boundaries, rotating leadership, and command rather than control (see chapter 2).

But that's not to say that standardization will disappear. It remains vitally important, even in all-edge adhocracies! The easier it is to transport information, the easier it is for people to become overloaded with information.

To function effectively, all-edge adhocracies must establish a standardization cycle—as Semoptco did. To understand this cycle, let's turn to the sociologist Manuel Castells and his distinction between generic and self-programmable labor.

STANDARDIZATION AND GENERIC LABOR

Standardization—that is, increased codification and abstraction—thrives when the environment is predictable and tasks are repeated. Tasks settle into routines supported by stable sets of tools and rules. Solutions that work well at one point will work well again, so we can optimize them and make them more efficient. In fact, once we solve a problem in such an environment, it will generally stay solved; we can rely on the same tool over again. Often *the expertise migrates into the tool*: once we solve the problem, we can make the solution into a standardized, generic routine with abstract, codified inputs and outputs, a routine that can be applied to similar problems. (This point has often been made in genre studies; see Spinuzzi [2003].) When we calculate our taxes with software, when we drive an automobile with an automatic transmission, and when we calculate SEO metrics with software, we are reaping the benefits of this generic labor.

Generic labor is a term used by Manuel Castells to describe labor that involves predictably transforming defined inputs into defined outputs. "Generic labor is assigned a given task, with no reprogramming capability, and it does not presuppose the embodiment of information and knowledge beyond the ability to receive and execute signals" (Castells 1998, p. 361). Such tasks can easily be automated—or outsourced. When Carl gave the task of social bookmarking to interns, and when Semoptco developed BRILLIANCE to track metrics and generate "report cards," they were both taking advantage of making labor generic. As Castells argues elsewhere, in terms of automation: "Generic labor is embodied in workers who do not have special skills, or special ability to acquire skills in the production process, other than those necessary to execute instructions from management. Generic labor can be replaced with machines, or by generic labor anywhere else in the world, and the precise mix between machines, on-site labor, and distant labor depends on ad hoc business calculation" (Castells 2003, p. 94).

As we saw in the previous section, standardization tends to involve codified, abstract information—information that is explicit, in the terms I used in chapter 8. That standardized kind of information is vital in cases that replace human, discretionary labor with automation. The more stable and predictable the environment, the more useful generic labor is—the more it can be made categorical, calculable, and easily recognizable. Generic labor can be controlled, ordered, and predicted. And as Warren Bennis and Philip Slater (1998) argue, bureaucracies exist to control, order, and predict (see chapter 2). But when the environment is more complex and contingent, labor has other requirements.

INNOVATION AND SELF-PROGRAMMABLE LABOR

Innovation thrives when the environment is unpredictable, complex, and contingent, often with decreased codification and abstraction. In such an environment, we cannot be confident that a solution will work from one time to the next; we must try it and find out. Solutions that work well at one point may not work well again, so although we can take them as reference points, we will likely have to customize them during each pulse; we also might need to incorporate new tools and procedures during each pulse. This creative process is not efficient, but it is agile and flexible, resulting in unique, customized solutions that cannot be wholly derived from a generic routine. So *the expertise remains with the specialist,* who must use her or his judgment to deal with these unique cases. These are the cases that can't be automated, built into a tool, or encapsulated in rigid procedures.

Castells describes this sort of labor as *self-programmable labor:*

> Self-programmable labor has the autonomous capacity to focus on the goal assigned to it in the process of production, find the relevant information, recombine it into knowledge, using the available knowledge stock, and apply it in the form of tasks oriented toward the goals of the process. The more our information systems are complex, and interactively connected to databases and information sources via computer networks, the more what is required from labor is the capacity to search and recombine information. This demands appropriate education and training, not in terms of skills, but in terms of creative capacity, as well as in terms of the ability to co-evolve with changes in organization, in technology, and in knowledge. (Castells 2009, p. 30)

Self-programmable labor is needed when the environment is more complex and contingent—that is, under the same conditions that require networks and adhocracies. That means less standardization: less codification and often less abstraction. Instead, it requires human discretion, expertise, and judgment in tacit, uncodified, and often concrete work.

But that's not to say that generic and self-programmable labor are mutually exclusive. Far from it: they're both necessary if we are to keep work integrated. As Boisot et al. (2011, p. 39) argues, organizations tend to undergo a social learning cycle that involves codifying and abstracting information to improve its diffusion, absorption, and impact. Semoptco underwent a remarkably rapid version of this cycle. The cycle was underpinned by the dynamic between generic and self-programmable labor, a dynamic that is characteristic of all-edge adhocracies.

GENERIC AND SELF-PROGRAMMABLE LABOR: A DYNAMIC

As we've seen, standardization and innovation—and their two types of labor, generic and self-programmable—are good for different things. As table 9.1 suggests, generic labor lends itself well to stable environments, in which explicit objects must be pulsed to meet predictable, efficient, and reliable outcomes: the sorts of outcomes at which bureaucratic hierarchies excel. In contrast, self-programmable labor lends itself well to complex, open-ended environments, in which tacit objects must be pulsed to meet innovative, creative outcomes: the sorts of outcomes at which adhocratic networks excel.

But as we've seen, objects have various aspects. And complex multiperspectival objects such as subcontractor networks, coworking, and SEO need both standardization and innovation, both generic and self-programmable labor, in order to succeed. In successful cases, the two reach a productive dynamic that keeps their object integrated.

To see why, let's return to the Semoptco case from chapter 7, specifically figure 7.1, which is duplicated here as figure 9.1. In this figure, we see that a lot of different kinds of information go into writing the monthly report. Even though the information itself changes from month to month, even though

TABLE 9.1. Contrasting generic and self-programmable labor

Generic (high standardization)	Self-programmable (low standardization)	Source
Low-skilled	Multiskilled	Castells (1998, p. 361)
Automated or low cost	Specialists	Castells (2003, p. 94)
Focus on tasks; receive and execute signals	Focus on goal; generate own tasks to achieve; autonomous	Castells & Cardoso (2006, p. 10)
Routine, repetitive tasks	Problem-solving, creating knowledge	Castells & Cardoso (1996, p. 242)
Predictably transform inputs to outputs (low discretion)	Coevolve (high discretion)	Castells (1998, p. 361; 2003, pp. 90–91; 2009, p. 30)
Formalizable (explicit)	Unformalizable (tacit)	Castells (1996, p. 242)
Low value	High value	Castells (1996, p. 243)
Terminal learning	Lifelong learning	Castells (1998, p. 361; 2003, pp. 90–91)

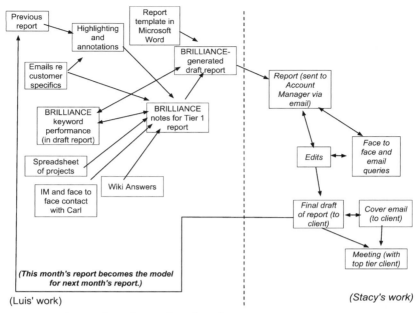

FIGURE 9.1. Semoptco's standing set of transformations

the clients' needs and the conditions constantly change, the basic set of trans-formations going into this cycle is relatively stable. The set of transformations depends on Semoptco's networked organization, in which each specialist has discretion over her or his own work. It's also stabilized by its institutional un-derpinnings: specialists are supported by a bureaucratic hierarchy, but (gen-erally) not hindered by it, as they make decisions.

This process is always changing, but it's also stable. Remember, adhocra-cies have certain strengths that are unmatched by other organizations: creativ-ity, innovation, and flexibility. But they also have considerable weaknesses: they're not good at reliably and efficiently producing the same outcome over and over. That's the sort of thing at which institutional bureaucracies excel. But in figure 9.1, we see a process that does both.

Why doesn't an organization like this fly apart under the stresses of con-stant change? How do adhocracies become stable? It appears that Semoptco's success turned on three integrations, three ways in which different kinds of information were brought together to produce something greater than their parts. Specifically,

- Semoptco's specialists were *integrated writers*, people who routinely com-bined knowledge, methods, and procedures as they pursued processes that they owned;

- Semoptco's specialists engaged in *integrated writing* in which the products of their work—reports—underwent a generic process, then were customized for individual clients; and
- Semoptco's specialists engaged in the *integration of distributed work*, in which they pulled information from different sources, crossing different domains, to provide value across different contexts.

Semoptco's workers aren't alone. As Eva-Maria Jakobs and I argue elsewhere (Jakobs & Spinuzzi 2014; Spinuzzi & Jakobs 2013), these interrelated trends show up in knowledge work across the developed world. And taken together, they help us to understand how all-edge adhocracies shore up their weaknesses and leverage their strengths.

INTEGRATED WRITERS: THE DIFFUSION OF KNOWLEDGE PRODUCTION

In all-edge adhocracies, specialists routinely combine knowledge, methods, and procedures as they pursue the processes that they own. They're integrated writers. Let's untangle that statement a bit, because it encapsulates several things that I've discussed in previous chapters.

Information as process and product of work   All-edge adhocracies are a recent phenomenon, powered by new information technology that lets them scale up to meet challenges (chapter 8). This information technology makes mutual adjustment practical and inexpensive across distances, organizations, and specializations. But it also allows the product of all-edge adhocracies, which is knowledge, to move easily across such boundaries. That is, information—especially writing—characterizes both the product and the process of their work.

Distributed control   Since all-edge adhocracies are composed of specialists, they aren't controlled by a single individual or point or hierarchy (chapter 2). They can be commanded but not controlled. That is, the individual specialists retain operational discretion over their work; they work with other specialists who might be able to tell them what's needed, but who don't have the expertise to tell them how to produce it. To do their work well, specialists must have the freedom, flexibility, and creative latitude to apply their specialization to the project.

Innovation and creativity   All-edge adhocracies, then, are well positioned to deliver on their key promises of innovation and creativity. That's because the specialists working in an all-edge adhocracy represent self-programmable labor: they set their own tasks, determine and own their own processes, apply their own creativity, and adjust and evolve nimbly to address new circumstances and unique problems (see Castells 1996, 1998, 2003, 2009; Castells & Cardoso 2006). When Bob and Tom tackle a graphic design problem (chapter 3), when Helen forms a team-for-today at Conjunctured (chapter 5), and when Daria reacts to a change in a search engine's algorithm (chapter 7), they are performing self-programmable labor, working nimbly to tailor unique solutions.

We've seen examples of integrated writers in various literatures. Integrated writers are knowledge workers who own processes and who routinely combine knowledge, methods, and information with their work on those processes. Such integrated writers (e.g., engineers, general managers, accountants, health technologists) do not see themselves as writing professionals, but nevertheless they integrate writing with their other tasks across their organizations. They often demonstrate deficient problem-solving strategies in their writing (e.g., intensive text planning, but weak revising and a weak addressee orientation; see Jakobs 2008). They perceive writing as a less important and unloved part of their work, yet these writing tasks are often vital, especially as work becomes increasingly textualized (Jakobs & Spinuzzi 2014). When veterinary students use various forms of infrastructure to write patient care narratives (Swarts 2007), when online gamers develop documentation for each other (Sherlock 2009), they do not consider themselves to be writers, yet their writing is vital to the success of their activities.

In such cases, *writing has become an essential skill*, more or less the first level of information standardization in an organization. With digital ICTs, writing is easier to produce, circulate, and store than before, making it less costly to communicate, coordinate, and collaborate across boundaries, even when information is relatively uncodified.

As we've seen throughout this book, and especially in figure 9.1, writing in all its forms is key to making knowledge work happen. As writing became a widely held skill, and as ICTs allowed it to diffuse more broadly, anyone in a given organization became a potential integrated writer: a potential processor, coordinator, and producer of information. *All-edge adhocracies are composed of integrated writers.* That's part of what makes these organizations all edge, able to produce information at any point and to connect any point to others in different organizations. Even though they consider themselves graphic writers and web developers (chapter 3), interior decorators and consultants (chapter 5), account managers and SEO specialists (chapter 7), as they work in their all-edge adhocracies, these workers are all integrated writers.

INTEGRATED WRITING: THE STANDARDIZATION CYCLE

But these all-edge adhocracies would fly apart without some sort of stan-dardization. As I discussed in chapter 6, without a pulse, an activity is dead; without some regular cycle to provide continuity, people don't learn, perfect, and retain a specialization. Yet adhocracies, as we saw in chapters 2 and 8, are weak at standardization. In emphasizing innovation and creativity, they give up the chief advantage of bureaucratic hierarchies: the ability to do the same thing over and over, reliably and efficiently. Without some sort of standard-ization, all-edge adhocracies might not be able to consistently deliver on their promises, making it impossible to provide a front stage (see chapters 3 and 5). And their members might lose the very expertise that makes them useful to the adhocracy.

But in practice, all-edge adhocracies do standardize. They do have a pulse—although that pulse is quite different from that of bureaucratic hier-archies. To pursue their goals of flexibility, freedom, and creativity, all-edge adhocracies paradoxically end up standardizing and automating a great deal. That standardizing tendency shows up throughout this book. For instance, in chapter 3, nonemployer firms settled on specific tools (such as Basecamp and e-mail) and rules (don't meet the client at your home office; do supply firm-branded e-mails to subcontractors). In chapter 5, coworking spaces de-veloped written and unwritten codes of conduct. And in chapter 7, SEO spe-cialists constantly embedded new solutions in templates, in blog posts, and in Semoptco's information system. Once they solved a problem, they automated it as soon as they could—so that they could get back to other problems that demanded their innovation and creativity.

In other words, what these specialists brought to all-edge adhocracies was their self-programmable labor; but once they found a solution, they would turn it into generic labor, labor that they could formalize, then offload to an intern, a rule set, a template, or an information system. This is a version of the social learning cycle that Boisot et al. (2011, p. 39) describe (see figure 9.2). Three things were involved in making that labor generic: standardization, customized solutions, and specialist interfaces.

Standardization   First, specialists standardized information and processes, giving shape and regulation to their work. They strengthened the pulse of their work activity, making it stronger and deeper; they allowed themselves room to be creative and innovative without having to reinvent the wheel each time. They shored up the great weakness of all-edge adhocracies without imperiling the strengths. (See Spinuzzi [2012b] for more on this standardization process.)

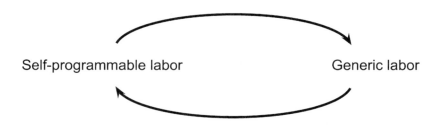

FIGURE 9.2. Turning self-programmable labor into generic labor

Customized solutions   Second, specialists allowed for customized solutions to emerge from a generic process. They made it possible to present a front stage. As Manuel Castells (2003) argues, knowledge work often involves a generic process that is then customized for a specific client. Especially at Semoptco (chapter 7), people worked hard to make their processes more generic, but their end products—the monthly reports—were customized for each client. When Sophie creates a logo or Benny creates a website (chapter 3), when Helen consults with a client or Tricia decorates a room (chapter 5), they are following an established process that provides their work with a structure and a pulse, but the end product is customized for each client.

Specialist interfaces   Third, specialists created interfaces (i.e., standard ways to share information) that allowed them to support their collaboration with proper coordination. Specialists in these all-edge adhocracies made sure to create stable interfaces with each other so that they could work together. Remember, these all-edge adhocracies had to be composed of people from different organizations, specializations, and locations (chapter 2), and these specialists had to be able to collaborate without fully understanding each other's work. That meant constant mutual adjustment via different technologies, but it also meant standard kinds of coordination for supporting collaboration. For instance, Semoptco's specialists coordinated in meetings and conversations, but also in notes in BRILLIANCE, in e-mails, and in IMs.

Such specialist interfaces are common in electronic environments. For instance, wikis provide complex mechanisms for coordinating work and hashing out differences involved in collaboration (e.g., Oxley, Morgan, Zachry &

Hutchinson 2010; Gokhman, McDonald & Zachry 2011; McDonald, Javanmardi & Zachry 2011), content management systems provide similar spaces
(McCarthy, Grabill, Hart-Davidson & McLeod 2011), social media often furnish a social layer to supplement other collaborations within and across organizations (Baehr & Alex-Brown 2010; McNely 2009; Zhao & Rosson 2009),
and publicly available online services sometimes furnish additional coordinative layers (Divine, Hall, Ferro & Zachry 2011; Ferro, Derthick, Morgan,
Searle & Zachry 2009).

THE INTEGRATION OF DISTRIBUTED WORK

As we've seen throughout this book, all-edge adhocracies are distributed:
across organizations, specialties, and geographic distances. And being distributed makes them stronger, since it means that they can pull their different
sets of expertise together to yield innovative, customized solutions to unique
problems. But being distributed also poses a huge challenge: it's not easy to
pool efforts across these boundaries. To realize their promise, all-edge adhocracies have to find ways to integrate distributed work (Spinuzzi 2007; Rainie
& Wellman 2012, p. 16). That integration happens in backstage areas.

Stable infrastructure   As we saw above, one way it happens is through generic labor, which provides stable infrastructure for specialists to interact
with each other: regular templates, tools, and avenues for mutual adjustment.
This infrastructure is stable in the sense that it allows consistent, well-known
practices to develop. Such infrastructure can include not only tools and protocols (such as Internet Protocol and telephony) but also genres (such as
user interfaces and report types) and information-sharing practices (such
as workstreaming, ambient awareness, and the social media layers that have
spread so quickly across organizations in the last decade). All of this stable
infrastructure provides standard and rapid ways to diffuse information (in
Boisot's sense), allowing users to "shift the curve" by sharing information
widely even when it is less abstract and codified than it would have had to be
in the past.

Weak ties   Another way, as we saw in all three of the cases, is to establish and
pursue weak ties, tenuous and far-flung connections (Granovetter 1973)—
to network, not just in the sense of professional networking, but also in the
sense of personal and affinity networking. When Sophie finds subcontractors
in her circle of friends and Cory finds them in Christian organizations (chapter 3), when Damon subcontracts someone at Conjunctured and Rhonda

bounces ideas off of other people at Link (chapter 5), and when Daria reaches out to friends in medical school (chapter 7), they are pursuing collaborative, interdependent relationships—relationships that are different from those provided through clan affiliation, hierarchical authority, or market competition (see chapter 8). Each unique problem might activate a unique set of connections, making the all-edge adhocracy extraordinarily flexible. As Lee Rainie and Barry Wellman (2012, pp. 27–30) argue, people's social networks have grown large and diverse while group boundaries have become weaker; as Paul Adler and Charles Heckscher (2007) argue, people who work in collaborative communities must develop swift trust with these weak ties throughout the collaboration.

Interdependence   And this brings us to a third way that all-edge adhocracies integrate distributed work: they function through interdependence, by bringing value to all in the adhocracy, tying the success of each to the success of all (Adler & Heckscher 2007; see also Heckscher 2007; Zuboff & Maxmin 2004). When an all-edge adhocracy is successful, it's successful for all of its interdependent, collaborative members. We see that collaborative success in the nonemployer firms of chapter 3, although we also see examples in which bad actors do not live up to their obligations. We see it in chapter 5, in which the coworking space helps people meet the needs of their front and back stages. And we see it especially in chapter 7, in which SEO was not considered successful unless it brought value to all stakeholders, from the clients to their customers to the search engines to Semoptco itself.

THE WORK OF ALL-EDGE ADHOCRACIES

The work of all-edge adhocracies, then, is not just to tie things together but also to integrate them: to integrate information aspects into the processes owned by each specialist, to integrate disparate bodies of knowledge to produce unique solutions, and to integrate the interests of everyone in the all-edge adhocracy. Even though each all-edge adhocracy lasts only as long as the project objective that it is assembled to solve, these three integrations allow them to work on a scale and with a level of success that they could not achieve otherwise. Without these three integrations, all-edge adhocracies would disintegrate, torn apart by the differences in their objects, pulses, and types of information.

Still, adhocracies are tactical, short-lived, reactive. They are project-oriented, arguably lacking a strategic outlook. Do they have a future? In the final chapter, I argue that they do, and I discuss what it looks like.

10

The Future of All-Edge Adhocracies

As we've seen, the new workplace networks have tremendous potential. But they also have limitations. We're not all ready to work in pure all-edge adhocracies—nor do we need to be. But we do need to know about all-edge adhocracies and the networks that underlie them, since we'll be interacting with them more and more frequently, and since other organizations will tend to take on at least a bit of their values, focuses, and logics.

Throughout this book, I've specifically examined cases that are grounded in communication and design work, which constitutes the leading edge for development of all-edge adhocracies. That's for three reasons. First, this work is focused on innovation, finding unique solutions to unique projects rather than mass-producing a product. Second, this work is centered on information: these unique solutions are informational solutions (such as designed logos, texts, and links), and thus people can communicate about them, coordinate work on them, and collaborate on them digitally. Third, this work is largely situated in service industries, which have become distributed via the long-term trend of shedding noncore assets.

But although all-edge adhocracies have flourished in communication and design work, they are making inroads in other activities as well. Innovation is an increasingly important part of work across many sectors (e.g., Castells 2003), work across the board is increasingly "informated" or overlaid with information (Zuboff 1988), and the trend of shedding noncore assets is hardly limited to communication and design work. Indeed, we see aspects of it in software development (e.g., Ducheneaut 2005; Fraiberg 2013; Grabher 2004; Hemetsberger & Reinhart 2009), health care (Spence & Reddy 2011), entertainment (Bilton 1999; Foster 2013); administration (Hart-Davidson, Zachry & Spinuzzi 2012; McCarthy, Grabill, Hart-Davidson & McLeod 2011), international development projects (Walton 2013), and the enterprise (Baehr & Alex-Brown 2010; Brzozowski, Sandholm & Hogg 2009; Divine, Hall, Ferro & Zachry 2011; Subramaniam, Nandhakumar & Baptista John 2013). New information and communication technologies have lowered the cost of informating and distributing work in multiple fields (Spinuzzi 2007, 2009; Swarts & Kim 2009), making all-edge adhocracies increasingly viable either as stand-alone organizational forms or as overlays over existing forms. Along with these changes come the challenges of addressing ambient awareness (Kolfschoten, Herrmann & Lukosch 2013), nomadic work (Czarniawska 2013; Mark & Su 2010; cf. Swarts & Kim 2009), multiple and contradictory stakeholders (Ducheneaut 2005; Walton 2013), and blurred work-life boundaries (Kylin & Karlsson 2008; Solomon 2012).

Beyond work, as we saw in chapter 1, the conditions for all-edge adhocracies have developed in nonwork activities as diverse as parenting and growing up, leisure and sociality, politics, disaster recovery, and warfare. Across these sectors, the conditions are right for all-edge adhocracies, both as the primary organizational structure and as one that overlays and amplifies existing ones (as we saw in chapter 7).

Yet all-edge adhocracies also have their drawbacks. The very things that make them agile, flexible, creative, and innovative also make them temporary, tactical, and reactive. They focus on temporary project objectives, not strategy. How do we get them to flourish? How do we support their strengths, minimize their weaknesses, and use them to their potential?

What We've Learned about All-Edge Adhocracies

In chapter 1, we saw developments in information and communication technologies (ICTs) that led to all-edge adhocracies. These developments laid the groundwork for the characteristics of communication, coordination, and cooperation that all-edge adhocracies demand.

Communication　Communication can be abstract or concrete, codified or uncodified, synchronous or asynchronous, textual or nontextual, and directed or ambient. As we've developed more ICTs, we generally have not simply substituted one for another—we've typically layered them, adding new ICTs, providing new channels for communication in more media, underpinning more genres. These ICTs have taken on different roles, allowing us extraordinary flexibility in our communication choices, but requiring us to learn an expanding repertoire of ICTs, media, and genres.

Coordination   Our broad and expanding range of ICTs allows us to coordinate in different ways, ordering and integrating our efforts—not just with people in our immediate vicinity or in our bureaucratic silo, but across organizations, specialties, occasions, and locations. Significantly, these ICTs have generally dropped in cost—both the cost to produce them and the cost to convey them. Between the rapid expansion of ICTs and their rapid drop in cost, we are finding it more and more practical to coordinate with others. Mutual adjustment, which was once practical only in small colocated groups, is now eminently practical across locations and boundaries.

Collaboration   The expanding repertoire of ICTs also makes cross-disciplinary, cross-organizational collaboration more practical. Shared objects can be discussed and negotiated practically and rapidly across disciplines, organizations, and distances. As a result, we see more shared objects and more temporary objects. Swarming becomes an effective tactic, allowing more-agile, flexible temporary collaborations.

In chapter 2, we saw how adhocracies developed to address these changes in communication, coordination, and cooperation—especially the drop in communication costs and the complexity of specializations. All-edge adhocracies took on these characteristics:

- *Project-oriented.* Whereas bureaucratic hierarchies locate work in parts of the hierarchy—departments, offices—all-edge adhocracies organize themselves around the temporary, shared project.
- *Agile.* All-edge adhocracies are flexible, reconfigurable, and mobile, and can change size and composition during a project.
- *Innovative.* All-edge adhocracies involve constant boundary crossing across disciplines, specialties, and organizations. Boundary crossing becomes a key part of their work, allowing them to tap into and combine the different parts, developing innovative solutions.
- *Allied.* An all-edge adhocracy is voluntarily joined in an alliance of different specialists with their own motivations, expectations, home organizations, and values.
- *Decentralized.* All-edge adhocracies rotate leadership among specialists; each team member tends to have very limited authority or leverage over the other members of the team.
- *Autonomous.* Team members in all-edge adhocracies are able to exercise their own freedom, flexibility, and creativity as long as they can produce

results. Whereas bureaucratic hierarchies imply a command-and-control mechanism, all-edge adhocracies coordinate and cultivate.

All-edge adhocracies are built on organizational networks. As we saw in chapter 4, organizational networks have these characteristics:

- *Flat structure.* In an organizational network, team members are connected nonhierarchically: no single node controls the rest of the network.
- *Changing composition.* Organizational networks tend to change composition frequently, bringing in specialists for particular phases and dropping them once their phase is finished. People circulate in and out of these networks, changing their composition and dynamic.
- *Flexibility.* Since organizational networks are often composed of "part-timer" specialists, the people who work in organizational networks tend to value flexibility and freedom over permanence. An outsider can easily become an insider—and vice versa.
- *Adaptivity.* Finally, because they are nonhierarchical, change in composition, and are built around flexibility, organizational networks are highly adaptive. Problems might scale and change rapidly, and are often ill-defined, requiring networks to adapt quickly to handle them.

Although all-edge adhocracies are temporary and ever changing, we can still understand them in terms of cyclical human activity. In chapter 6, we saw that these activities have certain characteristics:

- *Stable, structured, and pulsing.* In an all-edge adhocracy, each person's work focuses on a specific project or set of projects, which has to be transformed in a predictable way, using specific processes and tools. Each time someone takes on a project—each pulse of her work—she learnes more and applies what she learned to the next pulse.
- *Kinetic.* The work activities of all-edge adhocracies come into contact with other dynamically structured activities, all of which may be developing at different rates and in different directions. When they come into contact, these activities may conflict with each other, requiring dynamic adjustment.
- *Dynamic.* Finally, this work changes constantly because of tensions within and across these kinetic activities. These tensions can result in problems, disruptions, and strains, but they also can result in innovations and adaptations.

Activities are configured to pulse different objects in different ways. And, as we saw in chapter 8, sometimes—perhaps more often than not—those configurations overlap, causing internal contradictions in a given activity. These objects can be characterized as

- *hierarchies,* which excel at controlled, ordered, and predictable tasks that are explicitly and internally defined;
- *markets,* which excel at flexible tasks that are explicitly and externally defined;
- *clans,* which excel at value- and culture-oriented tasks that are tacitly and internally defined; and
- *networks,* which excel at interdisciplinary and interorganizational, emergent tasks that are tacitly and externally defined, and take advantage of new communication capabilities to generate new possibilities of interaction— and in the process, make all-edge adhocracies possible.

These different kinds of activities make it harder for people to coordinate and collaborate, since they have to address different pulses across different boundaries. In chapter 9, we saw three integrations that all-edge adhocracies use to keep this multiperspectival work together.

- *Integrated writers.* Specialists routinely combine knowledge, methods, and procedures as they pursue the processes that they own.
- *Integrated writing.* Specialists cyclically turn self-programmable labor into generic labor so that they can take up new problems.
- *The integration of distributed work.* Specialists pool their efforts across organizations, specialties, and geographic distances.

Given the above, how can we improve all-edge adhocracies? How can we support their strengths, shore up their weaknesses, and realize their potential?

Supporting the Strengths of All-Edge Adhocracies

Here, at the end of the book, you might be detecting all-edge adhocracies in your own life: at work, in civil organizations, in professional and networking organizations, in politics. In all these realms, all-edge adhocracies have definite strengths. How do we support and maximize those strengths?

The question is pressing, since as Charles Heckscher (2007, p. 191) argues, the mobility and flexibility of the US labor market has its limits—the system is facing increasing strains. Heckscher goes on to argue that "mobility could be a good thing for employees as well as for companies *if* there were good systems in place for supporting mobile careers. These systems were unneeded in a bureaucratic order, but they are crucial now—and weak" (p. 272; original emphasis). Manuel Castells and Gustavo Cardoso (2006, p. 9) similarly describe an increasing trend toward the erosion of stable and predictable careers and toward autonomous work "not necessarily to increase monetary gains but to enjoy greater freedom, flex-time, or more opportunity to create" (p. 10)—work that has definite trade-offs in terms of stability and earnings.

That is, all-edge adhocracies currently have substantial strengths, largely because they are relatively unstructured. But to excel, they depend on other structures, and those structures must be strengthened if all-edge adhocracies are to reach their potential.

Workplace structure   All-edge adhocracies need workplaces that allow them to make the serendipitous, wide-ranging connections that can expand people's personal networks. These networks need to cross specializations, organizations, and locations, and they need to be redundant so that the adhocracy has plenty of specialists to choose from. So all-edge adhocracies require a workplace that is very different from that of bureaucratic hierarchies: one that fosters connections across specialists from different contexts. When Benny attends jellies (chapter 3), when Logan attends a meetup at Cospace and Nina asks her Link coworkers questions about how to run her business (chapter 5), when Daria shares breakfast with someone at Semoptco's breakfast taco club (chapter 7), they're making these connections. They have to.

Physical infrastructure   But all-edge adhocracies also need physical infrastructure. As we saw in chapters 1 and 8, it's only with the advent of widespread telecommunications and digital technologies that networks have been able to scale and all-edge adhocracies have been able to flourish. So people working in all-edge adhocracies need reliable access to that physical infrastructure, including mobile telecommunications networks, broadband Internet access, and mobile computing devices. This infrastructure is typically erected and serviced via bureaucratic hierarchies such as telecommunications companies and manufacturers: as we saw in chapter 2, bureaucracies are well suited to efficiently providing reliable outcomes. As Heckscher (2007, p. 136) argues, to succeed at collaboration, an enterprise should not centralize structure but rather standardize infrastructure.

Service infrastructure   Along with that physical infrastructure, all-edge adhocracies need access to the service infrastructure that supports it. As my case studies demonstrate, people in all-edge adhocracies use slates of different services, including SMS, instant messaging, videoconferencing, social networking sites, publicly available online services, and e-mail. These services often overlap and are used opportunistically to connect with different collaborators: in chapter 3, Benny, for instance, coordinated via direct phone calls, conference calls, and videoconferencing, while Bob and Tom coordinated via Basecamp, instant messaging, phone calls, face-to-face meetings, and SMS. In all-edge adhocracies, members must access and develop a repertoire of different services. As Chiara Rossitto, Cristian Bogdan, and Kerstin Severinson-Eklundh (2013) argue, people must orchestrate constellations of different technologies if they are to be effective at nomadic work.

Collaborative and social infrastructure   People in all-edge adhocracies must be able to build "shared understandings and processes" by freely using the physical and service infrastructure to contact each other, to collaborate via associational links without going through the levels of their organization's bureaucratic hierarchy (Heckscher 2007, p. 92). This collaborative infrastructure can and should be "deliberately managed" in larger enterprises (Heckscher 2007, pp. 92, 136). But for loosely organized all-edge adhocracies, which extend beyond a particular enterprise, people need lightly managed or unmanaged collaborative infrastructure. For instance, when Daria wanted to tap the expertise of her friends in medical school, she was free to use Semoptco's physical and service infrastructure to do so.

This collaborative infrastructure includes support for collaborative writing: in wikis (Bhatti, Baile & Yasin 2011; Gokhman, McDonald & Zachry 2011; Morgan & Zachry 2010; Starke-Meyerring 2010; Wagner 2010), content management systems (Andersen 2008; D. Clark 2008; McCarthy et al. 2011), and other publicly available online services (Ferro, Derthick, Morgan, Searle & Zachry 2009; Ferro, Divine & Zachry 2012). It also includes support for developing social and coordinative links via instant messaging (Isaacs, Walendowski, Whittaker, Schiano & Kamm 2002; Pazos, Chung & Micari 2012) and social media (Backhouse 2009; Brzozowski et al. 2009; Jacobs & Nakata 2010; Muller, Shami, Millen & Feinberg 2010).

Benefits infrastructure   As mentioned above, all-edge adhocracies have developed from the erosion of stable and predictable careers (Castells & Cardoso 2006, p. 9) and from workers' desire to "enjoy greater freedom, flextime, or more opportunity to create" (p. 10). But these benefits come with trade-offs in terms of stability and earnings. Charles Heckscher & Françoise Carré (2006) describe the development of networked quasi unions such as the Freelancers' Union, in which freelancers can band together to buy group health insurance, and Working Today, which represents freelancers' rights in the digital publishing industry. Yet, Heckscher adds, "There is no organized and systematic effort to build the infrastructure for mobile careers" (2007, p. 190; cf. p. 272). Without a benefits infrastructure to provide stability, some people in all-edge adhocracies—such as the nonemployer firms we met in chapter 3 and the self-employed coworkers we met in chapter 5—will continue to worry about the stability of their working arrangements. They will be caught between large employers, over whom they have less and less leverage (see Spinuzzi [2005] for a historical discussion), and the freelance market, which promises autonomy and mobility but involves losing health insurance and other benefits.

The Patient Protection and Affordable Care Act (ACA) seems to take a step toward addressing this problem, promising a reasonably priced alternative to employers' health insurance and thus providing a benefits infrastructure for freelancers and part-timers. However, as of January 2014, it's unclear to what extent the ACA will deliver on this promise and what sorts of unintended effects will develop from it. Proponents argue that although the ACA had a disastrous rollout, it will soon stabilize, providing reasonable service at reasonable premiums. Opponents claim that the ACA, given its new requirements, will raise the cost of all insurance, accelerate the shift toward a part-time economy, and reduce mobility (since most of the networks on the exchanges are not national). The actual outcome will not be known for some time, but I speculate that the ACA will not be the last such proposal to attempt to decouple benefits from employers.

Self-structure   Finally, although they need workplace structure and infrastructure, all-edge adhocracies still won't form without individuals who can structure their own tasks, activities, and interactions so that they can plan, create, and innovate on an agreed time frame. These individuals must be able to effectively coordinate their tasks and projects with others, both in person and in virtual teams, as we saw in chapter 3 (see also Spinuzzi 2007, 2008, 2009). As the cases in this book demonstrate, people who form all-edge adhocracies constantly look for partners who can self-structure: Denise vetted subcontractors carefully (chapter 3); Damon and Helen treated their coworking space as an audition space for potential subcontractors (chapters 5 and 6), and Stan and Daria looked for "self-starters" when hiring (chapter 7). Without the ability to self-structure, team members can't be trusted, as Benny, Cory, Ed, and Bob and Tom complained in chapter 3, and the all-edge adhocracy can collapse.

These different kinds of structure allow all-edge adhocracies to unlock their strengths: innovation, creativity, flexibility. But all-edge adhocracies also have well-known weaknesses.

Shoring Up the Weaknesses of All-Edge Adhocracies

All-edge adhocracies are great for accomplishing unique problems, but their strengths are matched by weaknesses: they aren't strategic, they can appear chaotic, and they require trust between team members who do not always deserve it. To shore up and minimize those weaknesses, all-edge adhocracies must manage them.

Collaborative project management   All-edge adhocracies, as we've seen, tend to be reactive and tactical. They form around a project objective, staying together just long enough to swarm it, pulse it, and complete it. But to complete that project, all-edge adhocracies must collaboratively manage it: that is, figure out how specialists will contribute, on what time frame, with what measures of success. As we saw in chapter 6, this project objective shapes the all-edge adhocracy, especially its division of labor.

Much of the collaborative project management happens—and has to happen—reactively, through the constant mutual adjustment that characterizes all-edge adhocracies. But critical parts of project management have to be handled in planning meetings (such as Benny's Skype sessions and Sophie's session with a subcontractor at her dining room table in chapter 3) or in an established process (such as Semoptco's launch process in chapter 7). So members of all-edge adhocracies need basic project management skills. In fact, all members do, since any one of them could take the lead at different stages of the project.

Stage management   The constant mutual adjustment, rotating leadership, and hand-offs among specialties can appear chaotic to clients. So all-edge adhocracies also need to deploy stage management skills, establishing and managing a front stage to their work so it can look more stable and reliable. They must be able to perform stability, emphasizing the reliability and efficiency that are core values of bureaucratic hierarchies while de-emphasizing the temporary, ad hoc nature of their creative work.

We saw these stage management skills throughout the cases. In chapter 3, nonemployer firms deployed websites and social media, gave subcontractors branded e-mail, and managed conference calls. In chapter 5, people in the good-partners configuration of coworking performed their parts as professional coworkers. And in chapter 7, the monthly report emphasized Semoptco's reliable "secret sauce" while de-emphasizing the ad hoc elements of the work.

Team management   Finally, all-edge adhocracies run on trust and need to manage threats to that trust. So members of these adhocracies actively manage their team members, frequently (if not continually) coordinating and negotiating the object that the team will pulse. In doing this, they integrate the distributed work performed by the different members of the ad hoc team.

All-edge adhocracies manage their teams in several ways. Usually they select team members for trust, as when nonemployer firms held "casting calls" in chapter 3. Often they develop swift trust before the engagement, as coworkers did when observing how other coworkers worked in chapter 5. And frequently they promote interdependence among team members by bringing value to all stakeholders, as Semoptco did in chapter 7. That is, they exhibit techniques that are common in virtual teams (Bullock & Klein 2011; Ruppel, Gong & Tworoger 2013; Yoo & Alavi 2004).

These three types of management shore up some of the weaknesses of all-edge adhocracies. So at this point, we have some basic guidelines for fine-tuning an all-edge adhocracy to handle a job. But they excel only at certain kinds of jobs.

Realizing the Potential of All-Edge Adhocracies

Think of all-edge adhocracies as a special tool in your organizational toolbox. It's not enough for the tool to be good—it also has to be the right tool for the job. The best hammer in the world will still make a poor spatula. So how do we identify the right job for all-edge adhocracies?

The right projects All-edge adhocracies are custom built for special projects: unique problems that require a custom, creative solution involving different specialties. This unique project is the common focus, the point of the swarm, and it gives shape to the all-edge adhocracy. Like the solution, the all-edge adhocracy is custom built.

But this configuration, as we saw in chapters 2 and 9, isn't right for *all* jobs. Yes, it works well for unique projects that are bounded in time. But the very characteristics that make all-edge adhocracies unbeatable for creative, innovative projects also make them a poor fit for steady, repeated, efficient operations. I might turn to an all-edge adhocracy to design my website, decorate my living room, or increase my search engine optimization (SEO) score, but I wouldn't want one running my electric utility or guaranteeing my water supply. I also wouldn't want one to be in charge of maintaining a long-term strategic direction for my company—at least, not on its own.

The right people Similarly, all-edge adhocracies need the right people: independent-minded, self-directed, specialized, creative, entrepreneurial, and open to reaching out through informal networks that they've built. These people must also be willing and able to develop rapid trust through a shared, collaborative object in which they all have a stake (Adler 2001; Heckscher

2007, p. 95). If the project doesn't involve these sorts of people—especially if it's not cross-disciplinary, if it doesn't require a creative aspect, or if self-directed people aren't available—the all-edge adhocracy simply won't gel. Throughout this book, we have seen people assessing each other as potential collaborators that they could trust: nonemployer firms carefully screened subcontractors; coworkers treated their interactions as rolling job interviews; and SEO specialists got to know others across the organization.

The right combinations Even if you have the right project and the right people, they need the right combinations in order for the all-edge adhocracy to excel. The all-edge adhocracy itself needs to be a unique combination of specialists that can establish interdependence for the duration of the project. This interdependence takes the place of more traditional forms of leverage, such as tribal affiliation, institutional authority, and market incentives, all of which are sharply limited in all-edge adhocracies. To create that interdependence, the project has to provide value to everyone involved—to meet the needs of everyone in the alliance.

Following All-Edge Adhocracies into the Future

All-edge adhocracies have a function in our work, our civil society, and our lives. That function is still emerging, in fits and starts, under the radar of more established kinds of work. But it *is* emerging. And understanding all-edge adhocracies—their uses and implications, their strengths and weaknesses, their structure and organization, their care and feeding—will be key to understanding the new workplace networks in which they operate and thrive.

Appendix: Methodology

The case studies in this book are based on my previously published work (Spinuzzi 2010, 2012b, 2014). Each was approved by the institutional review board at the university where I worked at the time of the study. I grounded the studies in writing, activity, and genre research (WAGR; see Russell 2009), specifically fourth-generation activity theory, which examines how clusters of disparate activities are networked together to perform cross-boundary work in emergent work organizations (see Spinuzzi [2011] for an overview). In these case studies, I examined how participants mediated and co-constructed their ongoing work activities, primarily through written genres, but also through other interactions. Below, I describe my methodology for each study.

Chapter 3. Stage Management: The Case of Nonemployer Firms

RESEARCH QUESTIONS

In this study, I sought to answer the following research questions about how nonemployee firms (NEFs) represented their work to clients:

- *How did NEFs represent themselves to clients?* That is, what rules did NEFs establish to govern relationships between their subcontractor network and the client? More broadly, how did they describe the shared object to which the NEFs, subcontractors, and client were oriented?
- *How did NEFs find and establish relationships with subcontractors who could support their self-presentation to clients?* That is, what rules did NEFs establish to build and govern their relationships within the subcontractor network, particularly rules oriented toward the "front stage" facing the client?

- *How did NEFs coordinate subcontractors in ways that reinforced rather than disrupted their self-presentation to clients?* That is, how did NEFs establish and maintain a division of labor within the subcontractor network so that it did not threaten the link between that network and the client?

SITES AND PARTICIPANTS

In Study 1, a colleague and I visited two graphic design NEFs that initially had no employees and worked out of their residences. (By the second set of observations and interviews, one of the NEFs had rented office space and hired employees.) In Study 2, I interviewed five self-employed individuals who worked in various aspects of web development: developing interactive sites, managing site development projects, writing content, and designing site aesthetics.

DATA COLLECTION

Given the number of sites and the difficulty of setting up interviews with people who have busy and fluid schedules, I collected data snapshots rather than longitudinal data. These data snapshots focused on how the firms reported presenting themselves to clients and how they coordinated with subcontractors.

The word *reported* is important here, since much of the data come from my interviews with the NEFs rather than direct observations. Although I conducted short observations at work sites in Study 1, these proved impractical in Study 2 due to the participants' extremely flexible schedules and mobile work patterns. In no cases could I observe their meetings with clients, since my presence itself would threaten their performance. Consequently, I relied primarily on participants' statements, which I then triangulated with their self-representations in public artifacts (see the "Data Analysis" section below).

For Study 1, which spanned July 2007–August 2008, I collected the following qualitative data:

- *Interviews.* I interviewed participants twice; initial interviews took about 30 minutes and follow-up interviews took about 20 minutes.
- *Observations.* I observed each NEF twice, for one hour each. Given the brevity of these observations, I used them primarily as a way to spark interview questions.
- *Artifacts.* I collected 32 artifacts from the NEFs, including websites, photos (during observations), and LinkedIn and Twitter profiles. I used these

artifacts primarily to triangulate participants' interviews with how they represented themselves to clients.

For Study 2, which spanned August–October 2010, I collected the following qualitative data:

- *Interviews.* I interviewed each participant once; interviews ranged from 20 to 45 minutes, averaging 28 minutes.
- *Artifacts.* I collected 31 artifacts from the NEFs, including websites; LinkedIn and Twitter profiles' Yelp and Google Places pages, when available; and collateral materials related to how participants proposed, contracted, and managed projects.

DATA CODING

After collecting the data, I transcribed all interviews, resulting in paragraph-separated units: 281 for Study 1 and 837 for Study 2. I placed each study's data in a relational database, with tables for participants, interviews, artifacts, and (for Study 1) observations. Each datum (database entry) could be assigned multiple codes. For each study, I coded entries using the following procedures:

- *Starter codes.* I began coding deductively, using descriptive starter codes (Miles & Huberman 1994, pp. 57–58). For Study 1, the starter codes were based on activity theory's implications for knowledge work (Spinuzzi 2008, chap. 7). For Study 2, the starter codes were based on my semistructured interview questions, which in turn were grounded in activity theory concepts.
- *Open coding.* In open coding (Corbin & Strauss 2008), I inductively identified recurrent themes, based code definitions on them, then checked these codes deductively on the basis of these definitions. I first developed open codes on the basis of specific issues discussed during interviews, then applied them to related data in the other data types. For codes related to texts and tools, I initially autocoded (applied codes on the basis of keywords in the interview text), then added codes to applicable entries that did not share the keywords. I interspersed autocoding with developing open codes, treated as emergent and recursive (Corbin & Strauss 2008).
- *Axial coding.* Finally, I performed axial coding (Corbin & Strauss 2008) to draw connections across starter and open codes. To develop axial codes, I looked for codes that appeared together frequently, then used a single code to articulate the relationship among them, developing a specific description for that code. I then recoded all data for those axial codes, applying them to each piece of data that fit the description.

Study 1's axial codes, such as Face and Trust, informed open codes for Study 2. Similarly, after completing Study 2 coding, I recoded Study 1's data by applying some open codes from Study 2.

- *Data reduction.* In identifying recurrent themes, coding also allowed me to reduce the data by focusing on heavily coded data and on data related to key themes.

DATA ANALYSIS

As mentioned above, I primarily collected interview data, meaning that the participants were undoubtedly performing for me as well as the clients. Although I have no suspicion that they misled me, I recognize that I viewed their "front stage." Methodologically, I handled this issue by triangulating the interview data with artifacts such as collateral materials as well as (in Study 1) observations. To analyze the data, I followed the procedures outlined below.

Comparisons. I tested relationships between codes by examining whether they were supported by multiple data sources. I triangulated in the following ways:

- *Across data types, same NEF.* This comparison involved examining how the same phenomenon was treated in interviews, artifacts, and (for Study 1) observations at a given NEF. For instance, I examined how a given NEF represented itself to clients in its website and LinkedIn profile, then compared those with its interview statements about self-representation.
- *Within data types, across NEFs.* This comparison involved examining how the same phenomenon was treated within a given data type across sites. For instance, I examined how all the NEFs reported representing themselves to clients.

Member checks. After interviews were transcribed, I conducted a transcription check with each participant to gather comments and feedback. After writing a draft report, I gathered manuscript comments from participants.

Chapter 5. Working Alone, Together: The Case of Coworking

RESEARCH QUESTIONS

I sought to answer the following research questions, drawn from three parts of the activity system: the object, actors, and outcome.

- *What is coworking?* That is, how do these space proprietors and coworkers in their spaces define coworking in their interviews and texts, and to what extent do they agree? What metaphors and analogies do they use to describe coworking? What is the object of their activity, and what contradictions exist in their understanding of that object?

- *Who coworks?* That is, what potential coworkers are targeted by proprietors, and who actually decides to cowork in their spaces? Who are the actors of the activity, and what contradictions exist across them?
- *Why do people cowork?* What motivations do these space proprietors and coworkers in their spaces report in their interviews and texts? What outcomes do the actors desire, and what contradictions exist across those desired outcomes?

SITES AND PARTICIPANTS

I interviewed proprietors at nine Austin-area coworking sites and toured their facilities. One proprietor interview (Cospace) occurred the month before the facility was opened. Another proprietor (Link) was interviewed twice: once when she announced that she planned to open a coworking site, and again once the site was open. In the other cases, I interviewed as soon as I found out about each site and could persuade the proprietors to give an interview. Site names and proprietor names are not pseudonyms. I also interviewed 17 coworkers at the three most populated coworking sites. Coworker names are pseudonyms.

DATA COLLECTION

Data collection spanned July 2008–February 2011. Given the number of sites and the difficulty of setting up interviews with people who have busy and fluid schedules, I collected data snapshots rather than longitudinal data: the data represent points early in the life of the coworking spaces, not necessarily the current state of these spaces. Given the research questions, I focused not on how people lived coworking in their daily actions, but rather how they described the object of coworking, their own characteristics as workers, and their own motivations for coworking. Thus my data collection was built around collecting these self-descriptions rather than around observations. I collected the data described below.

Proprietor formal interviews. I conducted interviews with proprietors of the coworking spaces (see table 5.1). Interviews ranged from 29 to 77 minutes, averaging 48 minutes. When a space had multiple proprietors, I interviewed them together.

Proprietor informal interviews and space tours. I conducted informal interviews with the proprietors, which I then posted on my blog after soliciting proprietor feedback. I also toured the spaces and took photographs to record details such as layout, furniture, and amenities. Finally, I informally observed the most populated spaces (Conjunctured, Cospace, Link) by working at least six hours in each space.

Texts. I collected 84 texts, including collateral, membership agreements, member lists, business plans, Craigslist ads, and website pages for each site. I also collected social media related to each site, when available: Yelp and Google Places reviews, Foursquare and Gowalla check-ins, and each site's Facebook page.

Coworker interviews. I interviewed 17 members of the three most populated coworking spaces: Conjunctured, Cospace, and Link (see table 5.1). These members were selected in a convenience sample: I approached coworkers who were working in the spaces during my visits. Later, I compared the convenience sample to these sites' membership directories, verifying that it was roughly representative of each site's coworkers in terms of industry and gender. Interviews ranged from 9 to 45 minutes, averaging 21 minutes.

LinkedIn profiles. I collected all available LinkedIn profiles: all 17 coworkers and 13 of 16 proprietors. These profiles described participants' education, job history, industry, and job titles.

DATA STORAGE, CODING, AND REDUCTION

After collecting the data, I transcribed all interviews, resulting in 2,608 interview entries (paragraph-separated units) for proprietors and 1,893 interview entries (paragraph-separated units) for coworkers. I coded entire texts rather than text segments. I placed all data in a relational database, with tables for participants, proprietor interviews, coworker interviews, texts, and photos, and created summary characterizations for entries in each data type (Miles & Huberman 1994, pp. 54–55).

Coding was nonexclusive: each datum could be assigned multiple codes. I coded entries using the following procedures:

- *Starter codes.* I began coding deductively, using descriptive starter codes (Miles & Huberman 1994, pp. 57–58) based on my semistructured interview questions.
- *Open coding.* In open coding (Corbin & Strauss 2008), I inductively identified recurrent themes, based code definitions on them, then checked these codes deductively on the basis of these definitions. I first developed open codes on the basis of specific issues discussed during interviews,

then applied them to related data in the other data types. For codes related to texts and tools, I initially autocoded (applied codes on the basis of keywords in the interview text), then added codes to applicable entries that did not share the keywords. I interspersed autocoding with developing open codes, which I treated as emergent and recursive (Corbin & Strauss 2008): information in one set of data might yield hypotheses that I could then test by coding other data sets.

- *Axial coding.* Finally, I performed axial coding (Corbin & Strauss 2008) to draw connections across starter and open codes. To develop axial codes, I looked for codes that appeared together frequently, then used a single code to articulate the relationship among them, developing a specific description for that code. I then recoded all data for those axial codes, applying them to each piece of data that fit the description.
- *Data reduction.* In identifying recurrent themes, coding also allowed me to reduce the data by focusing on heavily coded data and on data related to key themes.

DATA ANALYSIS

To analyze the data, I followed the procedures outlined here.

Comparisons. I tested relationships between codes by examining whether they were supported by multiple data sources:

- *Across data types, same site.* I compared how the same phenomenon was treated in proprietor interviews, coworker interviews, texts, and photos at a given site. For instance, I examined whether a definition of coworking was consistent and supported across data types at a given site.
- *Within data types, across sites.* I compared how the same phenomenon was treated within a given data type across sites. For instance, I examined whether a definition of coworking was shared by all proprietors across sites.

Member checks. I enacted three levels of feedback. First, after informal interviews and site walk-throughs, I wrote blog profiles of each site (http://spinuzzi .blogspot.com /search /label /coworking). Site proprietors reviewed and gave feedback on these profiles before I posted them. Although this method resulted in positive, somewhat promotional profiles, it also allowed me to check accuracy and build trust with proprietors. Next, after interviews were transcribed, I conducted a transcription check with each participant to gather comments and feedback. Finally after writing a draft report, I gathered manuscript comments from site proprietors, which I included in later drafts.

Chapter 7. Lone Wolves: The Case of Search Engine Optimization

I sought to answer the following research questions:

- How do Semoptco's workers produce monthly reports? What tools and texts do they use?
- How do they share information and procedures as they produce reports?
- How do they ensure that the reports address critical rhetorical concerns such as audience analysis and ethos?

Data collection spanned September–November 2008, plus August 2009, when I had a follow-up interview with Stan. To develop a rich qualitative understanding of how the participants conducted their work and of the genres and media they used, I chose the qualitative ethnographic methods listed here.

Site interviews. I conducted one 40-minute semistructured interview with Stan in September 2008 before contacting the other participants, then a 30-minute follow-up interview in August 2009.

Pre-observational interviews. I conducted one short (20–30 minute) semi-structured interview with Daria, with Stacy, and with Luis and Carl (as a pair) in September 2008 to collect information about their professional biography and history with project management, collaboration, and related tools and practices.

Naturalistic observations. I conducted three one-hour observations of Daria, Luis, Carl, and Stacy in October–November 2008. I conducted clusters of observations at different times of the month. During observations, I took detailed field notes that focused on participants'

- work environment, particularly texts;
- interactions with others, including fellow workers and clients (when possible, I copied spoken and written interactions into the field notes verbatim; when not, I summarized and paraphrased);
- interactions with texts, broadly defined as symbolic inscriptions, including writing, reading, annotating and highlighting, juxtaposing, stacking and arranging, and posting; and
- movements from one space to another, along with any artifacts they took with them and artifacts they used in each space.

Post-observational interviews. I conducted individual, semistructured interviews (averaging 30 minutes each) with Stacy, Luis, and Carl immediately after all but one observation, and with Daria after all observations. These interviews focused on how the participants interpreted their own and others' actions during the observation; elicited contextual insights about the texts and procedures I had observed, particularly as they related to work cycles; and confirmed or disconfirmed my understanding of key events in the observation.

Artifact collection. I collected artifacts from Daria's, Luis's, Carl's, and Stacy's workspaces that were related to project management, collaboration, information sharing, teamwork, and training. Artifacts included

- photos of each participant's work environment and any environmental texts (such as posted materials); and
- copies or photos of project lists, to-do lists, reports, and marketing collateral.

In all, I collected 12 documents and 22 photos.

To ensure privacy of others, participants redacted artifacts as appropriate before turning them over to me. Consequently, although I was able to observe several participants writing reports, I was allowed to keep only two heavily redacted copies.

DATA STORAGE, CODING, AND REDUCTION

After collecting the data, I transcribed all field notes and paraphrased and partially transcribed interviews.

Field notes. I transcribed these as they were written, with paragraph breaks representing distinct actions or speaking turns within observations. In all, I generated 1,381 observation entries (paragraph-separated units).

Interviews. I initially paraphrased these, then transcribed parts that were critical to the emerging analysis. Paragraph breaks represented changes in speakers. In all, I generated 613 interview entries (paragraph-separated units).

I then placed all data in a relational database, with tables for participants, observations, interviews, and artifacts. I created summary characterizations for entries in each data type (cf. Miles and Huberman 1994, pp. 54–55).

Coding. Coding was nonexclusive: each datum could be assigned multiple codes. I coded entries using the following procedures.

- *Starter Codes.* I began coding deductively, using descriptive starter codes (Miles and Huberman 1994, p. 57–58): Time/Project Management, Understanding, Relationships, Strategy, and Training (these were based on Spinuzzi [2008, chap. 6]).

- *Open Coding.* In open coding (Corbin & Strauss 2008), I inductively identified recurrent themes, based code definitions on them, then checked these codes deductively on the basis of these definitions. I coded for tool and text use and production; search use; types of interactions; teams; and indications of planning and cycles.

  Creating open codes from pre-observation interview questions. I first developed open codes on the basis of specific issues discussed during pre-observation interviews, then applied them to related data in the other data types.

  Autocoding open codes. For codes related to texts and tools, I initially autocoded (applied codes on the basis of keywords in the observation notes and interview text), then added codes to applicable entries that did not share the keywords. I interspersed autocoding with developing open codes.

  Developing open codes. I treated open codes as emergent and recursive (Corbin & Strauss 2008): information in one set of data might yield hypotheses that I could then test by coding other data sets.

- *Axial Coding.* Finally, I performed axial coding, which was loosely based on Corbin and Strauss (2008), to draw connections across starter and open codes. To develop axial codes, I looked for codes that appeared together frequently, then used a single code to articulate the relationship among them, developing a specific description for that code. I then recoded all data for those axial codes, applying them to each piece of data that fit the description.
- *Data reduction.* In identifying recurrent themes, coding also allowed me to reduce the data by focusing on heavily coded data and on data related to key themes.

DATA ANALYSIS

To analyze the data, I followed the procedures given here.

Triangulating. I tested relationships between codes by examining whether they were supported by multiple data sources. I triangulated in the following ways:

- *Across data types, same incident.* This triangulation involved examining how the same incident was represented in two or more data types, such as an observation and the corresponding post-observational interview.

- *Across participants.* This triangulation involved examining how the same phenomenon was represented in two or more participants' data. This form of triangulation allowed me to confirm how idiosyncratic or shared that phenomenon was.
- *Across visits.* This triangulation involved examining how different actions were taken at different points of the work cycle.

In the analysis, I drew on all three kinds of triangulation; each incident, phenomenon, and action is supported by correspondingly triangulated data.

Conducting member checks. After drafting the completed analysis, I shared it with the participants for comments in October–November 2009. Participants offered no critical comments.

Works Cited

Adler, P. S. (2001). Market, Hierarchy, and Trust: The Knowledge Economy and the Future of Capitalism. *Organization Science, 12*(2), 215–234. doi:10.1287/orsc.12.2.215.10117

Adler, P. S. (2007). Beyond Hacker Idiocy: The Changing Nature of Software Community and Identity. In C. Heckscher & P. S. Adler (Eds.), *The Firm as a Collaborative Community: Reconstructing Trust in the Knowledge Economy* (pp. 198–258). New York, NY: Oxford University Press.

Adler, P. S., & Heckscher, C. (2007). Towards Collaborative Community. In C. Heckscher & P. S. Adler (Eds.), *The Firm as a Collaborative Community: Reconstructing Trust in the Knowledge Economy* (pp. 11–105). New York, NY: Oxford University Press.

Adler, P. S., Kwon, S.-W., & Heckscher, C. (2008). Perspective—Professional Work: The Emergence of Collaborative Community. *Organization Science, 19*(2), 359–376. doi:10.1287/orsc.1070.0293

Agarwal, S. D., Barthel, M. L., Rost, C., Borning, A., Bennett, W. L., & Johnson, C. N. (2014). Grassroots Organizing in the Digital Age: Considering Values and Technology in Tea Party and Occupy Wall Street. *Information, Communication & Society, 17*(3), 326–341. doi:10.1080/1369118X.2013.873068

Ahonen, T. (2012). Latest Mobile Numbers for End of Year 2012 - This Is Getting Humongous. *Communities Dominate Brands.* Retrieved July 11, 2013, from http://communities-dominate.blogs.com/brands/2012/12/latest-mobile-numbers-for-end-of-year-2012-this-is-getting-humongous.html

Alberts, D. S., & Hayes, R. E. (2003). Power to the Edge. DOD Command and Control Research Program. Retrieved September 11, 2009, from http://www.dodccrp.org/files/Alberts_Power.pdf

Andersen, R. (2008). The Rhetoric of Enterprise Content Management (ECM): Confronting the Assumptions Driving ECM Adoption and Transforming Technical Communication. *Technical Communication Quarterly, 17*, 61–87.

Anderson, N. (2009). Hidden Gay Slur, Search Terms, Get Campaign Site Blacklisted. *Ars Technica.* Retrieved August 3, 2009, from http://arstechnica.com/tech-policy/news/2009/08/hidden-gay-slur-search-terms-get-campaign-site-blacklisted.ars

Arquilla, J. (2011). *Insurgents, Raiders, and Bandits: How Masters of Irregular Warfare Have Shaped Our World*. Lanham, MD: Ivan R Dee.

Arquilla, J., & Ronfeldt, D. (1997). Cyberwar Is Coming! In J. Arquilla & D. Ronfeldt (Eds.), *In Athena's Camp: Preparing for Conflict in the Information Age* (pp. 23–60). Santa Monica, CA: RAND.

Arquilla, J., & Ronfeldt, D. (2000). *Swarming and the Future of Conflict*. Santa Monica, CA: RAND. Retrieved June 25, 2014, from http://www.rand.org/content/dam/rand/pubs/documented_briefings/2005/RAND_DB311.pdf

Artemeva, N., & Freedman, A. (2001). "Just the Boys Playing on Computers": An Activity Theory Analysis of Differences in the Cultures of Two Engineering Firms. *Journal of Business and Technical Communication, 15*(2), 164–194.

Austin Business Journal. (2011, December 1). Austin Led the Nation in Percentage of Small Business Growth. *Austin Business Journal*. Retrieved December 22, 2011, from http://www.bizjournals.com/austin/news/2011/12/01/austin-led-the-nation-in-percentage-of.html

Austin Business Journal. (2013, April 5). Austin Named Friendliest City for Small Business. *Austin Business Journal*. Retrieved June 25, 2014, from http://www.bizjournals.com/austin/blog/morning_call/2013/04/austin-the-friendliest-city-for-small.html

Autier, F. (2001). *Bureaucracy vs. Adhocracy : A Case of Overdramatisation ?* (Vol. 14). Lyon, France. Retrieved from http://www.em-lyon.com/en/faculty-research-education/faculty-research/entrepreneurship-research/Research-papers2/Bureaucracy-vs.-Adhocracy-a-case-of-overdramatisation

Backhouse, J. (2009). Social Media: Impacting the Enterprise? In *European and Mediterranean Conference on Information Systems (EMCIS) 2009*. Retrieved June 25, 2014, from http://www.iseing.org/emcis/CDROM%20Proceedings%20Refereed%20Papers/Proceedings/Presenting%20Papers/C15/C15.pdf

Baehr, C., & Alex-Brown, K. (2010). Assessing the Value of Corporate Blogs: A Social Capital Perspective. *IEEE Transactions on Professional Communication, 53*(4), 358–369.

Barabási, A.-L. (2003). *Linked: How Everything Is Connected to Everything Else and What It Means*. New York, NY: Plume.

Barr, G. (2013). Austin Retains Ranking as No. 1 Economy in the U.S. *Austin Business Journal*. Retrieved January 7, 2014, from http://www.bizjournals.com/austin/blog/at-the-watercooler/2013/11/austin-retains-ranking-as-no-1.html?ana=RSS&s=article_search&utm_source=feedburner&utm_medium=feed&utm_campaign=Feed:+bizj_austin+(Austin+Business+Journal)

Bazerman, C. (1999). *The Languages of Edison's Light*. Cambridge, MA: MIT Press.

Beniger, J. (1989). *The Control Revolution: Technological and Economic Origins of the Information Society*. Cambridge, MA: Harvard University Press.

Benkler, Y. (2006). *The Wealth of Networks*. New Haven, CT: Yale University Press.

Benkler, Y. (2011). *The Penguin and the Leviathan: How Cooperation Triumphs over Self-Interest*. New York, NY: Crown Business.

Bennis, W., & Slater, P. E. (1998). *The Temporary Society: What Is Happening to Business and Family Life in America Under the Impact of Accelerating Change* (30th Anniv.). San Francisco, CA: Jossey-Bass.

Bhatti, Z. A., Baile, S., & Yasin, H. M. (2011). The Success of Corporate Wiki Systems: An End User Perspective. In *WikiSym '11: Proceedings of the 7th International Symposium on Wikis and Open Collaboration* (pp. 134–143). New York, NY: ACM.

Bilton, C. (1999). *The New Adhocracy: Strategy, Risk and the Small Creative Firm*. Coventry, UK. Retrieved June 25, 2014, from http://www2.warwick.ac.uk/fac/arts/theatre_s/cp/research/publications/centrepubs/ccps_paper_4.pdf

Boisot, M., & Child, J. (1996). From Fiefs to Clans and Network Capitalism: Explaining China's Emerging Economic Order. *Administrative Science Quarterly, 41*(4), 600–628.

Boisot, M., & Child, J. (1999). Organizations as Adaptive Systems in Complex Environments: The Case of China. *Organization Science, 10*(3), 237–252. doi:10.1287/orsc.10.3.237

Boisot, M., MacMillan, I. C., & Han, K. S. (2001). *Explorations in Information Space: Knowledge, Agents, and Organization*. New York, NY: Oxford University Press.

Boisot, M., Nordberg, M., Yami, S., & Nicquevert, B. (2011). *Collisions and Collaboration: The Organization of Learning in the ATLAS Experiment at the LHC*. New York, NY: Oxford University Press.

Bonnet, Sophie. (2011, February 28). Number of Coworking Spaces Increases to 700 Worldwide. Retrieved May 23, 2011, from http://www.deskmag.com/en/number-of-coworking-spaces-worldwide-700

Botsman, R., & Rogers, R. (2011). *What's Mine Is Yours: How Collaborative Consumption Is Changing the Way We Live*. New York, NY: Collins.

Bradner, E., & Mark, G. (2002). Why Distance Matters: Effects on Cooperation, Persuasion and Deception. In *CSCW '02: Proceedings of the 2002 ACM Conference on Computer Supported Cooperative Work* (pp. 226–235). New York, NY: ACM Press.

Brafman, O., & Beckstrom, R. A. (2008). *The Starfish and the Spider: The Unstoppable Power of Leaderless Organizations*. New York, NY: Portfolio Trade.

Broadhead, G. J., & Freed, R. (1986). *The Variables of Composition: Process and Product in a Business Setting*. Carbondale: Southern Illinois University Press.

Brzozowski, M. J., Sandholm, T., & Hogg, T. (2009). Effects of Feedback and Peer Pressure on Contributions to Enterprise Social Media Categories and Subject Descriptors. In *GROUP '09: Proceedings of the ACM 2009 International Conference on Supporting Group Work* (pp. 61–70). New York, NY: ACM.

Bullock, C., & Klein, J. T. (2011). *Virtual Work Environments in the Post-Recession Era*. Retrieved June 25, 2014, from http://www.brandman.edu/files/attachments/virtual_teams_brandman_forrester_white_paper.pdf

Burt, R. S. (2010). *Neighbor Networks: Competitive Advantage Local and Personal*. New York, NY: Oxford University Press.

Burton-Jones, A. (2001). *Knowledge Capitalism*. New York, NY: Oxford University Press.

Büscher, M. (2014). Nomadic Work: Romance and Reality. A Response to Barbara Czarniawska's "Nomadic Work as Life-Story Plot." *Computer Supported Cooperative Work (CSCW), 23*(2), 223–238. doi:10.1007/s10606-013-9194-6

Callon, M., Lascoumes, P., & Barthe, Y. (2009). *Acting in an Uncertain World: An Essay on Technical Democracy*. Cambridge, MA: MIT Press.

Calnan, C. (2013). Dell Wants More Employees to Work Remotely. *Austin Business Journal*. Retrieved January 7, 2014, from http://www.bizjournals.com/austin/blog/techflash/2013/11/dell-wants-more-employees-to-work.html?ana=RSS&s=article_search

Cameron, K. S., & Quinn, R. E. (2011). *Diagnosing and Changing Organizational Culture: Based on the Competing Values Framework*. San Francisco, CA: Jossey-Bass.

Castells, M. (1996). *Rise of the Network Society*. Malden, MA: Blackwell.

Castells, M. (1997). *The Power of Identity*. Malden, MA: Blackwell.

Castells, M. (1998). *End of Millennium*. Malden, MA: Blackwell.

Castells, M. (2003). *The Internet Galaxy: Reflections on the Internet, Business, and Society*. New York, NY: Oxford University Press.

Castells, M. (2007). Communication, Power and Counter-Power in the Network Society. *International Journal of Communication, 1*(1), 238–266. Retrieved June 25, 2014, from http://www.itu.dk/stud/speciale/specialeprojekt/Litteratur/Castells_2007 - Communication power in the network society.pdf

Castells, M. (2009). *Communication Power*. New York: Oxford University Press.

Castells, M., & Cardoso, G. (Eds.). (2006). *The Network Society: From Knowledge to Policy*. Washington, DC: Center for Transatlantic Relations, Paul H. Nitze School of Advanced International Studies, Johns Hopkins University.

Castells, M., Fernández-Ardèvol, M., Linchuan Qiu, J., & Sey, A. (Eds.). (2007). *Mobile Communication and Society. A Global Perspective. Communication*. Cambridge, MA: MIT Press.

Chib, A., Malik, S., Aricat, R. G., & Kadir, S. Z. (2014). Migrant Mothering and Mobile Phones: Negotiations of Transnational Identity. *Mobile Media & Communication, 2*(1), 73–93. doi:10.1177/2050157913506007

Christiansen, E. (1996). Tamed by a Rose: Computers as Tools in Human Activity. In B. A. Nardi (Ed.), *Context and Consciousness* (pp. 175–198). Cambridge, MA: MIT Press.

CIA. (2013). Literacy. *CIA World Factbook*. Retrieved January 7, 2014, from https://www.cia.gov/library/publications/the-world-factbook/fields/2103.html#us

Clark, D. (2008). Content Management and the Separation of Presentation and Content. *Technical Communication Quarterly, 17*(1), 35–60.

Clark, M. A. (2000). *Teleworking in the Countryside: Home-Based Working in the Information Society*. Burlington, VT: Ashgate.

Clinton, H. R. (2010). Remarks on Internet Freedom. *U.S. Department of State*. Retrieved July 11, 2013, from http://www.state.gov/secretary/rm/2010/01/135519.htm

Cole, M., & Engeström, Y. (1993). A Cultural-Historical Approach to Distributed Cognition. In G. Salomon (Ed.), *Distributed Cognitions: Psychological and Educational Considerations* (pp. 1–46). New York: Cambridge University Press.

Collings, D., & Rohozinski, R. (2008). *Bullets & Blogs: New Media and the Warfighter*. Carlisle Barracks, PA: US Army War College.

Conjunctured. (2008a). Conjunctured >> Howdy. Retrieved April 14, 2008, from http://conjunctured.com/

Conjunctured. (2008b). Scouring the city for a space. Retrieved May 7, 2008, from http://conjunctured.com/blog/scouring-the-city-for-a-space/

Corbin, J., & Strauss, A. C. (2008). *Basics of Qualitative Research: Techniques and Procedures for Developing Grounded Theory* (3rd ed.). Thousand Oaks, CA: Sage Publications.

Cornejo, R., Tentori, M., & Favela, J. (2013). Ambient Awareness to Strengthen the Family Social Network of Older Adults. *Computer Supported Cooperative Work (CSCW), 22*(2–3), 309–344. doi:10.1007/s10606-012-9166-2

Costas, J. (2013). Problematizing Mobility: A Metaphor of Stickiness, Non-Places and the Kinetic Elite. *Organization Studies, 34*(10), 1467–1485. doi:10.1177/0170840613495324

Coworking Wiki. (n.d.). Retrieved May 23, 2011, from http://wiki.coworking.info/w/page/16583831/FrontPage

Cross, R., Parker, A., & Sasson, L. (Eds.). (2003). *Networks in the Knowledge Economy*. New York, NY: Oxford University Press.

Cummings, J., Massey, A. P., & Ramesh, V. (2009). Web 2.0 Proclivity : Understanding How Personal Use Influences Organizational Adoption. In B. Mehlenbacher, A. Protopsaltis, A. Williams, & S. Slattery (Eds.), *SIGDOC '09: Proceedings of the 27th ACM International Conference on Design of Communication* (pp. 257–263). New York, NY: ACM.

Czarniawska, B. (2013). Nomadic Work as Life-Story Plot. *Computer Supported Cooperative Work (CSCW)*. doi:10.1007/s10606-013-9189-3

De Jong, A., & Mante-Meijer, E. (2008). Teleworking Behind the Front Door: The Patterns and Meaning of Telework in the Everyday Lives of Workers. In E. Loos, E. Mante-Meijer, & L. Haddon (Eds.), *The Social Dynamics of Information and Communication Technology* (pp. 171–187). Burlington, VT: Ashgate.

Denning, P. J., & Dunham, R. (2010). *The Innovator's Way: Essential Practices for Successful Innovation.* Cambridge, MA: MIT Press.

Dicks, S. (2010). The Effects of Digital Literacy on the Nature of Technical Communication Work. In R. Spilka (Ed.), *Digital Literacy for Technical Communication: 21st Century Theory and Practice* (pp. 51–82). New York, NY: Taylor & Francis.

Ding, H. (2008). The Use of Cognitive and Social Apprenticeship to Teach a Disciplinary Genre: Initiation of Graduate Students into NIH Grant Writing. *Written Communication, 25*(1), 3–52. doi:10.1177/0741088307308660

Divine, D., Hall, S., Ferro, T., & Zachry, M. (2011). Work through the Web : A Typology of Web 2.0 Services. In A. Protopsaltis, N. Spyratos, C. J. Costa, & C. Meghini (Eds.), *SIGDOC '11: Proceedings of the 29th ACM International Conference on Design of Communication* (pp. 121–127). New York, NY: ACM.

Divine, D., Morgan, J. T., Ourada, J., & Zachry, M. (2010). Designing Qbox: A Tool for Sorting Things Out in Digital Spaces. In *GROUP '10: Proceedings of the 16th ACM International Conference on Supporting Group Work* (pp. 311–312). New York, NY: ACM.

Dixon, M., & Ross, P. (2011). *VWork: Measuring the Benefits of Agility at Work.* Kingston upon Thames: Unwired Ventures. Retrieved June 25, 2014, from http://www.regus.com/images/Regus-VWork-7-nocrops_tcm8-39506.pdf

Dolan, T. E. (2010). Revisiting Adhocracy: From Rhetorical Revisionism to Smart Mobs. *Journal of Futures Studies, 15*(2), 33–50.

Drucker, P. F. (1994). *Post-Capitalist Society.* New York, NY: Harper Paperbacks.

Ducheneaut, N. (2005). Socialization in an Open Source Software Community: A Socio-Technical Analysis. *Computer Supported Cooperative Work (CSCW), 14*(4), 323–368. doi:10.1007/s10606-005-9000-1

Duncan, W. R. (1996). *A Guide to the Project Management Body of Knowledge* (1st ed.). Newton Square, PA: Project Management Institute.

Dunn, E. C. (2012). The Chaos of Humanitarian Aid: Adhocracy in the Republic of Georgia. *Humanity: An International Journal of Human Rights, Humanitarianism, and Development, 3*(1), 1–23. doi:10.1353/hum.2012.0005

Durkheim, E. (1933). *The Division of Labor in Society.* New York, NY: Free Press.

Dwyer, C. J. (2011). *Contingent Labor Management: The Evolution of Contemporary Contingent Workforce.* Boston, MA.: Aberdeen Group. Retrieved August 5, 2012, from http://www.aberdeen.com/aberdeen-library/7023/RA-contingent-labor-workforce.aspx

Edwards, S. J. A. (2005). *Swarming and the Future of Warfare.* Santa Monica, CA: Pardee RAND Graduate School.

Eisenstein, E. L. (1980). *The Printing Press as an Agent of Change.* New York, NY: Cambridge University Press.

Ellis, C. A., Gibbs, S. J., & Rein, G. L. (1991). Groupware: Some Issues and Experiences. *Communications of the ACM, 34*(1), 38–58.

Ellison, N. B. (2004). *Telework and Social Change: How Technology Is Reshaping the Boundaries between Home and Work.* Westport, CT: Praeger.

Engeström, Y. (1999). Expansive Visibilization of Work: An Activity-Theoretical Perspective. *Computer Supported Cooperative Work, 8,* 63–93.

Engeström, Y. (2008). *From Teams to Knots: Studies of Collaboration and Learning at Work.* New York, NY: Cambridge University Press.

Engeström, Y. (2009). The Future of Activity Theory: A Rough Draft. In A. Sannino, H. Daniels, & K. Gutierrez (Eds.), *Learning and Expanding with Activity Theory* (pp. 303–328). New York, NY: Cambridge University Press.

Engeström, Y., Brown, K., Christopher, L. C., & Gregory, J. (1997). Coordination, Cooperation, and Communication in the Courts: Expansive Transitions in Legal Work. In M. Cole, Y. Engeström, & O. Vasquez (Eds.), *Mind, Culture, and Activity: Seminal Papers from the Laboratory of Comparative Human Cognition* (pp. 369–388). New York, NY: Cambridge University Press.

Engeström, Y., Engeström, R., & Karkkainen, M. (1995). Polycontextuality and Boundary Crossing in Expert Cognition: Learning and Problem Solving in Complex Work Activities. *Learning and Instruction, 5*(4), 319–336. doi:10.1016/0959-4752(95)00021-6

Engeström, Y., Engeström, R., & Vähääho, T. (1999). When the Center Does Not Hold: The Importance of Knotworking. In S. Chaiklin, M. Hedegaard, & U. J. Jensen (Eds.), *Activity Theory and Social Practice* (pp. 345–374). Aarhus, Denmark: Aarhus University Press.

Ericsson. *Ericsson Mobility Report: On the Pulse of the Networked Society.* (2013). Retrieved June 25, 2014, from http://www.ericsson.com/res/docs/2013/ericsson-mobility-report-june-2013.pdf

Ferro, T. (2012). The Rat City Rollergirls and the Potential of Social Networking Sites to Support Work. In *SIGDOC '12:Proceedings of the 30th ACM International Conference on Design of Communication* (pp. 157–166). New York, NY: ACM.

Ferro, T., Derthick, K., Morgan, J. T., Searle, E., & Zachry, M. (2009). Understanding How People Use Publicly Available Online Services for Work. In *SIGDOC '09: Proceedings of the 27th ACM International Conference on Design of Communication* (pp. 311–312). New York, NY: ACM.

Ferro, T., Divine, D., & Zachry, M. (2012). Knowledge Workers and Their Use of Publicly Available Online Services for Day-to-day Work. In *SIGDOC '12:Proceedings of the 30th ACM International Conference on Design of Communication* (pp. 47–53). New York, NY: ACM.

Foot, K. A. (2002). Pursuing an Evolving Object: A Case Study in Object Formation and Identification. *Mind, Culture, and Activity, 9*(2), 132–149.

Foster, P. C. (2013). Mobile Project Networks: Regional Dynamics in the U.S. Film and Television Industry. *Work and Occupations, 40*(4), 398–430. doi:10.1177/0730888413504766

Fraiberg, S. (2013). Reassembling Technical Communication: A Framework for Studying Multilingual and Multimodal Practices in Global Contexts. *Technical Communication Quarterly, 22*(1), 10–27. doi:10.1080/10572252.2013.735635

Fried, M. H. (1967). *The Evolution of Political Society: An Essay in Political Anthropology.* New York, NY: Random House.

Galbraith, J. R. (1983). Designing the Innovating Organization. *Organizational Dynamics, 10*(3), 5–25.

Galbraith, J. R. (2007). Mastering the Law of Requisite Variety with Differentiated Networks. In C. Heckscher & P. S. Adler (Eds.), *The Firm as a Collaborative Community: Reconstructing Trust in the Knowledge Economy* (pp. 179–197). New York, NY: Oxford University Press.

Geisler, C., Bazerman, C., Doheny-Farina, S., Gurak, L., Haas, C., Johnson-Eilola, J., . . . Yates, J. (2001). IText: Further Directions for Research on the Relationship between Information Technology and Writing. *Journal of Business and Technical Communication, 15*(3), 269–308.

Gelernter, D. (1991). *Mirror Worlds: Or the Day Software Puts the Universe in a Shoebox . . . How It Will Happen and What It Will Mean.* New York, NY: Oxford University Press.

Ghemawat, P., & Altman, S. A. (2012). *DHL Global Connectedness Index 2012.* Retrieved December 12, 2012, from http://www.dhl.com/en/about_us/logistics_insights/studies_research/global_connectedness_index/global_connectedness_index_2012.html#.Ud7Wk1NQ29g

Gibson, W. (1986). *Burning Chrome.* New York, NY: Arbor House.

Gladwell, M. (2002). *The Tipping Point: How Little Things Can Make a Big Difference.* New York, NY: Back Bay Books.

Goffman, E. (1959). *The Presentation of Self in Everyday Life.* New York, NY: Anchor.

Gokhman, S., McDonald, D. W., & Zachry, M. (2011). Wiki Architectures as Social Translucence Enablers. In *WikiSym '11: Proceedings of the 7th International Symposium on Wikis and Open Collaboration* (pp. 203–204). New York, NY: ACM. doi:10.1016/0950-7051(89)90039-7.

Grabher, G. (2004). Learning in Projects, Remembering in Networks? Communality, Sociality, and Connectivity in Project Ecologies. *European Urban and Regional Studies, 11*(2), 103–123. doi:10.1177/0969776404041417

Granovetter, M. (1973). The Strength of Weak Ties. *American Journal of Sociology, 78*, 1360–1380.

Guile, D. (2010). *The Learning Challenge of the Knowledge Economy.* Boston, MA: Sense Publishers.

Guile, D. (2012). Inter-professional Working and Learning: "Recontextualising" Lessons from "Project Work" for Programmes of Initial Professional Formation. *Journal of Education and Work, 25*(1), 79–99.

Gurstein, P. (2001). *Wired to the World, Chained to the Home: Telework in Daily Life.* Vancouver: University of British Columbia Press.

Haas, C., & Witte, S. (2001). Writing as Embodied Practice: The Case of Engineering Standards. *Journal of Business and Technical Communication, 15*(4), 413–457.

Hansen, M. (2009). *Collaboration: How Leaders Avoid the Traps, Build Common Ground, and Reap Big Results.* Boston, MA: Harvard Business School Press.

Hart-Davidson, W., Spinuzzi, C., & Zachry, M. (2007). Capturing & Visualizing Knowledge Work: Results & Implications of a Pilot Study of Proposal Writing Activity. In D. G. Novick & C. Spinuzzi (Eds.), *SIGDOC '07: Proceedings of the 25th Annual ACM International Conference on Design of Communication* (pp. 113–119). New York, NY: ACM. doi:10.1145/1297144.1297168

Hart-Davidson, W., Zachry, M., & Spinuzzi, C. (2012). Activity Streams: Building Context to Coordinate Writing Activity in Collaborative Teams. In *SIGDOC '12: Proceedings of the 30th ACM International Conference on Design of Communication* (pp. 279–287). New York, NY: ACM.

Heckscher, C. (2007). *The Collaborative Enterprise: Managing Speed and Complexity in Knowledge-Based Businesses.* London, UK: Yale University Press.

Heckscher, C., & Carré, F. (2006). Strength in Networks : Employment Rights Organizations and the Problem of Co-ordination. *British Journal of Industrial Relations, 44*(4), 605–628.

Hemetsberger, A., & Reinhardt, C. (2009). Collective Development in Open-Source Communities: An Activity Theoretical Perspective on Successful Online Collaboration. *Organization Studies, 30*(9), 987–1008. doi:10.1177/0170840609339241

Hernandez, D. J. (1995). *America's Children: Resources from Family, Government, and the Economy.* New York, NY: Russell Sage Foundation.

Holland, D., & Reeves, J. R. (1996). Activity Theory and the View from Somewhere: Team Perspectives on the Intellectual Work of Programming. In B. A. Nardi (Ed.), *Context and Consciousness* (pp. 257–282). Cambridge, MA: MIT Press.

Holt, R. (2008). Using Activity Theory to Understand Entrepreneurial Opportunity. *Mind, Culture, and Activity, 15*(1), 52–70. doi:10.1080/10749030701800957

Humphry, J. (2013). Officing: Mediating Time and the Professional Self in the Support of Nomadic Work. *Computer Supported Cooperative Work (CSCW).* doi:10.1007/s10606-013-9197-3

Hunt, T. (2009). *The Whuffie Factor: Using the Power of Social Networks to Build Your Business.* New York, NY: Crown Business.

Hyysalo, S. (2005). Objects and Motives in a Product Design Process. *Mind, Culture, and Activity, 12*(1), 19–36.

INRIX. (2009). *INRIX ® National Traffic Scorecard. Methodology.* Retrieved August 5, 2012, from http://scorecard.inrix.com/scorecard/pdf/INRIX National Traffic Scorecard MY2009 Special Report.pdf

iPass. (2011). *The iPass Global Mobile Workforce Report: Understanding Enterprise Mobility Trends and Mobile Usage.* Redwood Shores, CA: iPass. Retrieved August 5, 2012, from http://www3 .ipass.com/wp-content/uploads/2011/05/iPass_MWR_Q2_2011.pdf

Isaacs, E., Walendowski, A., Whittaker, S., Schiano, D. J., & Kamm, C. (2002). The Character, Functions, and Styles of Instant Messaging in the Workplace. In *CSCW '02: Proceedings of the 2002 ACM Conference on Computer Supported Cooperative Work* (p. 11–20). New York, NY: ACM.

Isaksson, A. (2010). *Telecommunications and Industrial Development.* Retrieved June 19, 2013, from http://www.unido.org//fileadmin/user_media/Publications/Research_and_statistics /Branch_publications/Research_and_Policy/Files/Working_Papers/2009/WP%2014 %20Telecommunications%20and%20Industrial%20Development.pdf

Jacobs, A., & Nakata, K. (2010). Evolving the Social Business: A Look at Stages of Growth for Web 2.0 Integration with Business Activities. In *IWCSC '10: First Interdisciplinary Workshop on Communication for Sustainable Communities.* New York, NY: ACM.

Jakobs, E.-M. (2008). Berufliches schreiben: Ausbildung, training, coaching. In E.-M. Jakobs & K. Katrin (Eds.), *Coaching und berufliches Schreiben* (pp. 1–14). Frankfurt/M. u.a., Germany: Peter Lang.

Jakobs, E.-M., & Spinuzzi, C. (2014). Professional Domains: Writing as Creation of Economic Value. In E.-M. Jakobs & D. Perrin (Eds.), *Handbook of Writing and Text Production* (pp. 359–384). Berlin: De Gruyter.

Johnson-Eilola, J. (2005). *Datacloud: Toward a New Theory of Online Work.* Cresskill, NJ: Hampton Press.

Jones, A. M. (2013). *The Fifth Age of Work: How Companies Can Redesign Work to Become More Innovative in a Cloud Economy.* Portland, OR: Night Owls Press.

Jones, D. L. (2012). *The User Experience of Participation: Tracing the Intersection of Sociotechnical Design and Cultural Practice in Digital Ecosystems.* Norfolk, VA: Old Dominion University.

Jones, D. L., & Potts, L. (2010). Best Practices for Designing Third-Party Applications for Contextually Aware Tools. In *Proceedings of the 28th ACM Conference on the Design of Communication* (pp. 95–102). New York, NY: ACM.

Jones, J. (2014). Switching in Twitter's Hashtagged Exchanges. *Journal of Business and Technical Communication, 28*(1), 83–108. doi:10.1177/1050651913502358

Kallio, K. (2010). The Meaning of Physical Presence: An Analysis of the Introduction of Process-Optimisation Software in a Chemical Pulp Mill. In H. Daniels, A. Edwards, Y. Engeström, T. Gallagher, & S. R. Ludvigsen (Eds.), *Activity Theory in Practice: Promoting Learning across Boundaries and Agencies* (pp. 25–48). New York, NY: Routledge.

Kaptelinin, V. (2005). The Object of Activity: Making Sense of the Sense-Maker. *Mind, Culture, and Activity, 12*(1), 4–18.

Kaptelinin, V., & Nardi, B. A. (2006). *Acting with technology: Activity theory and Interaction Design.* Cambridge, MA: MIT Press.

Karlsson, A.-M. (2009). Positioned by Reading and Writing: Literacy Practices, Roles, and Genres in Common Occupations. *Written Communication, 26*(1), 53–76. doi:10.1177/0741088308327445

Kent-Drury, R. (2000). The Nature of Leadership in Cross-Functional Proposal-Writing Groups. *Technical Communication,* (February/March), 90–98.

Kilgour, F. G. (1998). *The Evolution of the Book.* New York: Oxford University Press.

Killoran, J. B. (2009). Targeting an Audience of Robots: Search Engines and the Marketing of Technical Communication Business Websites. *IEEE Transactions on Professional Communication, 52*(3), 254–271. doi:10.1109/TPC.2009.2025309

Kjaerulff, J. (2010). *Internet and Change: An Anthropology of Knowledge and Flexible Work.* Aarhus, Denmark: Intervention Press.

Kolfschoten, G. L., Herrmann, T., & Lukosch, S. (2013). Differentiated Awareness-Support in Computer Supported Collaborative Work. *Computer Supported Cooperative Work (CSCW), 22*(2–3), 107–112. doi:10.1007/s10606-012-9185-z

Kotkin, J. (2013a). The Cities Creating The Most Middle-Class Jobs. *Forbes.* Retrieved January 7, 2014, from http://www.forbes.com/sites/joelkotkin/2013/10/24/the-cities-creating-the-most-middle-class-jobs/

Kotkin, J. (2013b). The Metro Areas with the Most Economic Momentum Going into 2014. NewGeography.com. Retrieved January 7, 2014, from http://www.newgeography.com/content/004111-metro-areas-most-economic-momentum-2014

Krackhardt, D., & Hanson, J. R. (2003). Informal Networks: The Company behind the Chart. In R. Cross, A. Parker, & L. Sasson (Eds.), *Networks in the Knowledge Economy* (pp. 235–247). New York, NY: Oxford University Press.

Kylin, C., & Karlsson, J. C. (2008). Re-establishing Boundaries in Home-Based Telework. In C. Warhurst, D. R. Eikhof, & Haunschild. Axel (Eds.), *Work Less, Live More? Critical Analysis of the Work-Life Boundary* (pp. 173–190). New York, NY: Palgrave Macmillan.

Latour, B. (1999). *Pandora's Hope: Essays on the Reality of Science Studies.* Cambridge, MA: Harvard University Press.

Latour, B. (2013). *An Inquiry into Modes of Existence: An Anthropology of the Moderns.* Boston, MA: Harvard University Press.

Law, J. (1986). On the Methods of Long Distance Control: Vessels, Navigation and the Portuguese Route to India. In J. Law (Ed.), *Power, Action and Belief: A New Sociology of Knowledge?* (pp. 234–263). Boston, MA: Routledge.

Lister, K., & Harnish, T. (2010). *Workshifting Benefits: The Bottom Line.* Retrieved August 5, 2012, from http://www.workshifting.com/downloads/downloads/Workshifting%20Benefits-The%20Bottom%20Line.pdf

Ludvigsen, S. R., Havnes, A., & Lahn, L. C. (2003). Workplace Learning across Activity Systems:

A Case Study of Sales Engineers. In T. Tuomi-Gröhn & Y. Engeström (Eds.), *Between School and Work: New Perspectives on Transfer and Boundary-Crossing* (pp. 291–310). Boston, MA: Pergamon.

Madden, M., & Lenhart, A. (2013). *Teens and Technology 2013*. Retrieved March 18, 2013, from http://www.pewinternet.org/Reports/2013/Teens-and-Tech/Summary-of-Findings.aspx

Malone, T. W. (2004). *The Future of Work: How the New Order of Business Will Shape Your Organization, Your Management Style and Your Life*. Boston, MA: Harvard Business School Press.

Mark, G., & Semaan, B. (2008). Resilience in Collaboration: Technology as a Resource for New Patterns of Action. In *CSCW '08: Proceedings of the 2008 Conference on Computer Supported Cooperative Work* (pp. 137–146). New York, NY: ACM.

Mark, G., & Su, N. M. (2010). Making Infrastructure Visible for Nomadic Work. *Pervasive and Mobile Computing, 6*(3), 1–12. doi:10.1016/j.pmcj.2009.12.004

McCarthy, J. E., Grabill, J. T., Hart-Davidson, W., & McLeod, M. (2011). Content Management in the Workplace: Community, Context, and a New Way to Organize Writing. *Journal of Business and Technical Communication, 25*(4), 367–395.

McDonald, D. W., Javanmardi, S., & Zachry, M. (2011). Finding patterns in Behavioral Observations by Automatically Labeling Forms of Wikiwork in Barnstars. In *WikiSym '11: Proceedings of the 7th International Symposium on Wikis and Open Collaboration* (pp. 15–24). New York, NY: ACM Press. doi:10.1145/2038558.2038562

McNely, B. J. (2009). Backchannel Persistence and Collaborative Meaning-Making. In B. Mehlenbacher, A. Protopsaltis, A. Williams, & S. Slattery (Eds.), *SIGDOC '09: Proceedings of the 27th ACM International Conference on Design of Communication* (pp. 297–303). New York, NY: ACM.

Mettler, A., & Williams, A. D. (2013). *The Rise of the Micro-Multinational: How Freelancers and Technology-Savvy Start-Ups Are Driving Growth, Jobs and Innovation*. Retrieved February 25, 2013, from http://www.lisboncouncil.net/publication/publication/67-the-rise-of-the-micro-multinational-how-freelancers-and-technology-savvy-start-ups-are-driving-growth-jobs-and-innovation.html

Midler, C. (1995). "Projectification" of the Firm: The Renault Case. *Scandinavian Journal of Management, 11*(4), 363–375.

Miettinen, R. (1998). Object Construction and Networks in Research Work: The Case of Research on Cellulose-Degrading Enzymes. *Social Studies of Science, 28*(3), 423–463.

Miettinen, R. (2008). Contradictions of High-Technology Capitalism and the Emergence of New Forms of Work. In A. Sannino, H. Daniels, & K. D. Gutierrez (Eds.), *Learning and Expanding with Activity Theory* (pp. 160–175). New York, NY: Cambridge University Press.

Mihailidis, P. (2014). A Tethered Generation: Exploring the Role of Mobile Phones in the Daily Life of Young People. *Mobile Media & Communication, 2*(1), 58–72. doi:10.1177/2050157913505558

Miles, M. B., & Huberman, A. M. (1994). *Qualitative Data Analysis: An Expanded Sourcebook*. Thousand Oaks, CA: Sage Publications.

Miller, C. R., & Selzer, J. (1985). Special Topics of Argument in Engineering Reports. In L. Odell & D. Goswami (Eds.), *Writing in Nonacademic Settings* (pp. 309–342). New York, NY: Guilford Press.

Mintzberg, H. (1979). *The Structuring of Organizations*. New York, NY: Prentice Hall.

Mintzberg, H., & McHugh, A. (1985). Strategy Formation in an Adhocracy. *Administrative Science Quarterly, 30*, 160–197.

Mol, A. (2002). *The Body Multiple: Ontology in Medical Practice*. Durham, NC: Duke University Press.

Mol, A., & Law, J. (1994). Regions, Networks and Fluids: Anaemia and Social Topology. *Social Studies of Science, 24*(1), 641–671.

Monroy-Hernández, A., Counts, S., Way, O. M., & Wa, R. (2013). The New War Correspondents : The Rise of Civic Media Curation in Urban Warfare. In *CSCW '13: Proceedings of the ACM 2013 Conference on Computer Supported Cooperative Work*. New York, NY: ACM.

Moore, R. J., Ducheneaut, N., & Nickell, E. (2006). Doing Virtually Nothing: Awareness and Accountability in Massively Multiplayer Online Worlds. *Computer Supported Cooperative Work (CSCW), 16*(3), 265–305. doi:10.1007/s10606-006-9021-4

Morgan, J. T., & Zachry, M. (2010). Negotiating with Angry Mastodons. In Wayne Lutters & Diane H. Sonnenwald (Eds.), *GROUP '10: Proceedings of the 16th ACM International Conference on Supporting Group Work* (pp. 165–168). New York, NY: ACM.

Mueller, M. L. (2010). *Networks and States: The Global Politics of Internet Governance.* Cambridge, MA: MIT Press.

Muller, M., Shami, N. S., Millen, D. R., & Feinberg, J. (2010). We Are All Lurkers : Consuming Behaviors among Authors and Readers in an Enterprise File-Sharing Service. In *GROUP '10: Proceedings of the 16th ACM International Conference on Supporting Group Work* (pp. 201–210). New York, NY: ACM.

Nardi, B. A. (2005). Objects of Desire: Power and Passion in Collaborative Activity. *Mind, Culture, and Activity, 12*(1), 37–51.

Nardi, B. A. (2010). *My Life as a Night Elf Priest: An Anthropological Account of World of Warcraft.* Ann Arbor: University of Michigan Press.

Nardi, B. A., Whittaker, S., & Schwarz, H. (2002). NetWORKers and Their Activity in Intensional Networks. *Computer Supported Cooperative Work, 11*, 205–242.

Nielsen. (2013). Mobile Majority: U.S. Smartphone Ownership Tops 60%. *Nielsen.* Retrieved July 11, 2013, from http://www.nielsen.com/us/en/newswire/2013/mobile-majority--u-s--smartphone-ownership-tops-60-.html

Novick, D. G., Elizalde, E., & Bean, N. (2007). Toward a More Accurate View of When and How People Seek Help with Computer Applications. In *SIGDOC '07: Proceedings of the 25th Annual ACM International Conference on Design of Communication* (pp. 95–102). New York, NY: ACM. doi:http://doi.acm.org/10.1145/1297144.1297165

Oh, O., Agrawal, M., & Rao, H. R. (2011). Information Control and Terrorism: Tracking the Mumbai Terrorist Attack through Twitter. *Information Systems Frontiers, 13*(1), 33–43. doi:10.1007/s10796-010-9275-8

O'Leary, M., Orlikowski, W., & Yates, J. (2002). Distributed Work over the Centuries: Trust and Control in the Hudson's Bay Company, 1670–1826. In P. J. Hinds & S. Kiesler (Eds.), *Distributed Work* (pp. 27–54). Cambridge, MA: MIT Press.

Olivieri, J. (2013). Economist Offers Sunny Forecast for Central Texas Region in 2014. *Community Impact.* Retrieved January 7, 2014, from http://impactnews.com/austin-metro/southwest-austin/economist-offers-sunny-forecast-for-central-texas-region-in-2014/

O'Neill, R. M., & Quinn, R. E. (1993). Editors' Note: Applications of the Competing Values Framework. *Human Resource Management, 32*(1), 1–7.

Ouchi, W. G. (1980). Markets, Bureaucracies, and Clans. *Administrative Science Quarterly, 25*(1), 129–141.

Oxley, M., Morgan, J. T., Zachry, M., & Hutchinson, B. (2010). "What I Know Is . . .": Establishing Credibility on Wikipedia Talk Pages. In *WikiSym '10: Proceedings of the 6th International Symposium on Wikis and Open Collaboration* (pp. 2–3). New York, NY: ACM.

Paretti, M. C., McNair, L. D., & Holloway-Attaway, L. (2007). Teaching Technical Communica-

tion in an Era of Distributed Work: A Case Study of Collaboration between U.S. and Swed-
ish Students. *Technical Communication Quarterly, 16*(3), 327–352.

Pazos, P., Chung, J. M., & Micari, M. (2012). Instant Messaging as a Task-Support Tool in Information Technology Organizations. *Journal of Business Communication, 50*(1), 68–86.
doi:10.1177/0021943612465181

Pennell, M. (2007). Fraternities and ITexts: Composing in the Post-Industrial Turn. *Computers
and Composition, 24*(1), 74–91. doi:10.1016/j.compcom.2006.12.007

Pew Research. (2013). A Quarter of Teens Mostly Access the Internet Using Their Cell Phones.
Pew Research Center. Retrieved July 11, 2013, from http://www.pewresearch.org/daily
-number/a-quarter-of-teens-mostly-access-the-internet-using-their-cell-phones/

Pogner, K.-H. (2003). Writing and Interacting in the Discourse Community of Engineering.
Journal of Pragmatics, 35(6), 855–867. doi:10.1016/S0378-2166(02)00122-4

Polanyi, M. (2009). *The Tacit Dimension.* Chicago, IL: University of Chicago Press.

Popham, S. L. (2005). Forms as Boundary Genres in Medicine, Science, and Business. *Journal of
Business and Technical Communication, 19*(3), 279–303.

Potts, L., Seitzinger, J., Jones, D., & Harrison, A. (2011). Tweeting Disaster: Hashtag Construc-
tions and Collisions. In *Proceedings of the 29th ACM Conference on the Design of Communication* (pp. 235–240). ACM. doi:10.1145/2038476.2038522

Quan-Haase, A., & Wellman, B. (2007). Hyperconnected Net Work: Computer-Mediated Com-
munity in a High-Tech Organization. In C. Heckscher & P. S. Adler (Eds.), *The Firm as a
Collaborative Community: Reconstructing Trust in the Knowledge Economy* (pp. 281–333).
New York, NY: Oxford University Press.

Quinn, R. E., & Rohrbaugh, J. (1981). A Competing Values Approach to Organizational Effectiveness. *Public Productivity Review, 5*(2), 122–140.

Quinn, R. E., & Rohrbaugh, J. (1983). A Spatial Model of Effectiveness Criteria: Towards a Competing Values Approach to Organizational Analysis. *Management Science, 29*(3), 363–377.

Rainie, L., & Wellman, B. (2012). *Networked: The New Social Operating System.* Cambridge, MA:
MIT Press.

Ramsower, R. M. (1985). *Telecommuting: The Organizational and Behavioral Effects of Working at
Home.* Ann Arbor, MI: UMI Research Press.

Rheingold, H. (2003). *Smart Mobs: The Next Social Revolution.* Cambridge, MA: Basic Books.

Rice, J. [Jeff]. (2012). *Digital Detroit: Rhetoric and Space in the Age of the Network.* Carbondale:
Southern Illinois University.

Rice, J. [Jenny]. (2012). *Distant Publics: Development Rhetoric and the Subject of Crisis.* Pittsburgh, PA: University of Pittsburgh Press.

Riemer, K., & Richter, A. (2010). Tweet Inside : Microblogging in a Corporate Context Micro-
blogging. In *The 23rd Bled eConference eTrust: Implications for the Individual, Enterprises
and Society Proceedings* (pp. 1–17). Retrieved June 25, 2014, from https://domino.fov.uni-mb
.si/proceedings.nsf/Proceedings/6D767B442CC0E928C12577570031A81A/$File/01_Riemer
.pdf

Robb, J. (2008). *Brave New War: The Next Stage of Terrorism and the End of Globalization.* Hobo-
ken, NJ: Wiley.

Ronfeldt, D. (1996). *Tribes, Institutions, Markets, Networks: A Framework about Societal Evolution.* Santa Monica, CA: RAND. Retrieved August 5, 2012, from http://www.rand.org/pubs
/papers/P7967.html

Ronfeldt, D. (2007). *In Search of How Societies Work: Tribes—The First and Forever Form.* Working paper, RAND, Santa Monica, CA. Retrieved August 5, 2012, from http://www.rand.org/pubs/working_papers/2007/RAND_WR433.pdf

Ronfeldt, D., Arquilla, J., Fuller, G. E., & Fuller, M. (1999). *The Zapatista Social Netwar in Mexico*. Santa Monica, CA: RAND.

Ronfeldt, D., and Varda, D. (2008). The Prospects for Cyberocracy (Revisited). Working paper. Retrieved July 10, 2014, from http://ssrn.com/abstract=1325809

Rosenwald, M. S. (2013, October 9). The Siren Call of the BlackBerry for Furloughed Federal Workers. *Washington Post*. Washington, DC. Retrieved October 9, 2013, from http://www.washingtonpost.com/local/the-siren-call-of-the-blackberry-for-furloughed-federal-workers/2013/10/09/62dc407c-3102-11e3-8627-c5d7de0a046b_print.html

Rossitto, C., Bogdan, C., & Severinson-Eklundh, K. (2013). Understanding Constellations of Technologies in Use in a Collaborative Nomadic Setting. *Computer Supported Cooperative Work (CSCW)*. doi:10.1007/s10606-013-9196-4

Ruppel, C. P., Gong, B., & Tworoger, L. C. (2013). Using Communication Choices as a Boundary-Management Strategy: How Choices of Communication Media Affect the Work-Life Balance of Teleworkers in a Global Virtual Team. *Journal of Business and Technical Communication*. doi:10.1177/1050651913490941

Russell, D. R. (1997). Rethinking Genre in School and Society: An Activity Theory Analysis. *Written Communication*, *14*(4), 504–554.

Russell, D. R. (2009). Uses of Activity Theory in Written Communication Research. In A. Sannino, H. Daniels, & K. D. Gutierrez (Eds.), *Learning and Expanding with Activity Theory* (pp. 40–52). New York, NY: Cambridge University Press.

Sarcevic, A., Palen, L., White, J., Starbird, K., Bagdouri, M., & Anderson, K. (2012). "Beacons of Hope" in Decentralized Coordination: Learning from On-the-Ground Medical Twitterers during the 2010 Haiti Earthquake. In *CSCW '12: Proceedings of the ACM 2012 Conference on Computer Supported Cooperative Work* (pp. 47–56). New York, NY: ACM.

Sauer, B. (2003). *The Rhetoric of Risk: Technical Documentation in Hazardous Environments*. Mahwah, NJ: Erlbaum.

Schmandt-Besserat, D. (1992). *Before Writing* (Vols. 1–2). Austin: University of Texas.

Schmandt-Besserat, D. (1997). *How Writing Came About*. Austin: University of Texas Press.

Schmandt-Besserat, D., & Erard, M. (2008). Origins and Forms of Writing. In C. Bazerman (Ed.), *Handbook of Research on Writing: History, Society, School, Individual, Text* (pp. 7–22). New York, NY: Erlbaum.

Schryer, C. F. (2003). Structure and Agency in Medical Case Presentations. (C. Bazerman & D. R. Russell, Eds.) *Writing Selves/Writing Societies: Research from Activity Perspectives*. Ft. Collins, CO: WAC Clearinghouse and *Mind, Culture, and Activity*. Retrieved from http://wac.colostate.edu/books/selves_societies

Schryer, C. F., & Spoel, P. (2005). Genre Theory, Health-Care Discourse, and Professional Identity Formation. *Journal of Business and Technical Communication*, *19*(3), 249–278.

Schuster, M. L., & Propen, A. D. (2011). *Victim Advocacy in the Courtroom: Persuasive Practices in Domestic Violence and Child Protection Cases*. Boston, MA: Northeastern.

Selby, W. G. (2009). Hutchison Site Is Loaded with Hidden Phrases—Including Two "Perry gay" References, Which the Campaign Says It's Removing. *Austin American-Statesman*. Retrieved July 30, 2009, from http://www.statesman.com/blogs/content/shared-gen/blogs/austin/politics/entries/2009/07/30/hutchisonoriented_site_luring.html/

Sherlock, L. (2009). Genre, Activity, and Collaborative Work and Play in World of Warcraft:

Places and Problems of Open Systems in Online Gaming. *Journal of Business and Technical Communication, 23*(3), 263–293.

Shirky, C. (2008). *Here Comes Everybody: The Power of Organizing without Organizations.* New York, NY: Penguin.

Shirky, C. (2011). *Cognitive Surplus: Creativity and Generosity in a Connected Age.* New York, NY: Penguin Books.

Small, M. L. (2009). *Unanticipated Gains: Origins of Network Inequality in Everyday Life.* New York, NY: Oxford University Press.

Snowden, D. J. (2005). Conference Papers Multi-ontology Sense Making: A New Simplicity in Decision Making. *Informatics in Primary Care, 13,* 45–53.

Snowden, D. J., & Boone, M. E. (2007). A Leader's Framework for Decision Making. *Harvard Business Review, 85*(11), 68–76.

Snyder, T. D. (1993). *120 Years of Education: A Statistical Portrait.* Washington, DC: National Center for Education Statistics, Office of Educational Research and Improvement, US Department of Education. Retrieved July 11, 2013, from http://0-nces.ed.gov.opac.acc.msmc.edu/pubs93/93442.pdf

Solomon, C. (2012). *The Challenges of Working in Virtual Teams* (pp. 1–40). New York, NY. Retrieved December 30, 2012, from http://www.google.com/url?sa=t&rct=j&q=&esrc=s&source=web&cd=2&cad=rja&ved=0CEIQFjAB&url=http://rw-3.com/2012VirtualTeamsSurveyReport.pdf&ei=SVtQUZzIA6O42gX1oYHYCw&usg=AFQjCNEg_cGhDwa3FTPJGjLe0P27IJEWkQ&bvm=bv.44158598,d.b2I

Spence, P. R., & Reddy, M. (2011). Beyond Expertise Seeking: A Field Study of the Informal Knowledge Practices of Healthcare IT Teams. *Computer Supported Cooperative Work (CSCW).* doi:10.1007/s10606-011-9135-1

Spinuzzi, C. (2003). *Tracing Genres through Organizations: A Sociocultural Approach to Information Design.* Cambridge, MA: MIT Press.

Spinuzzi, C. (2005). Lost in the Translation: Shifting Claims in the Migration of a Research Technique. *Technical Communication Quarterly, 14*(4), 411–446.

Spinuzzi, C. (2007). Guest Editor's Introduction: Technical Communication in the Age of Distributed Work. *Technical Communication Quarterly, 16*(3), 265–277.

Spinuzzi, C. (2008). *Network: Theorizing Knowledge Work in Telecommunications.* New York, NY: Cambridge University Press.

Spinuzzi, C. (2009). Starter Ecologies: Introduction to the Special Issue on Social Software. *Journal of Business and Technical Communication, 23*(3), 251–262.

Spinuzzi, C. (2010). Secret Sauce and Snake Oil: Writing Monthly Reports in a Highly Contingent Environment. *Written Communication, 27*(4), 363–409.

Spinuzzi, C. (2011). Losing by Expanding: Corralling the Runaway Object. *Journal of Business and Technical Communication, 25*(4), 449–486.

Spinuzzi, C. (2012a). Genre and Generic Labor. In C. Bazerman, C. Dean, J. Early, K. Lunsford, S. Null, P. Rogers, & A. Stansell (Eds.), *Advances in Writing Research: Cultures, Places, Measures* (pp. 487–505). Anderson, SC: Parlor Press and WAC Clearinghouse. Retrieved from http://wac.colostate.edu/books/wrab2011/chapter27.pdf

Spinuzzi, C. (2012b). Working Alone, Together: Coworking as Emergent Collaborative Activity. *Journal of Business and Technical Communication, 26*(4), 399–441.

Spinuzzi, C. (2013). *Topsight: A Guide to Studying, Diagnosing, and Fixing Information Flow in Organizations.* Austin, TX: Amazon CreateSpace.

Spinuzzi, C. (2014). How Nonemployer Firms Stage-Manage Ad-Hoc Collaboration: An Activity Theory Analysis. *Technical Communication Quarterly, 23*(2).

Spinuzzi, C. (Forthcoming). Toward a Typology of Activities: Understanding Internal Contradictions in Multiperspectival Activities. *Journal of Business and Technical Communication.*

Spinuzzi, C., & Jakobs, E.-M. (2013). Integrated Writers, Integrated Writing, and the Integration of Distributed Work. *Connexions: International Professional Communication Journal/Revista de Comunicação Profissional Internacional, 1*(1), 119–124. Retrieved June 13, 2013, from http://connexionsj.files.wordpress.com/2013/05/spinuzzi-jakobs.pdf

Starbird, K. (2011). "Voluntweeters": Self-Organizing by Digital Volunteers in Times of Crisis. In *CHI '11: Proceedings of the 2011 ACM Annual Conference on Human Factors in Computing Systems* (pp. 1071–1080). New York, NY: ACM.

Starbird, K. (2012). (How) Will the Revolution Be Retweeted? Information Diffusion and the 2011 Egyptian Uprising. In *CSCW '12: Proceedings of the ACM 2012 Conference on Computer Supported Cooperative Work* (pp. 7–16). New York, NY: ACM.

Starbird, K., & Palen, L. (2013). Working and Sustaining the Virtual "Disaster Desk." In *CSCW '13: Proceedings of the 2013 Conference on Computer Supported Cooperative Work* (pp. 491–502). New York, NY: ACM Press. doi:10.1145/2441776.2441832

Starbird, K., Palen, L., Hughes, A. L., & Vieweg, S. (2010). Chatter on *The Red*: What Hazards Threat Reveals about the Social Life of Microblogged Information. In *CSCW '10: Proceedings of the 2010 ACM Conference on Computer Supported Cooperative Work* (pp. 241–250). New York, NY: ACM.

Starke-Meyerring, D. (2010). Between Peer Review and Peer Production: Genres, Wikis, and the Politics of Digital Code in Academe. In C. Bazerman, R. Krut, K. Lunsford, S. McLeod, S. Null, P. Rogers, & A. Stansell (Eds.), *Traditions of Writing Research* (pp. 339–350). New York, NY: Routledge.

Su, N., & Mark, G. (2008). Designing for Nomadic Work. *DIS '08: Proceedings of the 7th ACM Conference on Designing Interactive Systems.* New York, NY: ACM Press.

Subramaniam, N., Nandhakumar, J., & Baptista John, J. (2013). Exploring Social Network Interactions in Enterprise Systems: the Role of Virtual Co-presence. *Information Systems Journal, 23*(6), 475–499. doi:10.1111/isj.12019

Sun, H. (2012). *Cross-Cultural Technology Design: Crafting Culture-Sensitive Technology for Local Users.* New York, NY: Oxford.

Swarts, J. (2000). Document Collaboration and Tacit Knowledge. In *IPCC/SIGDOC 2000: Technology and Teamwork. Proceedings. IEEE Professional Communication Society International Professional Communication Conference and ACM Special Interest Group on Documentation Conference.* (pp. 407–418). Piscataway, NJL IEEE. doi:10.1109/IPCC.2000.887298

Swarts, J. (2007). Mobility and Composition: The Architecture of Coherence in Non-places. *Technical Communication Quarterly, 16*(3), 279–309.

Swarts, J, & Kim, L. (2009). Guest Editors' Introduction: New Technological Spaces. *Technical Communication Quarterly, 18*(3), 211–223.

Tapscott, D., & Williams, A. D. (2006). *Wikinomics: How Mass Collaboration Changes Everything.* New York, NY: Portfolio.

Toffler, A. (1970). *Future Shock.* New York, NY: Random House.

Toffler, A. (1980). *The Third Wave.* New York, NY: Bantam Books.

Tuomi-Gröhn, T., & Engeström, Y. (Eds.). (2003). *Between School and Work: New Perspectives on Transfer and Boundary Crossing.* Boston, MA: Pergamon.

Ugander, J., Karrer, B., Backstrom, L., Marlow, C., & Alto, P. (2011). The Anatomy of the Facebook Social Graph. *Arxiv*. Retrieved May 14, 2012, from http://arxiv.org/pdf/1111.4503v1.pdf

US Census Bureau. (2011a). 51 Information. Retrieved July 25, 2011, from http://www.census.gov /econ /census02/naics/sector51/51.htm

US Census Bureau. (2011b). Nonemployer statistics. Retrieved July 25, 2011, from http://censtats .census.gov/cgi-bin /nonemployer/nonsect.pl

US Census Bureau. (2011c). Population Estimates Data Sets. Retrieved July 25, 2011, from http:// www.census.gov/popest /datasets.html

US Small Business Administration Office of Advocacy. (2011). Firm Data. Retrieved December 21, 2011, from http://archive.sba.gov/advo/research /data.html

Wagner, C. (2010). Capabilities and Roles of Enterprise Wikis in Organizational Communication. *Technical Communication, 57*(1), 68 – 89.

Walton, R. (2013). Stakeholder Flux: Participation in Technology-Based International Development Projects. *Journal of Business and Technical Communication, 27*(4), 409 – 435. doi:10.1177/1050651913490940

Waterman, R. H. (1993). *Adhocracy*. New York, NY: Norton.

Weber, M. (1978). *Economy and Society: An Outline of Interpretive Sociology*. Berkeley: University of California Press.

Weber, M. (2002). *The Protestant Ethic and the Spirit of Capitalism*. New York, NY: Penguin.

Weiner, M. S. (2013). *The Rule of the Clan: What an Ancient Form of Social Organization Reveals about the Future of Individual Freedom*. New York, NY: Farrar, Straus and Giroux.

Winsor, D. A. (1996). *Writing Like an Engineer: A Rhetorical Education*. Mahwah, NJ: Erlbaum.

Wu, A., DiMicco, J. M., & Millen, D. R. (2010). Detecting Professional versus Personal Closeness Using an Enterprise Social Network Site. In *CHI '10: Proceedings of the 28th International Conference on Human Factors in Computing Systems* (pp. 1955 – 1964). New York, NY: ACM. doi:10.1145/1753326.1753622

Xenos, M., Vromen, A., & Loader, B. D. (2014). The Great Equalizer? Patterns of Social Media Use and Youth Political Engagement in Three Advanced Democracies. *Information, Communication & Society, 17*(2), 1 – 17. doi:10.1080/1369118X.2013.871318

Yamazumi, K. (2009). Expansive Agency in Multi-activity Collaboration. In A. Sannino, H. Daniels, & K. D. Gutierrez (Eds.), *Learning and Expanding with Activity Theory* (pp. 212 – 227). New York, NY: Cambridge University Press.

Yamazumi, K. (2013). Inexpressible Memories and Learning for Reconstruction: Between the Major Earthquake Disasters in Postwar in Japan. *Educational Studies in Japan: International Yearbook, 7*, 21 – 35.

Yates, J. (1989). *Control through Communication: The Rise of System in American Management*. Baltimore, MD: Johns Hopkins University Press.

Yoo, Y., & Alavi, M. (2004). Emergent Leadership in Virtual Teams: What Do Emergent Leaders Do? *Information and Organization, 14*(1), 27 – 58. doi:10.1016/j.infoandorg.2003.11.001

Zhao, D., & Rosson, M. B. (2009). How and Why People Twitter : The Role that Micro-Blogging Plays in Informal Communication at Work. In *GROUP '04 Conference Proceedings* (pp. 243 – 252). New York, NY: ACM.

Zuboff, S. (1988). *In the Age of the Smart Machine: The Future of Work and Power*. New York, NY: Basic Books.

Zuboff, S., & Maxmin, J. (2004). *The Support Economy: Why Corporations Are Failing Individuals and the Next Episode of Capitalism*. New York, NY: Penguin Books.

Index

abstraction. *See* information: abstraction of
accounting, 7–8, 94, 158
activity, 98–111; as dynamic, 99–107, 111, 170, 181; as kinetic, 16–17, 99, 104–6, 181; and pulsing (*see* pulse); as stable, 99–106, 144, 168, 170–71, 181–82; as structured (*see* activity system)
activity network, 57, 105–6, 139, 143–44
activity system, 100–102, 105–7, 138, 192
activity theory, 15, 57, 100, 104–8, 143, 159, 189, 191
actors, 32, 57, 61, 64–65, 67, 100–101; as activity system component, 103, 105; in clans, 152–53; in coworking, 107–10; in hierarchies, 146; in markets, 149; in networks, 157
adaptation, 23, 100, 181
adhocracy. *See* all-edge adhocracy; institutional adhocracy
affinities. *See* all-edge adhocracy: tactics and
agility, 4, 28
agriculture, 7–8, 28
all-edge adhocracy: alliances and, 27, 34, 51, 53, 57, 106, 180, 188; autonomy and, 40–41, 46, 53, 64, 70, 112, 117, 119, 122, 125, 128, 137, 154–55, 185; dispersing, 1–2, 15, 31, 37, 61, 73, 128, 142, 153–54; division of labor (*see* division of labor: in all-edge adhocracies); forming, 1–3, 14–16, 28, 31, 33, 37, 48, 53, 70, 82–83, 95, 109–12, 126, 129, 136–37, 173, 185–86; performance in (*see* front stage); potential of, 17, 187–88; specialization (*see* specialization: in all-edge adhocracies); strengths of, 17, 35, 38, 68, 115–16, 119, 136–37, 162, 171–72, 174, 182–85, 188; tactics and, 14, 46–48, 64, 68, 177, 179–80, 186; weaknesses of, 17, 28, 35, 62, 68, 70, 171–72, 174, 179, 182, 185–88
alliance, 27, 34, 51, 53, 57, 106, 180, 188
ambient awareness, 12–13, 176
arbitrage, 47

associational relations, 25, 184
audience analysis, 121–22, 128–29, 131–33, 196
Austin, city of, viii–ix, 36, 40–41, 71–81, 83, 85, 87, 91–92, 104, 111, 193
authority: and hierarchy, 20–21, 32, 61, 141–42, 146–47, 158, 160, 163, 177, 188; and ICTs, 12; in NEFs, 70; and networks, 12, 32, 35, 70, 157, 180; and trust, 114, 130, 133; in a typology of activities, 144
autonomy: and all-edge adhocracies, 35, 53, 127, 180, 182; and contingencies, 122; and coworking, 70–71; and institutional adhocracies, 137; and knowledge work, 29; and NEFs, 37–38, 40–41, 46, 53, 64, 185; and networks, 31, 67, 154–55; and self-programmable labor, 169–70; and SEO, 112, 117–19, 122, 125, 127–28

back stage, 42, 44, 50–54, 62, 68, 90, 96–98, 107, 109–10, 119, 132, 165, 176
bandwidth effect, 167
belonging, 141–42, 152, 162
black hat SEO. *See* snake oil
boundary crossing, 33–34, 116, 122, 180
Brainstorm Coworking, viii, 76, 79
BRILLIANCE, 118–20, 124, 126, 134–35, 145–47, 168, 175
bureaucracy, 16, 36; as activity, 100, 103–4, 106; and all-edge adhocracies, 27–35; command-and-control structure, 2, 22, 35, 61, 157, 181; and coworking, 70–71, 98; defined, 21; efficiency, 2, 19, 21–23, 145–47, 183; and generic labor, 170–71, 174; and institutional adhocracies, 23–27; and long-distance communication, 10; and NEFs, 45, 47–48, 51, 61; in SEO, 112, 115–17, 119–20, 122, 134–37; in a typology of activities, 140, 142, 166–67